NAY

ALLEN COUNTY PUBLIC LIBRARY

3 1833 03063 6150

P9-ECL-652

005.369 Of2p
Perry, Greg M.        JUL 2 97
Teach yourself Microsoft
   Office 97 in 24 hours

ach
rself

OSOFT

E 97

Hours

**ALLEN COUNTY PUBLIC LIBRARY**
FORT WAYNE, INDIANA 46802

You may return this book to any location of
the Allen County Public Library.

DEMCO

# Teach Yourself
# MICROSOFT
# OFFICE 97
## in 24 Hours

*Greg Perry*

**SAMS**
PUBLISHING

201 West 103rd Street
Indianapolis, Indiana 46290

Allen County Public Library
900 Webster Street
PO Box 2270
Fort Wayne, IN 46801-2270

*For Mr. Ben Stein, a man who knows life, love, and what's right. I may never meet you but your writing makes you a dear friend of our family.*

# Copyright © 1997 by Sams Publishing

FIRST EDITION

All rights reserved. No part of this book shall be reproduced, stored in a retrieval system, or transmitted by any means, electronic, mechanical, photo-copying, recording, or otherwise, without written permission from the publisher. No patent liability is assumed with respect to the use of the information contained herein. Although every precaution has been taken in the preparation of this book, the publisher and author assume no responsibility for errors or omissions. Neither is any liability assumed for damages resulting from the use of the information contained herein. For information, address Sams Publishing, 201 W. 103rd St., Indianapolis, IN 46290.

International Standard Book Number: 0-672-31009-0

Library of Congress Catalog Card Number: 96-70719

2000    99    98    97            4    3    2    1

Interpretation of the printing code: the rightmost double-digit number is the year of the book's printing; the rightmost single-digit, the number of the book's printing. For example, a printing code of 97-1 shows that the first printing of the book occurred in 1997.

*Composed in AGaramond and MCPdigital by Macmillan Computer Publishing*

*Printed in the United States of America*

## Trademarks

All terms mentioned in this book that are known to be trademarks or service marks have been appropriately capitalized. Sams Publishing cannot attest to the accuracy of this information. Use of a term in this book should not be regarded as affecting the validity of any trademark or service mark. Microsoft Office 97 is a registered trademark of Microsoft Corporation.

**Publisher**    Richard K. Swadley

**Publishing Manager**    Dean Miller

**Managing Editor**    Cindy Morrow

**Director of Marketing**    John Pierce

**Assistant Marketing Managers**    Kristina Perry, Rachel Wolfe

**Acquisitions Editor**
Dean Miller

**Development Editor**
Brian-Kent Proffitt

**Production Editor**
Kate Shoup

**Indexer**
Benjamin Slen

**Technical Reviewer**
Susan Teague

**Editorial Coordinator**
Katie Wise

**Technical Edit Coordinator**
Lynette Quinn

**Editorial Assistants**
Carol Ackerman
Andi Richter
Rhonda Tinch-Mize

**Cover Designer**
Tim Amrhein

**Book Designer**
Gary Adair

**Copy Writer**
Peter Fuller

**Production Team Supervisors**
Brad Chinn
Charlotte Clapp

**Production**
Cyndi Davis
Dana Rhodes
Janet Seib
Mary Ellen Stephenson

# Overview

# Contents

# Acknowledgments

Once again, I'm thanking Mr. Dean Miller for providing me with this writing opportunity. Dean, you must have been desperate for an author when you chose me! You are surely a major inspiration to Sams Publishing and Sams is extremely fortunate that you are there.

The people at Sams Publishing all take their jobs seriously. They want readers to have the best books possible. They accomplish that goal. Among the Sams editors and staff who produced this book, I want to send special thanks to Brian Proffitt and Kate Shoup.

Although they did not have a direct hand in this book, I must thank Sams' two most outstanding team members, Rosemarie Graham and Gayle Johnson. Rosemarie and Gayle are friends I've made from past books and I want them to know I appreciate the jobs they do.

My lovely and gracious bride stands by my side day and night. Thank you once again. You, precious Jayne, are everything that matters to me on earth. The best parents in the world, Glen and Bettye Perry, continue to encourage and support me in every way. I am who I am because of both of them. Two or three states of separation do not seem to hinder my best friendship with Bob and Cheryl Enyart, two people who have dramatically changed our lives in only two years. My deep thanks goes to them always for their continued encouragement and enlightenment.

*Greg Perry*

# About the Author

**Greg Perry** is a speaker and a writer on both the programming and the application sides of computing. He is known for his skills at bringing advanced computer topics to the novice's level. Perry has been a programmer and a trainer since the early 1980s. He received his first degree in computer science and a master's degree in corporate finance. Perry is the author or co-author of more than 40 books, including *Teach Yourself Windows 95 in 24 Hours*, *Absolute Beginner's Guide to Programming*, *Absolute Beginner's Guide to C*, and *Moving from C to C++*. He also writes about rental-property management and loves to travel. In his spare time, he helps produce a nationally-syndicated television talk show. His favorite place to be when away from home is either at New York's *Patsy's* or in Italy because he enjoys only the best pasta!

## Tell Us What You Think!

As a reader, you are the most important critic and commentator of our books. We value your opinion and want to know what we're doing right, what we could do better, what areas you'd like to see us publish in, and any other words of wisdom you're willing to pass our way. You can help us make strong books that meet your needs and give you the computer guidance you require.

Do you have access to CompuServe or the World Wide Web? Then check out our CompuServe forum by typing GO SAMS at any prompt. If you prefer the World Wide Web, check out our site at http://www.mcp.com.

 **NOTE**

> If you have a technical question about this book, call the technical support line at (800) 571-5840, ext. 3668.

As the publishing manager of the group that created this book, I welcome your comments. You can fax, e-mail, or write me directly to let me know what you did or didn't like about this book—as well as what we can do to make our books stronger. Here's the information:

Fax:     317/581-4669

E-mail:  opsys_mgr@sams.mcp.com

Mail:    Dean Miller
         Sams Publishing
         201 W. 103rd Street
         Indianapolis, IN  46290

# Introduction

Microsoft Corporation's Office products have an installed base of more than 22 million licensed users. Over 90 percent of Fortune 500 companies use Microsoft Office. When developing Office 97, Microsoft conducted more than 25,000 hours of customer research. Based on that research and user feedback, Microsoft designed Office 97 to be more user-friendly as well as more integrated between applications. You won't regret your decision to learn and use Office 97.

You probably are anxious to get started with your 24-hour Office 97 tutorial. Take just a few preliminary moments to acquaint yourself with the design of this book, as described in the next few sections.

## Who Should Read This Book

This book is for *both* beginning and advanced Office 97 users. Readers rarely believe that lofty claim for good reason, but the design of this book and the nature of Office 97 make it possible for this book to address such a wide audience. Here is why: Office 97 is a major improvement over the previous Office products.

Readers unfamiliar with the Windows 95-style of windowed environments will find plenty of introductory help here that brings them quickly up to speed. This book teaches you how to start and exit Office 97 as well as how to manage many of the Windows environmental elements that you need to use Office 97 effectively.

For those readers tired of the plethora of quick-fix computer titles cluttering today's shelves, you'll find a welcome reprieve here. This book talks to beginners but does not talk *down* to beginners.

For readers who presently use a Microsoft Office product, this book also addresses you. Here is how: There are several sidebars labeled *Step-Up* that explain how a specific Office 97 feature improves upon or replaces a previous Office feature. With your fundamental Office understanding, you'll appreciate Office 97's new features and added power. Keep in mind that Office 97 is similar to previous Office versions, but Office 97 includes plenty of new features and improvements to keep Office gurus intrigued for a long time.

## What This Book Will Do for You

Although this book is not a complicated reference book, you'll learn almost every aspect of Office 97 from the user's point of view. Office 97 includes many advanced technical details that most users will never need, and this book does not waste your time with those. This book knows that you want to get up to speed with Office 97 in 24 hours, and helps you fulfill that goal.

This book presents both the background and descriptions that a new Office 97 user needs. In addition to the background, this book is practical and provides more than 100 step-by-step tasks that you can work through to gain practical hands-on experience. The tasks guide you though all the common Office 97 actions you'll need to make Office 97 work for you.

## Can This Book *Really* Teach Office 97 in 24 Hours?

Yes. You can master each chapter in one hour. (By the way, chapters are referred to as "hours" in the rest of this book.) The material is balanced with mountains of tips, shortcuts, and traps to avoid that will make your hours productive and will hone your Office 97 skills.

## Conventions Used in This Book

Each hour ends with a question-and-answer session.

This book uses several common conventions to help teach the Office 97 topics. Here is a summary of those typographical conventions:

- ☐ Commands, computer output, and words you type appear in a special monospaced computer font.
- ☐ If a task requires you to select from a menu, the book separates menu commands with a vertical bar. Therefore, this book uses File | Save As to select the Save As option from the File menu.

In addition to typographical conventions, the following special elements are included to set off different types of information to make them easily recognizable:

**NOTE**

Special notes augment the material you read in each hour. These notes clarify concepts and procedures.

**TIP**

You'll find numerous tips that offer shortcuts and solutions to common problems.

**WARNING**

The warnings warn you about pitfalls. Reading them will save you time and trouble.

## Step-Up

Users of previous Office products will advance quickly by reading the step-ups provided for them.

Each hour contains new-term definitions to explain important new terms. New-term icons make those definitions easy to find.

# PART

# I

## Working with Office 97

## Hour

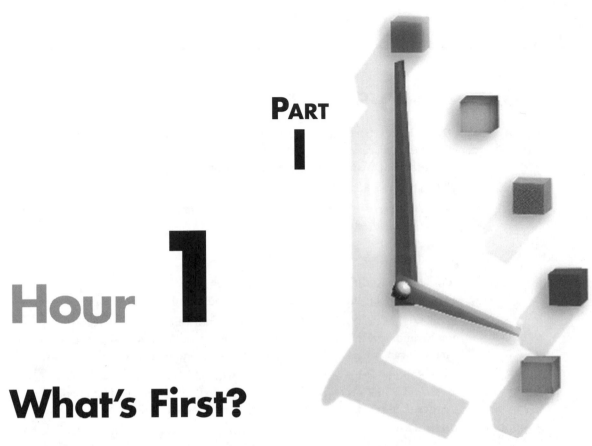

# Hour 1

# What's First?

Office 97 promises to improve your work environment by giving you integrated software tools that are easy to learn and simple to use while being powerful at the same time. Offices large and small can use Office 97–based applications for many of their computer needs.

If you've used previous versions of Office, Office 97 will take you to the next step by adding more power and more automatic editing aids. Office 97 tackles your software problems by providing many kinds of software that work in unison. In this hour, you'll see the big picture, which shows how Office 97 tackles many of the standard software requirements of today's offices.

The highlights of this hour include

- ☐ What Office 97 contains
- ☐ Why Office 97 provides synergy
- ☐ How the *Getting Results* book gives you a good Office 97 overview
- ☐ Which Office 97 products perform tasks you need
- ☐ How the Binder tracks project data for you

# What's in Office 97?

Office 97 includes Microsoft's most powerful applications. In the past, Microsoft sold versions of these applications separately. However, the programs work so well together that Microsoft combined them in the Office 97 collection of programs. Office 97 is often called a *suite of programs*.

**NEW TERM**  A *suite of programs* is a collection of programs that work together and have a similar interface.

Here is a quick overview of each Office 97 program:

- Word 97 is a word processor with which you can create notes, memos, letters, school papers, business documents, books, and even Internet Web pages.
- Excel 97 is an electronic worksheet program with which you can create charts, graphs, and worksheets for financial and other data. After you enter your financial data, you can analyze it for forecasts and generate numerous what-if scenarios.
- PowerPoint 97 is a presentation program with which you can create presentations for seminars and meetings. Not only can PowerPoint 97 create the presentation overheads, it can also create the presentation's speaker's notes.
- Access 97 is a database program with which you can organize data collections. No matter what kind of and how much data you must organize, Access 97 can analyze, sort, summarize, and report on that data.
- Outlook 97 is a contact manager that organizes your contact addresses, phone numbers, and other information in an address-book format. Use Outlook 97 to track your appointments, to schedule meetings, to generate to-do lists, and to keep a journal of your activities.
- Bookshelf Basics contains online reference materials that provide definitions, synonyms, and quotations.

---

**Step-Up**

Outlook 97 replaces Schedule+'s appointment and contact management features. Outlook 97 is a completely new program that adds new personal information features but retains all of Schedule+'s features.

---

Not only are all these products part of Office 97, but they *work together*, sharing data and features. If you create a financial table with Excel 97, you can put that table in a Word 97 letter that you send to your Board of Directors.

1

**TIP**

All the Office 97 products share common features and common menu choices. For example, Figure 1.1 shows Word 97's screen, and Figure 1.2 shows Excel 97's screen. Both screens display the open File menu. As you can see, the two program interfaces look virtually identical even though the programs accomplish entirely different goals.

**Figure 1.1.**

*Word 97's interface behaves like Excel 97's.*

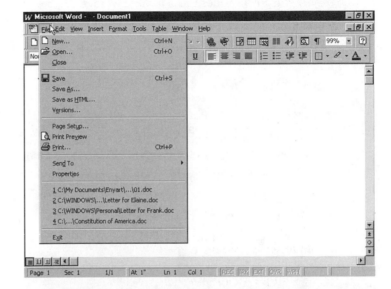

**Figure 1.2.**

*Excel 97's interface behaves like Word 97's.*

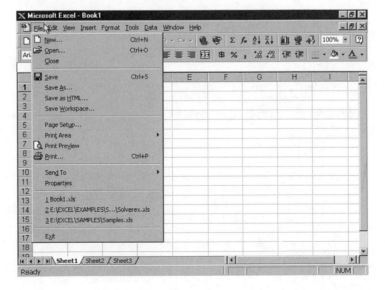

The Office 97 products are general purpose, meaning that you can customize applications to suit your needs. For example, you can use Excel 97 as your checkbook-balancing program and as your company's interactive balance-sheet system.

**NOTE**    You can integrate Office 97 into your network account. This way, Office 97 provides useful features whether you are networked to an intranet, to the Internet, or to both.

## Introducing Word 97

When you need to write any text-based document, look no farther than Word 97. Word 97 is a word processor that supports many features, including

- ☐ Wizards and templates that create and format documents for you
- ☐ Integrated grammar, spelling, and hyphenation tools
- ☐ Automatic corrections for common mistakes as you type
- ☐ Advanced formatting capabilities
- ☐ Numbering, bulleting, and shading tools
- ☐ Multiple document views
- ☐ Web-page development for the Internet
- ☐ Mail merge for creating personalized form letters
- ☐ Outlining tools

Figure 1.3 shows a Word 97 editing session. The user is editing a business letter to send to a client.

## Introducing Excel 97

Although Excel 97 can be used for non–numeral-based worksheets, Excel 97's primary goal is to help you organize financial information such as income statements, balance sheets, and forecasts. Excel 97 is an electronic worksheet program that supports many features, including

- ☐ Automatic cell formatting
- ☐ Proofing tools, such as spell checking
- ☐ Powerful maps, charts, and graphs that can analyze your numbers and turn them into simple trends
- ☐ Automatic row and column completion of value ranges

**1**

□ Tools to generate multiple what-if scenarios that help you decide between courses of action

□ Automatic worksheet formatting to turn your worksheets into professionally produced reports.

**Figure 1.3.**
*Word 97 helps you create, edit, and format letters.*

Figure 1.4 shows an Excel 97 editing session. The user is getting ready to enter invoice information for a sale. As you can see, Excel 97 can start with a pre-designed form. If you've worked with other worksheet programs, you might be surprised at how fancy Excel 97 can get.

## Introducing PowerPoint 97

Before PowerPoint 97, users had no way to generate presentations without making a tedious effort to design each color slide using some kind of graphics-drawing program. Although presentation products similar to PowerPoint 97 now exist, PowerPoint 97 is recognized as the leader. PowerPoint 97 is a presentation program that supports many features including

□ Automatic proofing tools such as spelling, grammar, and hyphenation

□ Sample presentation slides and slide collections that provide you with a fill-in-the-blank presentation

□ The capability to turn Word 97 document outlines into presentation notes

□ A slide projector that shows you the results of your presentation design

□ Complete color and font control of your presentation slides

**Figure 1.4.**

*Excel 97 helps you create, edit, and format numeric worksheets.*

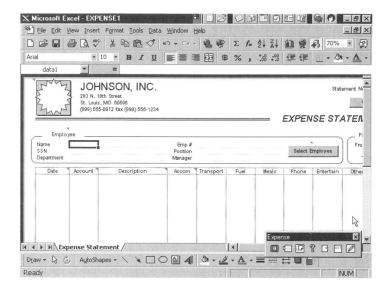

Figure 1.5 shows a PowerPoint 97 editing session. The user is getting ready for a presentation and has only a few minutes to prepare ten color slides for the meeting. With PowerPoint 97, a few minutes is more than enough!

**Figure 1.5.**

*PowerPoint 97 helps you create, edit, and format presentations.*

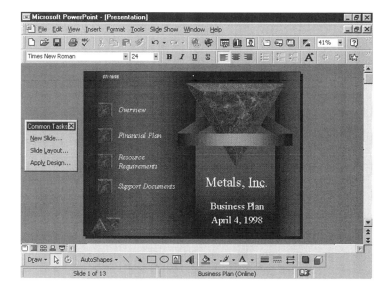

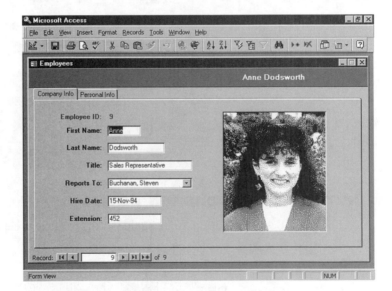

## Introducing Access 97

Access 97 provides one of the most comprehensive database systems available today. Access 97 goes far beyond other databases and supports many features, including

☐ Automatic proofing tools such as spelling, grammar, and hyphenation of data

☐ The capability to filter data rows and columns so you see only data you want to see

☐ Sorting of data by any value

☐ Report-generation that allows you to track and publish your data

☐ Complete relational database support to reduce data redundancies

☐ The capability to produce custom labels for any printer

☐ Automatic summary provisions such as totals, averages, and statistical variances

Figure 1.6 shows an Access 97 editing session. The user is editing employee records. Notice that Access 97 accepts and tracks all kinds of data, including numbers, text, and even pictures embedded as objects.

**Figure 1.6.**

*Access 97 manages your database data.*

## Introducing Outlook 97

Outlook 97 is a simple tool to manage your business and personal meetings, to-do lists, contacts, and appointments. Outlook 97 provides many features, including

☐ The capability to track your computer activities in a journal

☐ Management of your to-do lists

☐ The capability to track your contact information, including multiple phone numbers and computerized e-mail addresses

☐ The capability to schedule appointments

☐ The capability to plan people and resources you'll need for meetings

☐ The capability to sound an alarm before an important event

Figure 1.7 shows an Outlook 97 calendar screen. The user is getting ready to schedule a meeting on a particular day. As with all the Office 97 programs, you can modify Outlook 97's screen elements so they appear in a format most helpful to your needs.

**Figure 1.7.**

*Outlook 97 tracks appointments and events.*

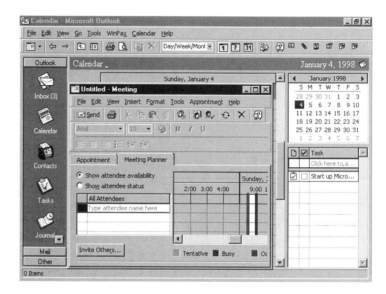

## Introducing Bookshelf Basics

Bookshelf Basics provides an online guide to the following references:

☐ The American Heritage Dictionary

☐ The Original Roget's Thesaurus

☐ The Columbia Dictionary of Quotations

The power of Bookshelf Basics becomes obvious when you're working in one of the other Office 97 products and you need a definition. Call Bookshelf Basics from the Word 97 menu, and Bookshelf Basics provides a definition for whatever word you need. Figure 1.8 shows a Bookshelf Basics screen. The user is looking up a reference for Italy.

1

**Figure 1.8.**
*The Bookshelf Basics dictionary provides more than simple definitions.*

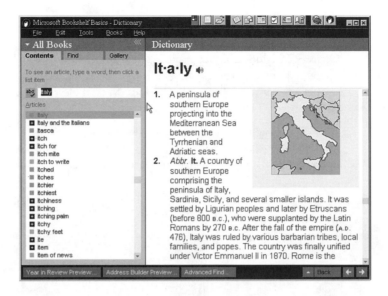

**NOTE**

Microsoft unabashedly supplied Bookshelf Basics in Office 97 as a sales preview for the full version of Microsoft Bookshelf, which includes nine reference works including an encyclopedia, Internet reference, and an online atlas. You might want to join Microsoft's subscription program that sends you a new Microsoft Bookshelf each year.

**TIP**

If you click the speaker icon next to the word *Italy*, you hear the word *Italy* spoken. Bookshelf Basics provides full multimedia support.

**Step-Up**

If you've mastered some of the advanced programming techniques behind earlier versions of Office 97 products, you'll be glad to know that every program in the Office 97 suite supports Visual Basic for Applications (VBA), Microsoft's standard application programming language compatible with Visual Basic for Windows. Word 97 does not, however, support Word Basic (the programming language that Microsoft included with previous versions of Word) due to Word Basic's incompatibility with other applications.

# How to Get Results

Office 97 includes an electronic version of *Getting Results*. This electronic book does not operate like an electronic manual; *Teach Yourself Office 97 in 24 Hours* teaches you far more about Office 97 than *Getting Results* does. Nevertheless, *Getting Results* shows you graphically what Office 97 is all about.

If you want to take a few minutes to browse *Getting Results*, click the Getting Results button on the Office Shortcut bar. The Office Shortcut bar is the row of buttons you see at the top of your Windows screen (Figure 1.9 shows the location of the Getting Results button).

**Figure 1.9.**

*The Office Shortcut bar gives you access to Office 97 products.*

The Getting Results button

**WARNING**

Depending on your installed options, your Office Shortcut bar might look different from Figure 1.9's.

Hour 2, "For Windows Newcomers," explains more about the Office Shortcut bar. For now, you do not need to understand the rest of the buttons on the bar. When you click the Getting Results button, Office 97 displays the first page of the electronic *Getting Results* book. Click a topic to see it in more detail.

As you move your mouse pointer over the screen, the pointer changes to a hand cursor, which lets you know when you can click for additional information. When you click a topic, Office 97 automatically turns the electronic page to show you more of the book's information.

# Binding your Work

If you've ever used a PC program you've probably created *data files* that hold information. For example, Word 97 data files hold documents and Access 97 data files hold databases.

 A *data file* is a disk file that contains related information.

If you want to use one of the Office 97 products to create multiple data files, you have these options:

☐ Create your files one at a time, saving the files to disk before clearing your workspace and creating the next file.

1

☐ Create your files one at a time, but keep each file in memory. For example, you can edit multiple documents at the same time in Word 97 (Ctrl+F6 switches between the documents).

The common theme in these multiple-file options is that you use the same program to create and edit the files. A problem can arise when working with a suite of programs such as Office 97. Suppose you're working on a project requiring two worksheets, three proposal documents, a database, and a color presentation. Office 97 includes a *binder* that lets you keep track of all work within a particular project, even if you must use separate Office 97 programs to create each of the project's files.

**NEW TERM**  A *binder* tracks Office 97 data files that you want grouped together in a project even when different Office 97 programs created each data file.

As you'll learn in Hour 22, "Office 97's Synergy," the Office 97 Binder is critical for holding multiple jobs that you want to track as a single group. When you start the Microsoft Binder program, you can add existing data files from any Office 97 product as well as create new Office 97 data files.

Figure 1.10 shows a binder that includes five data files (three Word 97 files, one Excel 97 file, and one PowerPoint 97 file). The icon next to each data file indicates the type of the file. To work with any file in the binder, click that file; Office 97 opens the program that you need to edit the file.

**Figure 1.10.**

*The Office 97 Binder keeps track of your project's data files.*

The icons let you know the owner program —

Selected Binder file —

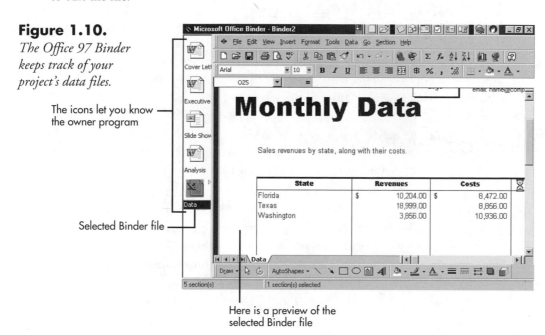

Here is a preview of the selected Binder file

# Summary

This hour introduces the Office 97 programs by showing you a little of what each program can accomplish. Before learning Office 97 specifics, you need to get the "big picture." This hour provides that big picture as well as introduces the Office 97 tools that you'll use.

All Office 97 programs share a common interface. After you learn one Office 97 program, the others are easy to master. Some users find that they can use Office 97 for all of their computer needs.

The next hour covers the Windows basics you need for Office 97. Take a moment to browse the next hour even if you've used Windows before because much of the material is specific to the Office 97 environment.

# Q&A

**Q  I've used Word and Excel. Do I need the other Office 97 products?**

**A**  Only you can answer that question because only you know whether you need a program to keep track of your appointments and contacts (Outlook 97) or your database (Access 97). Only you know whether you'll be called to present a topic in a meeting or at a conference (PowerPoint 97).

If you only need word-processing and worksheet computing, you may not need the other Office 97 products and you only need to install those programs you want to use. However, if you've truly mastered Word and Excel, you'll be glad that Microsoft kept the same uniform interface throughout all the Office 97 products. This allows you to use what you already know in those other products.

**Q  Why don't I see the Office Shortcut bar?**

**A**  Your Office 97 installer probably failed to install the Office Shortcut bar. Simply re-run the Office 97 Setup program and install the Office Shortcut bar. The Setup program acts like most other Windows-based installation programs, but if you feel uncomfortable running the setup program, ask whoever installed your Office 97 to help you.

**Q  Isn't a dictionary easier to use than Bookshelf Basics?**

**A**  If you had to start a Bookshelf Basics program every time you needed a definition, a paperback dictionary would probably be easier to use than Bookshelf Basics.

As you'll see in Hour 3, "Office 97's Neatest Features," when you're working on a Word 97 document (or any other Office 97 data file) and you need an extended definition for the word you just typed, you only need to click the word and press a

1

Bookshelf Basics button to read Bookshelf's definition for the word. This online reference is much quicker than going to a dictionary every time you need a definition.

**Q** **Suppose I want to keep track of names and addresses. Which Office 97 product would I use?**

**A** This is actually a trick question. Word 97, Excel 97, Access 97, and Outlook 97 track names and addresses! Word 97 keeps track of names and addresses for mail merging (sending the same letter to many people), Excel 97 includes a simple database feature that can track items such as names and addresses, Access 97's primary purpose is to track virtually any data in an organized list, and Outlook 97 records all your name and address records. Generally, use Outlook 97 for your names and addresses (all the other Office 97 products can read Outlook 97's data) and save the other Office 97 products for their primary purposes.

**Q** **Why are Office 97 products simple once I learn one well?**

**A** The Office 97 programs share common interfaces.

**Q** **How can I keep track of four Word 97 documents that belong together for a project?**

**A** Either create the four documents and save them in the same directory or create a new binder for the documents. If there's a chance that you'll need to add a different kind of Office 97 file (other than a word-processed file) at a later time, use a binder to bind Office 97 documents that require different Office 97 programs.

# Hour 2

# For Windows Newcomers

In case Office 97's Windows environment is new to you, this hour briefly covers some of the fundamentals you'll need to use Office 97 effectively. This hour does not give you an in-depth Windows tutorial because plenty of other books do a better job with that. This book reviews the tasks and features that directly relate to Office 97.

Although the Windows 95 interface has been around for a while, many companies are slow to change from older Windows interfaces (such as Windows for Workgroups 3.11) to Windows 95 or Windows NT (the Office 97 operating environments). Therefore, even if you have used previous versions of Windows, you might need this hour's refresher so that you hit the ground running with Office 97.

The highlights of this hour include

- [ ] What the Windows 95 interface provides
- [ ] How to access the Start menu's power

☐ Why the Open dialog box is so critical to your Office 97 work

☐ What improvements Office 97 brings to the Windows 95 interface

☐ Where to find ToolTips

☐ How to use tabbed property sheets

☐ How the Print dialog box produces a preview to save you time and paper

☐ Why you should master consistent Windows terminology when learning Office 97 with *Teach Yourself Office 97 in 24 Hours*

 **NOTE**

> You might be able to save time by skimming through this material if you've already seen many of this hour's topics, such as ToolTips. By presenting all the required Windows interface elements in one location, the remaining chapters can concentrate on Office 97 without taking time for Windows reviews throughout the book. This hour is designed to bring the Windows newcomer closer to your level, so you don't have to wade through review material throughout the book. You'll be better able to concentrate on Office 97's differences and improvements.

# The Overall Windows 95 Interface

If you use Windows NT 4.0, Windows 95, or any later version of those operating systems, the interface that your Windows version uses is called the *Windows 95 interface* because it has been around since the first version of Windows 95. The most prominent features of the Windows 95 interface are the Start button and the Start menu (see Figure 2.1).

 The *Windows 95 interface* is the user interface all versions of Microsoft operating systems have used since Windows 95 was released.

 The *Start button* is the button labeled Start from which you display the Windows 95 Start menu.

 The *Start menu* is the menu from which you can start any Windows program.

Your Windows screen might differ slightly from Figure 2.1 due to the programs and icons you have installed on your computer. In addition, the *wallpaper*, or screen's background picture, might differ from the figure's. Two things should be similar: You should see the Start menu when you click the Start button, and you should see two commands, New Office Document and Open Office Document, at the top of your Start menu.

**2**

**Figure 2.1.**

*Click the Start button to see the Windows 95 Start menu.*

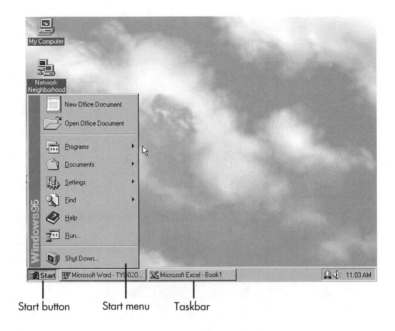

Start button    Start menu    Taskbar

 **NEW TERM** *Wallpaper* is the graphic background on your Windows 95 interface.

The Start menu provides all access to your computer's programs. If you want to start any program, click the Start button, select Programs, and follow the Start menu path to the program. You can start more than one program if you want to share work between two or more programs, such as between Word 97 and Access 97. As you start and run programs, the Windows 95 *taskbar* displays all the program icons on taskbar buttons. Click the taskbar buttons to switch between running programs just as you click the remote control to switch between television programs.

**NEW TERM** The *taskbar* at the bottom of your screen displays all programs currently running.

> **TIP**
>
> You can also switch between running programs by pressing Alt+Tab.

When using Office 97, you have a shortcut to all the Office 97 programs. Select New Office Document if you want to create a new Office 97 document (as you'll learn in Part II, "Processing with Word 97," an Office 97 *document* is any data file you create or edit with Office 97) using any of the Office 97 programs. Select Open Office Document if you want to work on an existing Office 97 document. To *open* a document means that you want to work with the document somehow, just as when you open a file cabinet drawer you want to work with a file from the cabinet.

 A *document* is any Office 97 data file.

 To *open* a document is to load it into your program workspace so you can work with it.

When you open an Office 97 document, Windows displays an Open dialog box such as the one in Figure 2.2.

**Figure 2.2.**

*The common Open dialog box.*

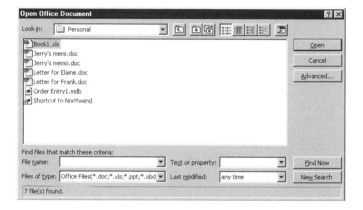

 **NOTE**

All Office 97 programs, and most other recent Windows programs, use an Open dialog box that resembles Figure 2.2's. This common interface lets you more quickly learn new programs.

 **TIP**

As you use Office 97 more and more, you'll learn which *icons* (pictures that represent items on your screen) go with which Office 97 products. When you display the Open dialog box, the icons indicate which Office 97 program created the document listed. For example, the flying W icon represents documents created by Word 97.

**NEW TERM** *Icons* are small colorful pictures that represent items on your Windows screen.

**2**

The Open dialog box is simple or complex, depending on what you need to do with it. Most of the time, you'll see the Office 97 document that you want to open and double-click the document's name to load it. The Open dialog box is smart enough to know which Office 97 product created the document; therefore, if you click a PowerPoint 97 document, the Open dialog box starts PowerPoint 97 and loads the selected document into PowerPoint 97 for you.

Each time a new Office 97 product is introduced in a lesson in this book, that lesson explains the specific ways you can start that particular program. For now, concentrate on getting an overall feel for the Windows 95 interface.

Here is a summary of other common tasks you can perform from the Open dialog box:

☐ If you want to open a document located in a directory or disk drive other than the one showing, or even on a different computer on a network across the Internet, click the Look in drop-down list box and select the location.

☐ You can limit the files shown to specific Office 97 programs by selecting from the drop-down list box labeled Files of type. For example, the Open dialog box displays only Access 97 documents if you select Databases.

☐ The toolbar buttons across the top of the Open dialog box display the files in a different format, giving you more or less detail about the documents that appear.

**NOTE**

As you use Office 97, you'll notice that it consistently maintains a chiseled appearance on its menus and toolbar buttons that previous Office products did not show. For example, as you move your mouse pointer over menu bar items, Office 97 indents the menu bar item to show the depression that would occur if you clicked the item. You'll notice small changes in the design that improve the distinctness of the screen elements. If you've used Internet Explorer 3.0, you'll notice that the Office 97 products often have an Internet Explorer-like look and feel. As you'll learn throughout this book, Office 97 integrates well with the Internet, so that Internet Explorer similarity is intentional.

# ToolTips

As you work with the Office 97 products and dialog boxes, such as the Open dialog box, you'll need to use the toolbar buttons across the top (and sometimes the bottom and sides) of your screen. Office 97 fully supports ToolTips. *ToolTips* are floating toolbar button descriptions that appear when you rest your mouse pointer over any toolbar button. Figure 2.3 shows an Excel 97 ToolTip describing the button to which it is pointing.

**Figure 2.3.**

*ToolTips tell you what
the buttons do.*

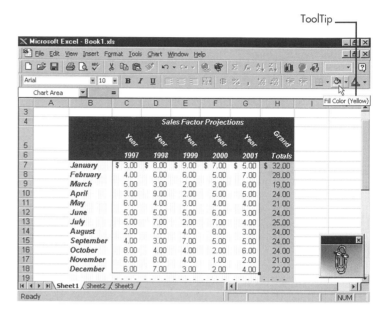

As you read this book, you won't find long boring tables that describe every toolbar button.
Let the ToolTips guide you! Although many of the buttons are obvious, you might need to
use ToolTips to locate a particular button.

# The Office 97 Shortcut Bar

The Start menu is not the only way to start an Office 97 product. In fact, you'll probably
forsake that stand-by menu and select from the *Office 97 Shortcut bar*. Figure 2.4 shows a
typical Office 97 Shortcut bar, which automatically appears at the top of most Office 97 user
screens.

The Office 97 Shortcut bar offers push-button access to any Office 97 product by letting you
open or create an Office 97 document by clicking the appropriate buttons. The Office 97
Shortcut bar always stays active and appears on your screen even if you work in programs that
are not Office 97 programs. Therefore, you'll always be able to access Office 97 programs and
documents from wherever you are.

 The *Office 97 Shortcut bar* displays a toolbar on your screen at all times from which
you quickly can start Office 97 programs and open Office 97 documents.

**2**

**Figure 2.4.**

*Start Office 97 programs quickly with the Office 97 Shortcut bar.*

Click here for options ⎯        ⎯ Office 97 Shortcut bar

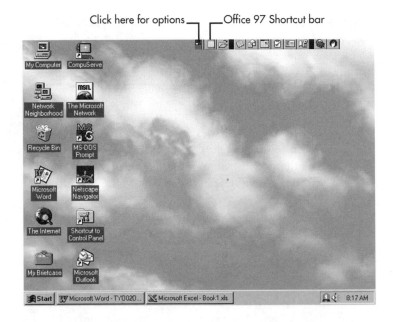

If you click the four-colored icon button on your Office 97 Shortcut bar (no ToolTip exists for this button), the Office 97 Shortcut bar displays a menu from which you can modify the Office 97 Shortcut bar's appearance or remove it from your screen altogether.

**TIP**

If you use certain Office 97 programs more often than others, you might want to select the Shortcut bar's Customize option and add those specific program icons to the Office 97 Shortcut bar. If the Office 97 Shortcut bar contains buttons you rarely use, such as the New Journal Entry button, use Customize to remove one of the existing buttons.

To get rid of the Office 97 Shortcut bar, perform these steps:

1. Click the Office 97 Shortcut bar's colored control icon to display the drop-down menu.

2. Click Exit. Windows displays Figure 2.5's dialog box.

3. If you want to remove the Office 97 Shortcut bar just for this session, click Yes. If you want to keep the Office 97 Shortcut bar from appearing in subsequent Windows sessions, click No.

**Figure 2.5.**
*You control when the
Office 97 Shortcut bar
appears.*

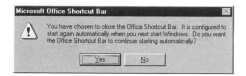

The Office 97 Shortcut bar appears automatically (until you remove it) because Office 97 installs the Office 97 Shortcut bar startup command in your Start menu's Startup folder. If you click Yes to keep the Office 97 Shortcut bar from reappearing, Windows removes the command from your Startup folder. You can add the command back to your Startup folder by selecting from the Start menu's Settings|Taskbar menu's advanced options.

# Dialog Boxes

You've probably worked with dialog boxes before. Earlier in this hour, you saw the Open dialog box. Dialog boxes give you access to a set of related controls and selection options.

Starting with Windows 95, many dialog boxes took on an added dimension. Instead of containing a single set of controls, such as command buttons and text boxes, dialog boxes contain several sets of controls. Each set appears on a tabbed page in the dialog box. Figure 2.6 shows one such dialog box. Notice the tabs across the top of the dialog box. When you click a tab, you'll see an additional set of dialog box controls.

**Figure 2.6.**
*Windows 95 dialog boxes
often contain several
pages.*

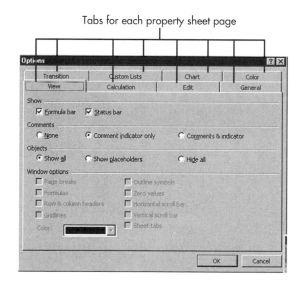

Tabs for each property sheet page

2

Dialog boxes that contain the tabbed pages are often called *property sheets*. When you click your mouse over one of the property sheet tabs, you display a different sheet, or page, within the dialog box. The property sheet dialog box style lets you control much more information from a single menu command.

**NEW TERM** *Property sheets* are the tabbed dialog boxes that are so common in Office 97 and other Windows 95 programs.

# Printing from Office 97

Being a Windows program, Office 97 uses the Windows *printer subsystem* for printing so you'll always see the same print options throughout the Office 97 suite of products. The Windows printer subsystem controls all printing from Windows programs. Therefore, no matter what kind of printer you connect to Windows, Office 97 only requires you to inform Office 97 of the print type or location of the printer.

**NEW TERM** The *printer subsystem* is the Windows printer interface that all your Windows programs write to.

The Windows printer subsystem lets you direct printed output to any printer device, including fax/modems that you might have connected to your computer. Therefore, you can print or fax an Office 97 document at any time. Your Windows system always defaults to your system's primary printer, but you can override the default printer by selecting a different target printer.

The most common way to initiate the print process is to select File|Print. Office 97 opens Figure 2.7's Print dialog box.

**Figure 2.7.**
*The Print dialog box controls all Office 97 printing.*

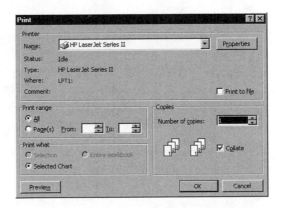

**WARNING**

Your print dialog box might look different depending on your printer hardware.

The Office 97 products always contain a Print toolbar button that you can use to print, but the Print toolbar button does not display the Print dialog box. Therefore, if you want to select a printer that differs from your usual Windows default printer, or if you want to select different print options, you'll need to use the Office 97 File | Print menu command to display the Print dialog box before you print.

From the Print dialog box you can change several options, including

- ☐ The number of copies
- ☐ The range you want to print, such as selected pages or only a portion of text from a single page
- ☐ The collation selection of output papers
- ☐ The target printer

None of the lessons in this book discuss the Print dialog box because you now know everything you need to print from all the Office 97 products. Before printing, however, you'll almost always want to preview your printed output on the screen. Although Office 97 products are generally *WYSIWYG*-based (What You See [on the screen] Is What You Get [on the page]), you rarely see an entire page at once unless you use an extremely high-resolution monitor and graphics adapter. Therefore, when you click the Print dialog box's Preview button (or select File | Print Preview from the menu bar), Office 97 displays the printed page on your screen, as shown in Figure 2.8. If your output looks correct, you can send the output to paper.

**NEW TERM** *WYSIWYG* (pronounced *wizzy-wig*) is an acronym for *What You See Is What You Get*, and refers to the concept that your screen shows your output as it will look on paper.

**TIP**

When previewing any Office 97 document, your mouse pointer will change to a magnifying glass. If you click the glass over any of the preview, Office 97 will magnify the preview to make the text more readable (at the expense of displaying less of the preview). Click the magnifying cursor once again, and the preview will revert back to its original full-page state.

**Figure 2.8.**

*Preview your output before printing it.*

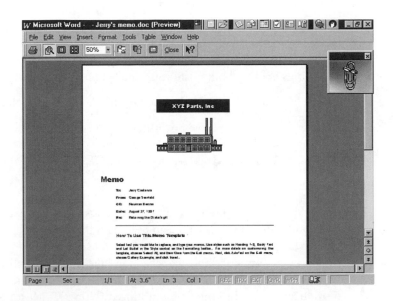

# A Word on Shortcut Keys

Often, a menu option or toolbar button has an associated *shortcut key* (sometimes called an *accelerator key*) that you can press to trigger the same operation. For example, if you display Word 97's File menu, you'll see that Ctrl+S is an equivalent shortcut key for the File | Save option. The Office 97 suite of applications uses a consistent shortcut key interface across all programs. Therefore, Ctrl+S opens the Save dialog box in every Office 97 program. When you learn one Office 97 program's shortcut key, you will know the other program's equivalent key as well.

 A *shortcut key* is a keystroke, often combined with the Ctrl key, that triggers a menu option of the toolbar button's operation.

 *Accelerator key* is another name for *shortcut key*.

The primary goal of this book is to acquaint you with Office 97 as quickly as possible, showing you the basics as well as useful shortcuts and tricks to make your Office 97 life simple. Ideally, you will learn in such a way that your mastery stays with you. Generally, Office 97 offers several ways to do the same thing. This book will not discuss a lot of the shortcut-key equivalents. You'll see shortcut-key equivalents when selecting from Office 97 menus, and you'll learn those shortcut keys as you use Office 97.

If a shortcut key seems obvious (for example, Ctrl+S for the Save operation) and generally easier to use (as opposed to an equivalent menu option or toolbar button), this book will teach you the shortcut key for the task. If, however, the shortcut-key is not the best way to trigger a task, this book will not waste your time with the shortcut-key description.

As you use Office 97, you'll discover the shortcut keystrokes that you prefer. Everybody has different preferences.

# A Final Word on Windows

Although this book does not assume you are a Windows guru, and although this book teaches Office 97 from the ground-up, this book does assume you possess those basic Windows skills that you can pick up in less than an hour with the Windows Tour (available from the Start menu's Help option). Therefore, you won't find any instructions for using the mouse except where the mouse specifically works in a unique way with Office 97. (Appendix A, "Bonus Hour: Using the IntelliPoint Mouse," covers the IntelliPoint mouse, a new mouse Microsoft introduced about the time they introduced Office 97. Most people are newcomers to the IntelliPoint mouse, so you'll want to check out its features to determine whether you want to switch to using it.)

Just to keep terminology straight throughout the book, take a moment to study the callouts in Figure 2.9. When this book mentions the Control menu or the window's Close button, you'll know exactly what the book is discussing.

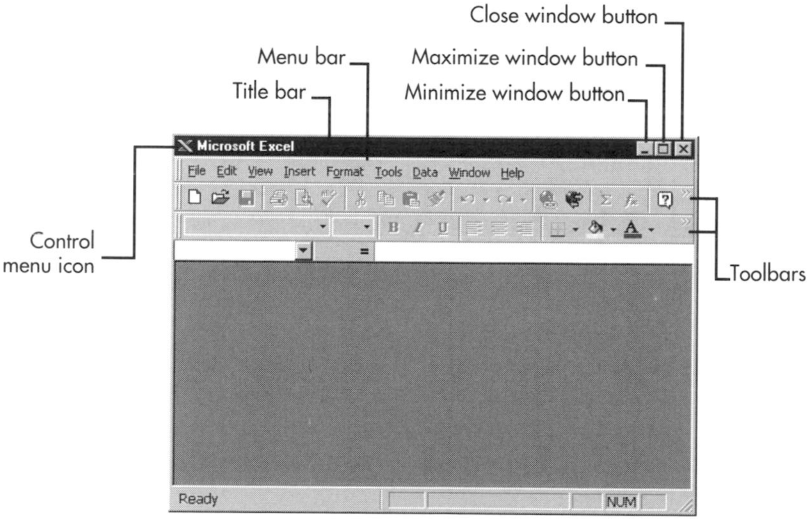

**Figure 2.9.**

*Common window element descriptions.*

**2**

**NOTE**
When you maximize a window's size by clicking the Maximize Window button, that button changes to the Resize Window button.

## Summary

This hour quickly summarizes the fundamental Windows skills that you'll need before diving into Office 97. If you've used the Windows 95 interface before, you'll feel right at home with Office 97. One of the primary reasons for covering this material early in the book is so that the rest of the book can use a level of terminology that all readers will understand.

The next hour moves from the standard (the Windows 95 interface) to the superstandard by explaining and demonstrating Office 97's neatest features. Whether you're an Office 97 novice or expert, you'll be blown away by what Office 97 can do!

## Q&A

**Q  I'm used to Windows 3.1, so can I begin using this book?**

**A**  Yes. Although the Windows 95 interface is new, most of your Windows 3.1 skills will still work for you. You'll see the Windows 95 improvements as soon as you begin to use Office 97.

However, you will lack skills to use some of the more useful Windows 95 interface features, such as Explorer, until you learn more about the Windows 95 interface than this book can cover. (The Windows 10-minute online tour, available from the Start menu's Help option, should explain enough to get started.) Nevertheless, you don't need to know any more about the Windows 95 interface than you'll learn in this hour's lesson to use Office 97 to its fullest.

**Q  I'm brand new to Windows. What are some good introductory Windows books?**

**A**  *Teach Yourself Windows 95 in 24 Hours* and *Windows 95 Unleashed,* both published in 1995 by Sams Publishing.

2

# Hour 3

# Office 97's Neatest Features

This hour previews some of Office 97's coolest features. If you're new to the Office environment, this hour will whet your appetite for Office 97. Office 97 provides some rather unusual help with the Office Assistant and the plain-language Answer Wizard. Every product in the suite of Office 97 programs includes these helpful guides.

Office 97 attempts to move beyond the normal Windows-based help system. If you've used Windows programs in the past, you've probably read online documentation, clicked hypertext links to other related topics, and searched for keywords you need help with. Office 97 includes all these standard online help tools, but takes that help to a new level of functionality. In a way, Office 97 looks over your shoulder and offers advice when it sees a better way to do something.

In addition to improving the routine Windows online help system, Office 97 helps disabled users by providing several accessibility options. These options magnify the screen's views and offer keyboard shortcuts that the user can define and control.

Perhaps the biggest add-on that Office 97 provides is Bookshelf Basics. Bookshelf Basics gives you an online reference to several reference books and includes several multimedia options. In this hour you'll learn how to run Bookshelf Basics as a standalone application (later in the book you will learn how to integrate the Bookshelf Basics entries into other Office programs).

The highlights of this hour include

- [ ] What Office Assistant is
- [ ] How to select a different Office Assistant style
- [ ] When Office Assistant offers help that you didn't even know you needed
- [ ] Which group-related document options Office 97 supports
- [ ] How Office 97 supports several data types
- [ ] Which accessibility options Office 97 supports
- [ ] How to select from the Bookshelf Basics books
- [ ] Where to look for Bookshelf Basics' multimedia entries

# The Office Assistant

When you start any Office 97 program, the first feature you'll notice is the *Office Assistant*, an online cartoon character that hangs around as you work. Figure 3.1 shows the Office Assistant (named *Clipit*), which appears when you start Office 97.

**NEW TERM**   *Office Assistant*, an animated cartoon character, offers advice as you use Office 97.

**Figure 3.1.**
*The Clipit Office Assistant helps you use Office 97.*

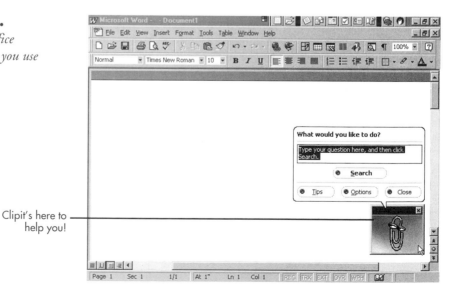

Clipit's here to
help you!

**3**

**NOTE**

If you see a different cartoon character, your Office Assistant is set to display a different character. The next section explains how to change the Office Assistant's animated character.

**Step-Up**

The Office Assistant replaces the TipWizard found in earlier Office products.

Keep your eyes on the Office Assistant as you work because you'll be amused at the contortions it goes through as it provides advice. If you have your speakers turned on, the Office Assistant makes noises when offering help to keep your attention.

Move the Office Assistant to a different screen location by dragging its window. If the Office Assistant notices that it is about to cover an area in which you are typing, it moves out of the way.

Suppose you want help italicizing Word 97 text. You can search through the online help system (via the Help menu), or you can click Office Assistant and type a question such as How do I italicize text? and press Enter. Office Assistant analyzes your question and displays a list of related topics (as shown in Figure 3.2). Click the topic that best fits your needs, and Office Assistant locates that help topic and displays the Help dialog box.

**Figure 3.2.**

*Office Assistant offers lots of advice.*

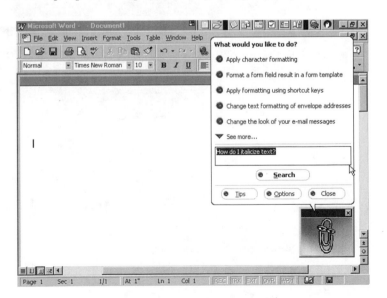

The Office Assistant looks over your shoulder and watches your actions. If you do something and Office Assistant knows a better way, a yellow light bulb that you can click for shortcut information is displayed. For example, if you create a numbered list using menus, Office Assistant displays the light bulb to let you know that you can create a numbered list by clicking a button on the toolbar.

# Customizing Office Assistant

If you work on a slow computer, you might want to disable Office Assistant to keep things moving a little faster. When you right-click Office Assistant, a pop-up menu appears with these options:

- Hide Assistant—Gets rid of Office Assistant. Display Office Assistant again by clicking the toolbar's Office Assistant button.

- See Tips—Displays a tip of the day. Click the Back and Next buttons to read additional tips.

- Options—Displays Figure 3.3's Office Assistant dialog box, from which you can control the behavior of the Office Assistant (such as Office Assistant's response to an F1 key press).

**Figure 3.3.**

*Control the way that Office Assistant behaves.*

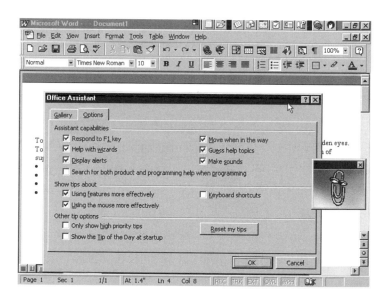

- Choose Assistant—Lets you change to a different animated Office Assistant character. As you work with Office 97, check out all the Office Assistants because they are fun to see.

☐ Animate—Causes Office Assistant to dance around its window; Office Assistant likes to show off! Select Animate a few times to see Office Assistant's contortions. As Office Assistant offers advice, it is likely to move through these animations while helping you. For example, if you attempt to exit a program without saving your work, Office Assistant is likely to knock on its window to get your attention (you'll even hear the knocking!).

Office 97 includes several Office Assistants to help you do your job. They differ in their animations, but not in their advice. Suppose you get tired of Clipit and decide that you want to see a different Office Assistant. Try this:

1. Right-click Office Assistant.

2. Select Choose Assistant. Office Assistant displays an Office Assistant Gallery screen.

3. Click Next to cycle through the Office Assistants. Each Office Assistant goes through a song and dance to convince you that it's the best. Figure 3.4 shows the Power Pup Office Assistant.

**Figure 3.4.**

*The Power Pup Office Assistant sniffs out answers for you.*

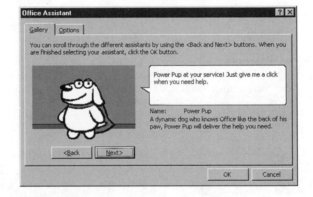

4. When you come to an Office Assistant you like, click the OK button to begin using that Office Assistant.

Here are the Office Assistants from which you can choose:

☐ Clipit—An animated paper clip that contorts in all shapes to point you to solutions.

☐ The Dot—A bouncing happy dot that keeps your attention.

☐ The Genius—An Einstein-like 3D character.

☐ Hoverbot—A futuristic robot.

☐ Office Logo—A twirling colorful Office 97 logo that spins when your attention is needed.

- [ ] Mother Nature—An environmentally correct guide for erasing mistakes and answering questions.
- [ ] Power Pup—A super-hero puppy that sniffs out answers for you.
- [ ] Scribble—A feline guide that purrs when you (not she) need attention.
- [ ] Will—A Shakespearean bard whose ancient advice still works for today's computers.

# Working in Groups

Although many people will use Office 97 on single-user computers, Microsoft understands the needs of today's office worker. Today's computers are often networked to other computers, either through a local area network, an Internet connection, or an *intranet* connection.

 An *intranet* is an internal network system that uses an Internet browser, such as Microsoft's Internet Explorer, to access information from other computers on the local area network.

As long as you use Microsoft Exchange, Microsoft Mail, or cc:Mail, you can create a Word 97 document and send it to users on your mail system. When you send a document, the receivers can read the document and even make changes to the document. Word 97 keeps track of revisions. Each reviewer's notes appear separate from the others. Using Word 97's Revision menu, you'll be able to accept or reject any of the reviewer's comments when the document gets back to you.

 **TIP** Office 97 lets you integrate all Office 97 products. Therefore, if you want to send an Excel 97 worksheet graph to someone over the network, embed that graph into a Word 97 document (as explained in the last part of this book) and send the Word 97 document. The graph will travel along with the document.

Office 97 supports these three document-routing options:

- [ ] Send a document—Sends a copy of your document to your list of reviewers. Each reviewer can make changes and return the document to you.
- [ ] Route a document—Sends a single copy of your document to each reviewer in turn. Every subsequent reviewer is able to read the previous reviewer's comments and add his own. The document finally gets back to you after the final reviewer makes revisions.

☐ Post a document—Sends a copy of your document to a public folder that everyone on your receiver list can read. Posting is useful when you have a company-wide policy or message that you want everyone to read. Posting requires that Microsoft Exchange Server be run with a Public Folder shortcut. Your network administrator should be able to help set up a public folder.

Word 97 keeps track of who made each revision. You can have the reviewers make changes to a copy or to the original document.

**TIP**

If the reviewers insert sound objects into the routed document, they can review the document with speech as well as with editing marks!

# The New View of Data

Office 97 understands today's data needs. In the past, you worked primarily with text in word processors and primarily with numbers in electronic worksheets. Today's multimedia computers require much more data support from programs. For example, a database might hold text, numbers, pictures, sounds, and even Internet hyperlink connections! Using OLE, COM, and ActiveX technologies (the advanced data-sharing and linking tools Office 97 uses to track all kinds of data), your documents will really come alive. You are no longer bound by outdated data limitations.

# Accessibility Features

The accessibility features of Office 97 let people with limited vision or limited dexterity use Office 97 products. Here are a few Office 97 accessibility features:

☐ The Change document magnification option magnifies documents for easier viewing (see Figure 3.5). Even the toolbar buttons are larger to make them easier to find.

☐ The Office 97 programs contain many *AutoComplete* features with which you can begin typing items such as dates, times, days of the week or month, names, and any other AutoText entries you set up. Office 97 will complete the entry for you. For example, if you begin typing a month name such as Nov, Word 97 will display a small box with November above your month abbreviation. If you press Enter, Word 97 completes the month name for you! If you type a full month name, such as

March, Word 97 offers to complete your entry with the current date such as March 7, 1997. You can accept the complete date by pressing Enter or ignore it by typing the rest of the sentence as you want it to appear.

☐ You can rearrange toolbar buttons and customize toolbars so they contain only the buttons you need most frequently.

☐ You can apply shortcut keys to just about any task in any Office 97 product. Suppose you need to colorize and boldface an Excel 97 value often; create a shortcut keystroke and press it whenever you need the special formatting.

**Figure 3.5.**

*Magnify your document to make it easier to read.*

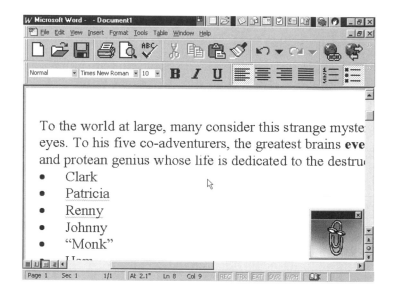

# Bookshelf Basics

Office 97 comes with Bookshelf Basics, which is a three-volume electronic reference set. Bookshelf Basics is a subset of the complete Microsoft Bookshelf product, which you can purchase separately.

**NOTE**

Previous versions of Office did not come with Bookshelf Basics; even though Bookshelf Basics supplies only a subset of Microsoft Bookshelf, the subset is a welcome and free add-on Office 97 product.

Bookshelf Basics is less of a standalone program than Word 97, Excel 97, Access 97, PowerPoint 97, and Outlook 97. In Hour 22, "Office 97's Synergy," you'll learn how to

**3**

access Bookshelf Basics from the primary Office 97 programs. Sometimes, however, you'll want to use Bookshelf Basics by itself, for research or just to pass the time.

To start Bookshelf Basics, click the Office Shortcut bar's Bookshelf Basics button or select Bookshelf Basics from the Microsoft Reference option on your Windows Start menu. Bookshelf Basics opens with a screen similar to Figure 3.6.

**Figure 3.6.**

*The opening Bookshelf Basics screen.*

**NOTE**
Depending on how your version of Office 97 is set up, Bookshelf Basics might present you with a Preview of the Day screen, much like the screen shown in Figure 3.7. The previews give you glimpses of the full-featured Microsoft Bookshelf product. You can order the full version by clicking the preview's Subscribe/Upgrade hypertext link or by phone, fax, mail, or modem. Click the Main hypertext link to return to Bookshelf Basics.

When you start Bookshelf Basics, you'll see the All Books label in the upper-left corner of the screen. Bookshelf Basics is letting you know that the search list of articles is a collection of all topics from all books within Bookshelf Basics (Bookshelf Basics includes a dictionary, a thesaurus, and a book of quotations, as well as a preview of the other Microsoft Bookshelf books). If you search for a subject, Bookshelf Basics will look through all the books.

If you want to limit the search to one of the three primary books within Bookshelf Basics, such as *Columbia Dictionary of Quotations*, click the All Books label and select Quotations from the list that appears to convert the article list to a set from that book only.

**Figure 3.7.**

*The Preview screen shows you a glimpse of the full Microsoft Bookshelf program.*

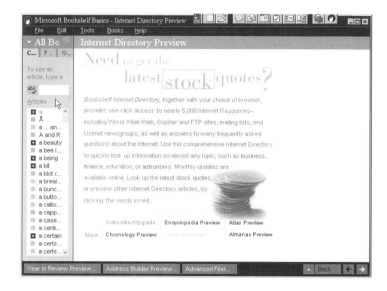

## Getting a Definition

Suppose you want to know the definition of the word *amerce*. Perform these steps:

1. Update the article list to show only entries from the dictionary (as described on the previous page).

2. Type the letters of the search word. As you type, the article list updates to show words from the dictionary that begin with the typed letters. As soon as you type the first four letters, you will see an article entry for *amerce*. Although you can scroll the article list to search, scrolling is not precise due to the large number of dictionary entries.

3. Click the plus sign next to amerce to display both entries. When multiple entries appear, the plus sign expands the article list to show all details. If only a single entry appears, click the green box next to the entry to see that definition.

4. Click amerce on the expanded list to see the definition shown in Figure 3.8.

When searching for multiple definitions, you can click Back to look through the list of words you've found. Print the definition by selecting File | Print Article. Listen to the word by clicking the speaker icon next to the entry.

**3**

**Figure 3.8.**

*Finding a definition for amerce.*

**TIP**

If you need help with the pronunciation symbols, click the phonetic spelling (which appears in red) next to the word's entry to display Figure 3.9's Pronunciation Key dialog box.

**Figure 3.9.**

*The dictionary offers standard pronunciation help.*

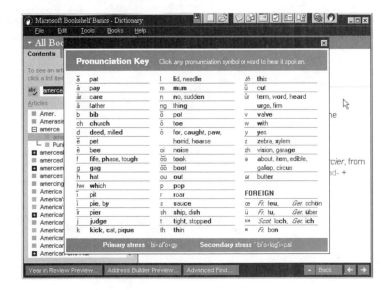

## Getting a Synonym

To search the Bookshelf Basics thesaurus for a synonym, such as all words related to the word *tactile*, perform these steps:

1. Select Thesaurus from the All Books item to limit your search to *Original Roget's Thesaurus*. Bookshelf Basics updates the article list to show only entries from the thesaurus. If you looked up the definition for *amerce* in the previous section, you'll notice that Bookshelf Basics automatically selects to find synonyms for the word *amerce*.

2. Type the word whose synonym you want to find (in this case, tactile). Like the dictionary, the Bookshelf Basics thesaurus updates the article list to display thesaurus entries for your search word as you begin typing the word.

3. Click tactile to display the synonym entry (see Figure 3.10).

If you click any of the red synonyms in the list, Bookshelf Basics displays that entry's synonym list.

**NEW TERM**     A *synonym* is a word with a meaning similar to that of another word.

**Figure 3.10.**

*Seeing the synonyms for tactile.*

**3**

## Getting a Quotation

To search the Bookshelf Basics book of quotations for a quote by author (John Adams, for example) or by subject, perform these steps:

1. Select Quotations from the All Books item to limit your search to the *Columbia Dictionary of Quotations*. Bookshelf Basics updates the article list to show only entries from the quotations book. If you looked up the synonyms for *tactile* in the previous section, you'll notice that Bookshelf Basics automatically selects to find quotations relating to the word *tactile*.

2. Type Adams, John to select the article of quotes by John Adams. Notice that more than one quotation by Adams appears.

3. Click the plus sign to expand the quotes by John Adams.

4. Click the third entry to see what John Adams said about democracy. You'll see Figure 3.11's screen.

**Figure 3.11.**
*Reading a quote.*

**NOTE**

The Bookshelf Basics quote always displays the quotation's source.

## Other Bookshelf Basics Options

The previous sections explain how to access specific topics within Bookshelf Basics. If you want to search for *all* occurrences of a subject, click the Find tab and type an entry to uncover every indexed location of a Bookshelf Basics topic.

Perhaps even more interesting if you are new to Bookshelf Basics is the Gallery tab. When you click the Gallery tab, Bookshelf Basics displays all the sound, image, and multimedia video entries that appear in Bookshelf Basics.

When you begin to explore Bookshelf Basics, search through the gallery to see and hear the multimedia entries. Figure 3.12 shows a volcano demonstration that you can watch.

**Figure 3.12.**

*The Bookshelf Basics multimedia entries are fun to watch.*

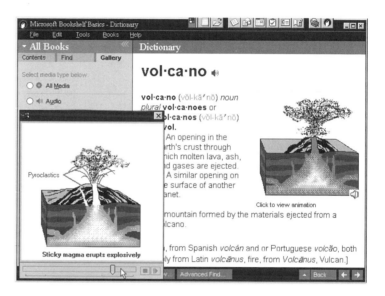

All the gallery entries appear under their particular article list when you search for them from the Bookshelf Basics books. The gallery, however, presents the sounds, images, and multimedia entries in a single place so you can browse.

**TIP**

> The full retail version of Microsoft Bookshelf provides many more gallery entries than does Bookshelf Basics.

**3**

# Summary

This hour introduces some of the more fun features of Office 97, including the Office Assistant and the Bookshelf Basics. In addition, you learned how Office 97 works in a shared office environment. By routing documents to your co-workers over your local area network (or over the Internet using Office 97's built-in Internet support), you can all work on the same documents and track revisions as each of you review Office 97 material.

Office 97 is available to all users, including those with limited vision and dexterity. Office 97 supports all the Windows 95 interface accessibility options and adds a few of its own.

Office 97's goal is not to be pretty, tricky, or cute (even though Office 97 often is each of those things). Office 97's goal is to help you get your work done as quickly and as accurately as possible. As you progress through these 24 hours, you'll discover that Microsoft achieved its goal for Office 97.

The next hour, "The Power Within Office 97," discusses some of Office 97's more powerful features.

**3**

# Q&A

**Q  What help functions does Office 97 support?**

**A**  Office 97 supports all the help features you've come to expect from a Windows program, including tying help to the F1 function key. This hour showed you the Office Assistant because the Office Assistant is new to Office 97 and provides functionality you've probably never seen in a help system.

Perhaps the best thing about Office Assistant is that it provides help when you don't even request it. If Office Assistant sees a better way to do something, it quietly lets you know by displaying the yellow light bulb. You can ignore Office Assistant's help or you click the light bulb to see what Office Assistant is talking about.

**Q  How can I see Office Assistant only when I need help?**

**A**  Right-click Office Assistant to display the pop-up menu, then select Hide Assistant. The Office Assistant window disappears. When you want to use Office Assistant again, click the toolbar's Office Assistant button. You might want to display the Office Assistant's Options dialog box (right-click Office Assistant and select Options) to change the way Office Assistant responds to you. The Options dialog box lets you modify the timing of Office Assistant's responses.

**Q  Why does Office 97 provide accessibility options when the accessibility options already appear in Windows?**

**A**  Office 97 extends Windows accessibility options. In addition to offering Windows accessibility options, Office 97 provides more advanced keyboard shortcuts such as the capability to finish typing common entries and entries that the user defines. You can also increase the size of the Office 97 icons on the toolbars as well as increase the viewing area of the data.

When you read about the IntelliPoint mouse in Appendix A, you'll learn about its zoom feature, which lets you increase the screen's viewing area with a click and a roll.

**Q  What is the name of the new Office 97 online help guide?**

**A**  Office Assistant.

**Q  How can I prevent Office Assistant from getting in the way when I enter data in an Office 97 product?**

**A**  You can drag the Office Assistant window out of the way or close it completely. Keep in mind, though, that Office Assistant automatically moves if it notices that you are about to enter data at its current screen location.

**Q  Why would I *route* a document instead of *sending* a document if co-workers needed to make revisions?**

**A**  Use the document routing option when you want to send the same document to multiple co-workers and let each co-worker see the revisions made by all the previous co-workers. When you send a document, Office 97 sends a copy to each of the recipients, who then make revisions to that single copy and return it to you. Office 97 users often route when they have more time to wait for revisions and when they want to send a document through a predetermined chain of organizational command.

**3**

# Hour 4

# The Power Within Office 97

This hour offers a glimpse into Office 97's most powerful features. You'll find out that these features do not necessarily have to be difficult to use or hard to understand. As a matter of fact, two of the most powerful Office 97 features, templates and wizards, exist solely to *reduce* your workload.

In addition to templates and wizards, this hour demonstrates how Office 97 integrates with the Internet. Throughout Office 97 you'll find Internet connections that let you support Office 97 with Internet files almost as easily as if the Internet were part of your own computer system.

The highlights of this hour include

- ☐ What templates are
- ☐ When templates are not the best approach
- ☐ What wizards are
- ☐ Where you access wizards
- ☐ How to follow the wizard's construction

☐   Where the Internet fits in with Office 97

☐   How to send your Office 97 data files via faxes and Internet e-mail addresses

# Templates and Wizards

*Templates* and *wizards* simplify your Office 97 work. Microsoft scattered many templates and wizards throughout Office 97. When you use templates and wizards, you can concentrate more on problem solutions and less on problem details.

 A *template* is an outline that holds the format of a document, database, or other Office 97 data file.

 A *wizard* is a step-by-step set of dialog boxes that guides you through the creation of a document or through a complicated selection process (such as a report's design).

The next sections further introduce you to templates and wizards.

**WARNING**

Although templates and wizards are great for Office 97 newcomers, you will not *always* want to start with them. Sometimes, its easier to *understand* an Office 97 program if you create your first few data files (documents, databases, electronic worksheets, and so on) from scratch. For example, until you've created an Access 97 database from scratch and until you've learned all the terminology related to such data, the Access 97 templates and wizards will not make a lot of sense to you. After you master the fundamentals of the Office 97 programs, you can leverage the power that templates and wizards provide.

This hour provides only a preview of Office 97 power. The next part of the book, "Processing with Word 97," begins coverage of the details you need to start creating Office 97 documents. Nevertheless, because templates and wizards are covered in this hour, the rest of the hours can refer to specific templates and wizards without discussing their definitions or explaining how templates and wizards work.

# Templates

A *template* is nothing more than a formatted outline of a document. Suppose you work in the oil-and-gas industry, and you prepare monthly royalty statements. Due to the royalty

**4**

percentage calculations, you correctly determine that Excel 97 will function well as the creation tool for your statements.

When you create your monthly statements, you have three options:

1. Create each royalty statement from scratch
2. Modify a saved royalty statement to change the details for each subsequent statement
3. Create a royalty statement template and fill in the details for each statement

Obviously, the first option requires the most work. Why create a new statement for each royalty holder, adding the titles, date, time, details, summaries, addresses, and footer information? Much of those details will remain the same from statement to statement.

The second option is not a bad idea if the statements are fairly uniform in design and require only slight formatting and detail changes. Some people would feel more comfortable changing an existing statement's details than creating statements from scratch or using a template. New Office 97 users might prefer to change an existing statement until they get accustomed to Office 97's programs.

When you get used to Office 97, however, you'll discover that the template method makes the most sense for long-term statement creation. The template literally provides a fill-in-the-blank statement. You won't have to format the same information from statement to statement, and you're guaranteed a uniform appearance.

## Creating New Templates

The only problem with templates is creating them from scratch. Office 97 comes with several templates for most of the Office 97 programs. You'll find templates for Word 97 letters, faxes, and memos, as well as for Excel 97 expense statements, purchase orders, and other financial documents. Access 97 and PowerPoint 97 also provide templates.

Although Office 97 supplies several pre-designed templates, you won't find an oil-and-gas statement template anywhere in Office 97. Such a statement is too specific, and Microsoft would waste the disk space of the Office 97 users who aren't in the oil-and-gas industry.

 **TIP**

Many companies provide Office 97 templates. For example, several accounting firms provide accounting templates for Word 97 and Excel 97, and you can often find Office 97 templates on the Internet as well as on other online services and *BBS*s.

**NEW TERM** *BBS* stands for *bulletin board system* and refers to dedicated online computers that you can dial into to access files and forums. The Internet and online services such as CompuServe have reduced the importance of dedicated BBSs, but many still exist. Almost every town supports one or more local BBSs.

Given the fact that your oil-and-gas template does not exist in Office 97, you'll have to create your own. To do so, follow these guidelines:

1.  Create a properly formatted sample data file, such as an oil-and-gas statement, so you'll know what design the template is supposed to produce.

2.  Print the sample statement for reference later when you design the template from the sample.

3.  Create a new Office 97 data file such as an Excel 97 worksheet or a Word 97 document. When you do so, Office 97 provides a template option that you can check to let Office 97 know you're creating a template file and not a normal data file. You'll learn the specifics of Office 97 documents throughout this book.

4.  Looking at the document you created in Step 1, add all titles, formatting, and footer information that does not change from statement to statement. Leave blank space for details.

5.  Save the template.

As you can see, the initial template takes some work. After spending the time to create the template, however, subsequent statements will be extremely simple. Instead of creating a statement from scratch, you can create the statement from the template; all you need to do is enter the details. The template supplies the proper formatting and the information that doesn't change from statement to statement.

 **TIP**

> As you learn more about the Office 97 products, you'll learn how to add specialized *fields* to the template to make the creation of your monthly oil-and-gas statements even easier.

**NEW TERM** A *field* is an area of a template you can click to enter information. The field contains all necessary formatting and spacing, so you need only be concerned with the data.

Office 97 supports a template-creation shortcut that you can use after you become more acquainted with Office 97. After you create the initial sample statement (or any other kind of file you want to use as the basis for a template), you can save that file as a template.

Remember that you can save a template at any time after the creation of an Office 97 data file. You might not always start out thinking you need a template. Suppose you create a fax

**4**

cover letter, and then decide that you like the letter enough to use it as a template for subsequent faxes; you can load the fax cover letter file and save the file as a template (putting two versions of the file on your disk: a final specific fax cover sheet and a template for future faxes).

# Using Existing Templates

Office 97 supplies several common templates; each Office 97 product also contains templates of its own. For example, when you want to create a new Excel 97 electronic worksheet, you can select from a blank worksheet or you can click the Spreadsheet Solutions tab to see four icons that represent templates. When you click a template icon, Office 97 shows you a preview of that template (as shown in Figure 4.1).

**Figure 4.1.**
*Office 97 provides several templates that you can preview.*

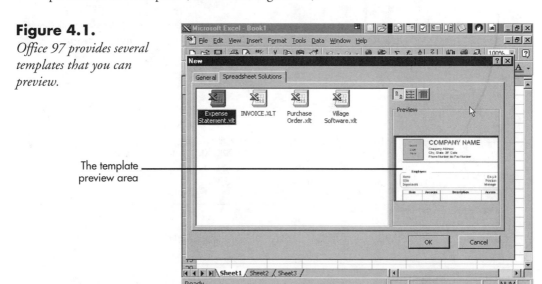

The template preview area

**NOTE**    An Excel 97 electronic worksheet is often called a *spreadsheet*, hence the name on the tab when you select from an Excel 97 template.

After you select a template, the Office 97 program opens it and presents the file (as shown in Figure 4.2). Edit the template and save the details in a separate file to create the data file you require.

**Figure 4.2.**

*You can now fill in the template details.*

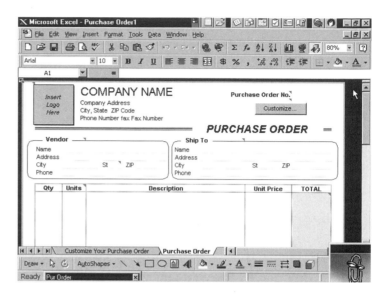

 **TIP**

If you use the same template for the majority of your work, each Office 97 program lets you specify a template that you want to be the basis for *all new files you create*. For example, if you create an Excel 97 template, save the template under the name BOOK.XLT, and store it in the XLSTART directory, Excel 97 automatically loads that template every time you create new worksheets.

# Wizards

One reason so many users have switched to Microsoft-based Office products is Microsoft's wizard technology. Wizards are step-by-step guides that walk you through the development of a document or through a complicated process such as creating an Internet Web page from scratch. (You'll learn more about Office 97's Internet integration later this hour.)

You probably don't have the means to create Office 97 wizards from scratch unless you have an extremely advanced programming background. However, you probably won't ever need to create a wizard yourself; Office 97 can usually supply one for you.

Although each wizard differs in its goal, all follow a similar pattern. Wizards display dialog boxes one at a time, and each dialog box asks for a set of values. As you fill in the dialog boxes, you answer questions to help the program perform a specific job.

**4**

Generally, each dialog box within a wizard contains Next and Back buttons, which you can click to move back and forth through the wizard. If you change your mind after leaving one dialog box, you can back up to that dialog box and change its values.

You'll find several Microsoft-supplied wizards as you create Office 97 documents. For example, if you use Word 97 to create a resume, you can select the Resume Wizard. Figure 4.3 shows the Resume Wizard's opening dialog box.

**Figure 4.3.**

*The opening Resume Wizard dialog box.*

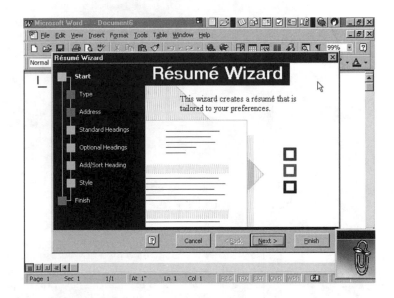

Many wizards contain opening dialog boxes that display information about the wizard. Figure 4.3 informs you that you selected the Resume Wizard. If you click the Next button, the wizard asks which of the following kinds of resumes you want to create:

- ☐ Entry-level resume
- ☐ Chronological resume
- ☐ Functional resume
- ☐ Professional resume

Clicking Next again displays a dialog box that requests your name and address information for the top of the resume. Office 97 is smart enough to automatically pull your name from the Office 97 registration information, but you can change the name if you create resumes for other people.

Continue through the wizard, clicking Next after you fill in each dialog box. Often, wizard dialog boxes present you with a selection of styles, such as the ones shown in Figure 4.4.

**Figure 4.4.**

*Wizards help you determine which styles you want to use.*

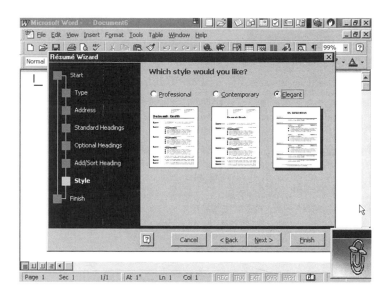

Every wizard's final dialog box include a Finish button. Click this to complete the wizard and generate the document based on the wizard.

**WARNING**

Don't worry if you have no idea how to use the Word 97 Resume Wizard! The goal of this section is simply to familiarize you with wizards so you'll know what to expect. The next part of the book explains how to use Word 97 to create and edit documents. When you become familiar with Word 97's environment, you'll be able to run the Word 97 Resume Wizard, and any other wizard available from Word 97.

Generally, wizards create shells of documents, such as Word 97 template documents or Access 97 databases, that contain no data. It's your job to enter the details.

Sometimes, Office Assistant (covered in Hour 3, "Office 97's Neatest Features") lends a hand and asks whether you want help (as shown in Figure 4.5). Even though the wizard is finished and your resume is ready for details, the Office Assistant offers a few services to make your resume complete.

Notice that the wizard applies formatting to the resume in response to your dialog-box answers. You don't have to center titles or format different parts of the resume. The wizard designs exactly the kind of resume you need.

**Figure 4.5.**

*The Office Assistant lends a hand after you complete a wizard.*

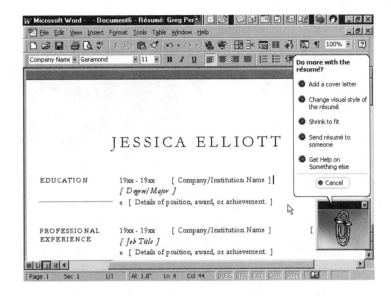

 **NOTE** A document created with a wizard ends up being no different from any other documents, including those you create from scratch. After a wizard designs a document, you are free to make whatever changes you need.

Some wizards are less complicated than Word 97's Resume Wizard. For example, Access 97's Table Wizard creates a single table of data within a much larger database. The Table Wizard asks you fewer questions than the Resume Wizard.

# Get Ready for the Internet and Office 97

Microsoft did not make the Internet interface really stand out; instead, the Internet interface appears as just one of a long line of Office 97 features. The Internet interface between the various Office 97 products differs a little, but the Internet interface is always underneath Office 97, ready to handle the connection.

Office 97 programs contain a Web Toolbar button that you can click to display Figure 4.6's Office 97 Web toolbar. The buttons give you Web access from within an Office 97 program.

**Figure 4.6.**

*Access the Internet from this Office 97 Web toolbar.*

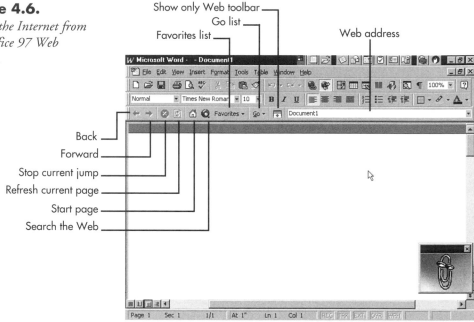

 **TIP**   If you've used Internet Explorer, you'll recognize the format Microsoft uses for the Web toolbar. Several of the Web toolbar buttons match those in Internet Explorer, and the drop-down list box contains a list of your most recently accessed Web *URL* addresses.

**NEW TERM**   *URL*, short for *Uniform Resource Locator*, uniquely identifies an Internet site.

If you're logged on to the Internet when you click a Web toolbar button such as the Start Page button, Office 97 takes you directly to your Start page, substituting your Web browser for the current Office 97 program on your screen. If you're not logged on to the Internet before using the Web toolbar buttons, Office 97 initiates your logon sequence (see the Internet Explorer dialog box shown in Figure 4.7) for you.

As you create Word 97 documents, Excel 97 worksheets, Access 97 databases, and PowerPoint 97 presentations, you'll be able to use the Insert | Hyperlink menu command (an Insert Hyperlink toolbar button also appears on the Web toolbar) to display Figure 4.8's Insert Hyperlink dialog box.

**4**

**Figure 4.7.**

*Office 97 helps you log on to the Internet.*

The Insert Hyperlink dialog box lets you insert a hyperlink to another file on your disk, on your network, or on the Internet. A *hyperlink* is an electronic address within one document that describes a separate, specific Internet location. If the file is an Office 97 document with a named bookmark, specify that location at the bottom of the Insert Hyperlink dialog box to jump directly to that location in the document. The jump takes place when the user of your document clicks the hyperlink.

**NEW TERM**   A *hyperlink* is an electronic address within one document that describes a separate specific Internet location.

**Figure 4.8.**

*Create a hyperlink location to jump to.*

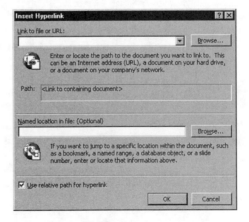

**TIP**   If you're giving a PowerPoint 97 presentation and need to reference something on the Web, simply insert a hyperlink jump to that Web site and click that jump during the presentation. PowerPoint 97 jumps to the Web and displays the page.

4

If you use Internet Explorer as your Web browser, type the name of any Office 97 data file in the URL Address drop-down list and Internet Explorer will display your properly formatted Office 97 data file.

You can even use the Internet as your Office 97 data repository. If you want to edit a document located on an FTP or HTTP site, just enter the document's URL when you open the document. You can also save to HTTP and FTP sites with any of the Office 97 save commands.

 **NOTE**

> A Web site does not have to exist yet for you to insert a hyperlink to it.

One of the major improvements to Word 97 is its capability to effortlessly create Web pages. Just use Word 97's formatting and text-entry capabilities to create a Web page. Select File | Save as HTML to save the file as a fully compatible Web page. For help creating your Web page, start Figure 4.9's Web Page Wizard.

**Figure 4.9.**

*Use the Web Page Wizard for help with Web-page design.*

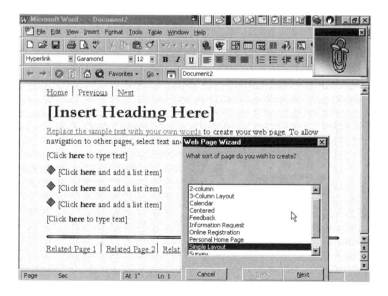

**NEW TERM** *HTML* stands for Hypertext Markup Language, and refers to a formatting language used to display Web pages.

When creating Web pages with Word 97, the Show Web Page Preview toolbar button shows a preview of the Web page with all the HTML codes displayed.

**4**

# The Send To Menu

Some Office 97 products present you with a File | Send To option that sends your data to one of the several locations listed below:

☐ Mail Recipient—Produces Figure 4.10's Send dialog box, in which you can select an e-mail recipient from your Microsoft Exchange address book.

**Figure 4.10.**

*Send a letter or worksheet to someone via e-mail.*

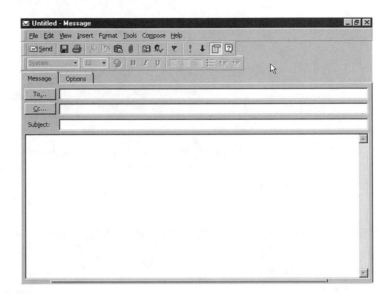

☐ Routing Slip—Produces Figure 4.11's Routing Slip dialog box, in which you can select one or more recipients from your Microsoft Exchange or Outlook 97 address book to send the data file to.

☐ Send To Exchange—Sends your data file to a Microsoft Exchange public folder.

☐ Fax Recipient—Faxes your data file to whatever fax recipient (or recipients) you select. You must have Microsoft fax or a compatible faxing software available on your computer to fax an Office 97 data file to someone.

**TIP**

Say you're writing a business proposal in Word 97, and you realize that you're missing a sales figure that you need. Without leaving Office 97 and starting your regular e-mail program, you can create a note asking for the sales figure. Send that note to your corporate office's e-mail address with Word 97's File | Send To | Mail Recipient menu option.

**Figure 4.11.**

*Route a letter or worksheet to several people for their review.*

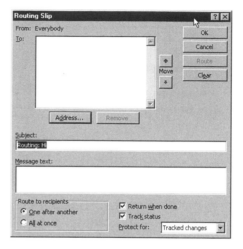

Even Office 97's online help extends far beyond your disk and Office 97 CD-ROM. When you want to know something about Office 97 (or any other Microsoft product), select Help | Microsoft on the Web, then select from one of the several Web sites Office 97 locates for you. Figure 4.12 shows the list of Web-based help areas that Office 97 provides.

**Figure 4.12.**

*Need more help? Office 97 takes you to the Web for additional Microsoft resources.*

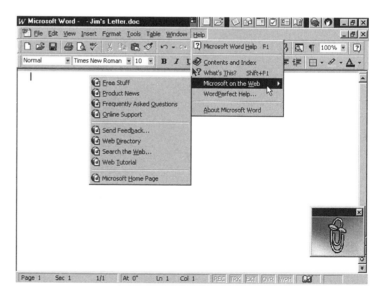

4

# Summary

This hour explores three of the most powerful features in the suite of Office 97 products: templates, wizards, and Office 97's Internet interface.

Previous versions of Office supported templates and wizards, but Office 97 expands and improves the templates and wizards. With Office 97, you have more of a selection. Some of the newer wizards help you create Web-based home pages.

Office 97 doesn't stop with just home pages. To Office 97, your computer is not limited by your hard disk and CD-ROM drive. You can work with any document on any computer connected to yours, whether the other computer is on your local area network or across the globe on the Internet. Office 97 also provides direct links to several Web sites and offers a Web toolbar, from which you can access the Internet's HTTP and FTP sites.

Hour 5, "Welcome to Word 97," introduces Word 97. You'll soon see why Word 97 is considered to be the most powerful word processor available.

# Q&A

**Q  What is the difference between a template and a wizard?**

**A**  A *template* is a formatted shell, design, or empty data file. For example, an Excel 97 accounts-receivables template would contain no data but would contain all the necessary titles and fields necessary for an accounts-receivable worksheet. After you load the template, you'll be able to add specific data easily without having to format titles and totals.

A *wizard* is more than a formatted shell. A wizard is a step-by-step guide that presents a series of dialog boxes. As you fill in each dialog box, the wizard builds a data file for you. You can create complex documents like professional resumes, newsletters, and Web pages, and you need only answer a few simple questions within the dialog box series.

**Q  What if I don't have Internet access?**

**A**  If you don't, you're the only person in the free world without it! Seriously, you will not be any worse off when using Word 97 than those with Internet access except that you will not be able to access Internet sites or send e-mail through Office 97's Internet mail. If you want to get Internet access, there are plenty of companies that would gladly sign you up. Microsoft offers Internet access through the Microsoft Network, and you can access everything you need using Microsoft's Internet Explorer that comes with Office 97.

4

**Q  Why is using a template or wizard not always the best approach when an Office 97 newcomer needs to create a data file?**

**A**  Sometimes you need to understand the Office 97 products a little before understanding the needs of templates and wizards. For example, if you've never created an Access 97 database and do not know the common terms related to database work, you might want to create your first Access 97 database from scratch. After you better understand Access 97 (as you will after completing this book's Part VI, "Tracking with Access 97"), the templates and wizards will make more sense.

**Q  True or False: A template is a file.**

**A**  True.

**Q  True or False: A wizard is a file.**

**A**  False; a wizard often generates a file.

**Q  True or False: A wizard generates a template file.**

**A**  False, but that's a trick question for two reasons. First of all, you haven't learned enough about using Office 97 to know the answer. In addition, *sometimes* a wizard creates a template, but not always. If you use a wizard to generate a data file from scratch, the wizard generally creates a template-like data-file shell that contains no data but contains all the formatting you'll need to create the final detailed document. Many wizards, however, simply walk you through a series of dialog boxes to complete a task such as logging you on to the Internet.

**4**

# PART

# II

## Processing with Word 97

# Hour

# Hour 5

# Welcome to Word 97

This hour introduces Word 97. If you've never used a previous version of Microsoft Word, you'll soon see why Word is the most popular word processor on the market. With Word 97, you'll create documents of any kind with amazing ease. Word 97 helps you painlessly create letters, proposals, business plans, resumes, novels, and even graphics-based multicolumn publications, such as fliers and newsletters.

The highlights of this hour include:

- ☐ How to start Word 97
- ☐ Why quitting Word 97 properly is important
- ☐ Which fundamental editing skills you need to get started
- ☐ How to edit multiple documents at once
- ☐ What the document-centric concept means to all Office 97 products
- ☐ When to find and replace text
- ☐ Where to modify Word 97's automatic editing tools

# Getting Acquainted with Word 97

You start Word 97 when you do one of these things:

- ☐ Click the Office 97 Shortcut bar's New Office Document button and double-click the Blank Document icon to create a new document. (Click the General tab to see the Blank Document icon.)
- ☐ Click the Office 97 Shortcut bar's New Office Document button and click one of the Word 97-based tabs to open a Word 97 template or start a Word-related wizard. (A *template* is a preset document layout that you can modify to create a particular kind of document.)

**NEW TERM** A *template* is a preset document layout that you can edit to create a customized document.

- ☐ Click the Office 97 Shortcut bar's Open Office Document button and select an existing document you want to edit.
- ☐ Use the Windows Start menu to start Word 97 by clicking Microsoft Word from the Program menu.
- ☐ Select a Word 97 document from the Windows Start menu's Documents option. Windows recognizes that Word 97 created the document, and will start Word 97 and load the document automatically. (The Start menu's Document option holds a list of your most recent work.)
- ☐ Click the Office 97 Shortcut bar's Word 97 button to create a blank document. (Depending on your Office 97 Shortcut bar's setup, you might not see the Word 97 button there.)

Figure 5.1 shows the opening Word 97 screen. (Your screen might differ slightly depending on the options that the installer set.)

When you're finished with Word 97, you can quit by performing any of the following:

- ☐ Select File|Exit.
- ☐ Press Alt+F4.
- ☐ Double-click the Control icon.
- ☐ Click Word 97's Close Window button.

**WARNING**

Always quit Word 97 and shut down Windows before turning off your computer, or you might lose your work.

**5**

**Figure 5.1.**

*Word 97's opening screen.*

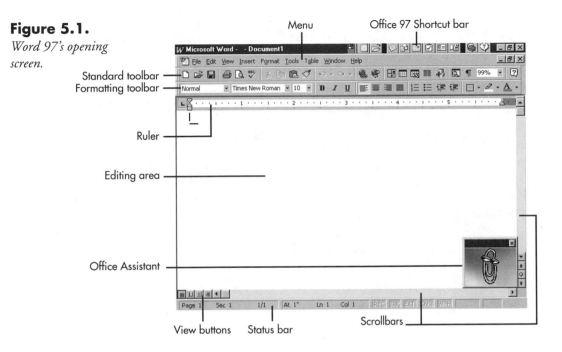

Standard toolbar
Formatting toolbar
Menu
Office 97 Shortcut bar
Ruler
Editing area
Office Assistant
View buttons
Status bar
Scrollbars

# Basic Editing Skills

Just a few years ago, complete word-processing books dedicated themselves to teaching typing, correcting, inserting, erasing, and over-typing skills. Today, tutorials assume you already have these basic skills. This section takes a few minutes to review fundamental Word 97 editing skills and bring you up to speed in case you are new to word processing

If you happen to be someone who is brand new to word processing, Word 97 will certainly be different from whatever else you're used to. If you have used other word processors, hang on to your hat because Word 97's features will knock you over.

---

### Step-Up

Microsoft did not completely revamp Word 95 to create Word 97; rather, Microsoft honed Word 95's environment to sew more Internet and cross-Office 97 hooks into Word 97. You'll like the slicker Word 97 look. For example, you'll wonder why nobody thought to show menu bar selections as push-buttons before (point your mouse to the File menu bar command to see this) or why nobody previously thought to label menu commands with their corresponding toolbar icons.

5

**NOTE**

> Remember the ToolTips described during Hour 2, "For Windows New-comers." If you forget what a toolbar button does, rest the mouse pointer over any button to learn the toolbar button's name.

## Acquaint Yourself with Document Files

Word 97, like all Office 97 products, uses a *document-centric* model. Whether you write a letter or a book (or create an Access 97 database or an Excel 97 worksheet), the text you write appears in a document. *Document* is just an Office 97 term for file. Figure 5.2 shows the many kinds of Office 97 documents that you'll work with.

 A *document* is an Office 97 file.

 *Document-centric* is the notion that Office 97 products work with documents instead of the traditional data files. The document-centric concept lets Office 97 products work uniformly with each other's files.

**Figure 5.2.**

*All Office 97 products interact with documents.*

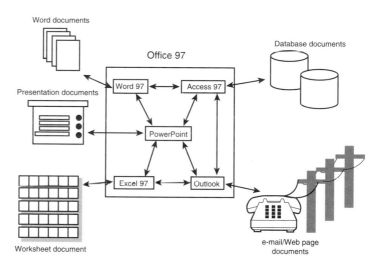

When you create a document, name it just as you label a file folder before you put it in a file cabinet. The document file's extension tells Office 97 which application (Word 97, Excel 97, or something else) works with that particular document. This book often uses the terms *documents* and *files* interchangeably.

**5**

**NOTE**
> Word 97 documents end with the .doc filename extension, as in
> Proposal.doc and Sales Notes.doc (filenames can have spaces in them).
> You don't have to type the extension when opening or saving documents;
> Office 97 automatically attaches the correct extension when needed.

You can use either uppercase or lowercase letters for your document names. Although neither Windows nor Office 97 considers Proposal.doc to be different from PROPOSAL.DOC, the document names are easier to read when you mix the case. If you let Office 97 add the extension, as you should usually do when you name documents, Office 97 adds a lowercase extension, such as .doc.

# Entering Text

When you start Word 97, it displays a blank editing area in which you can type text to create a new document. You also can load an existing Word 97 document and make changes to that document. If you've started Word 97 through the Start menu's Documents option, Word 97 starts with the open document you selected.

**NOTE**
> When you want to work with a document from any Office 97 program,
> you must open that document. The term *open* means to transfer an existing
> document file from disk into the Office 97 editing area. You *save* the
> document to transfer your work to disk for long-term storage. You can
> *close* a document if you want to clear that document from the editing
> area; if you have not first saved changes, Office 97 gives you a chance to
> save your work before closing the document.

**NEW TERM**    *Open* means to transfer a document file from disk into memory.

**TIP**
> If you open an existing document, press Shift+F5 to jump directly to the
> last edit you made. Keep pressing Shift+F5 to jump to each of your
> previous edits.

5

The text you write appears in the editing area. The flashing vertical bar (called the *text cursor* or *insertion point*) shows where your next character will appear. As you type, remember these basic editing points:

- Don't press Enter at the end of a line. As you type close to the right edge of the screen, Word 97 wraps the text to the next line for you.
- Press Enter at the end of each paragraph. Each subsequent Enter key press adds an extra blank line before the next paragraph.
- Press the Backspace key to reverse the text cursor and erase the previous character.
- Use the four arrow keys to move the text cursor around the editing area.
- Click your mouse pointer anywhere inside the editing area to move the text cursor to that location.
- If you type more text than will fit in the editing area, use the scrollbars, arrow keys, PageUp, PageDown, Ctrl+Home, and Ctrl+End keys to scroll to portions of text you want to see.

**NEW TERM** The flashing vertical bar that shows where your next typed character will appear is called the *text cursor*.

**NEW TERM** Another name for text cursor is *insertion point*.

If you write a lot of text, press Ctrl+G (the shortcut for Edit | Go To) to display Figure 5.3's Find and Replace dialog box with a Go To page. When you type a page number and press Enter, Word 97 immediately takes you to that page.

**Figure 5.3.**

*Quickly jump to any page.*

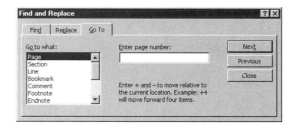

The Office Assistant will always be around if you need help. When you click the small Office Assistance window, Office Assistant displays a list of subjects related to what you're currently trying to do. If you don't want Office Assistant's help, close the Office Assistant's window by clicking the close button. Office Assistant stays out of your way; if your typing starts to get close to Office Assistant, Office Assistant moves to another area of the screen.

**WARNING**

If a red wavy line appears right below any word, Word 97 believes that word is misspelled. If a gray wavy line appears, Word 97 suspects a grammar mistake. Hour 7, "Managinng Documents and Customizing Word 97" illustrates how to correct such errors quickly. If the word is really not misspelled (perhaps you typed a foreign word), you will learn how to teach Word 97 the word so that Word 97 will not flag the error again.

Sometimes you might not know if you pressed Enter two or three times, pressed the spacebar enough, or pressed Tab when you meant to press spacebar to indent some text. If you click the Show/Hide toolbar button, Word 97 displays nonprinting characters (as shown in Figure 5.4). The nonprinting characters show you exactly where paragraph marks, tab presses (indicated by right arrows), and spaces (small dots) occur in your document.

Some writers prefer to show nonprinting characters during the entire editing session, while others prefer to keep the screen clear of the clutter. You can customize Word 97 to show only a subset of the nonprinting characters. Hour 7 shows you how to customize Word 97.

**Figure 5.4.**

*Display nonprinting characters.*

Show/Hide toolbar button

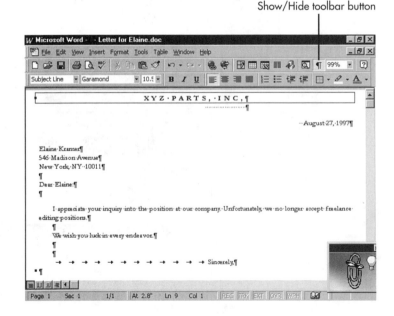

## Edit Multiple Documents at Once

At any point, you can work with multiple documents. For example, you could be typing a letter to a friend and remember that you've got to send a memo to your out-of-state office before the mail runs. Instead of closing your letter, click the toolbar's New button to create a blank document (or select File|New, which runs a new document wizard). The new document appears on top of your letter. Switch between the letter and your memo by selecting from the menu bar's Window option. In most instances, only one document is active (visible on the screen) at one time. When you issue a Close or Save command, Word 97 closes or saves the active document.

**TIP**

Select Window | Arrange All to show *both* (or as many as you currently have open) documents at once, as Figure 5.5 shows. When you display both documents, you can scroll each document individually, rearrange the window sizes to give more or less space to one of the documents, and copy and paste text between the documents. (The section that appears later this hour titled "Copying, Cutting, and Pasting" explains how to copy, cut, and paste text within a document, between windows, and between applications.)

**Figure 5.5.**

*Word 97 lets you edit two or more documents at once.*

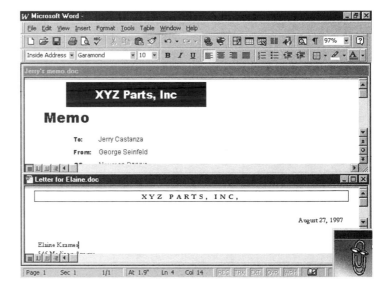

**5**

If you display multiple document windows, the window with the highlighted title bar and window buttons is the active window. It often helps to hide the ruler (View | Ruler) to allow more room for your documents within multiple windows.

## Inserting and Deleting Text

Your Word 97 Status bar will indicate Word 97's insertion mode. If the letters OVR are visible, Word 97 is in *overtype mode*. If OVR is grayed out, Word 97 is in *insert mode*.

 Word 97 uses *overtype mode* when you want typed characters to replace existing characters.

 Word 97 uses *insert mode* when you want to insert newly typed characters before existing characters.

Insert mode is Word 97's default start-up mode. When in insert mode, new typing appears at the text cursor, and new text pushes existing characters to the right (and down the page if needed). When in overtype mode, new text replaces existing text.

To change modes, click the status bar's OVR indicator or select the Tools | Options Edit page and click the Overtype mode option.

---

### Step-Up

Unlike previous Microsoft Word products, Word 97 does *not* let you toggle between insert and overtype modes by pressing the Insert key!

---

**5**

No matter which mode you're in, press Delete to delete any character at the text cursor's position. Any characters to the right of the deleted character will shift left to close the gap.

 **TIP** Here's a tip that even advanced Word 97 gurus often forget: Ctrl+Backspace erases the word to the left of your text cursor, and Ctrl+Delete erases the word to the *right* of your text cursor.

**WARNING**

The Del key on your numeric keypad's period is identical to the Delete key. On some keyboards, no Delete key appears, so your only option is to press Del. Make sure NumLock is off (the keyboard's indicator light will be off) before pressing Del; otherwise, a period will appear where you wanted to delete a character.

Not only can you insert text, but Word 97 also lets you insert blanks. Suppose you forget a space or want to insert three spaces before the start of a paragraph. Move the text cursor to the place you want the blanks (to the left of text that you want to shift right) by pointing and clicking the mouse cursor to anchor the text cursor in position. Press the spacebar as many times as you need to shift the existing text right.

The section found later this hour titled "Selecting Text" illustrates how to select multiple characters. After selecting multiple characters, press Delete to delete the entire selection.

## Locate Text Fast

Word 97 locates text for you. When writing extremely long documents, Word 97's search capabilities come in handy. For example, suppose you're writing a political letter and you want to correct a congressional district's seat name. Ask Word 97 to find all occurrences of the word *district* by following these steps:

1. Select Edit|Find. Word 97 displays Figure 5.6's Find and Replace dialog box. Some people prefer the Ctrl+F shortcut key, while others click the Select Browse Object on the vertical scrollbar and click the binoculars to display the Find and Replace dialog box. The Select Browse Object button has a round dot to distinguish it from the scrolling arrows. Use whatever method you can remember because you'll search (and replace) text quite a bit in word-processing sessions.

**Figure 5.6.**

*Enter text that you want Word 97 to locate.*

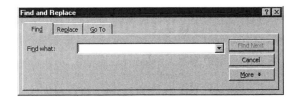

2. Type the word or phrase you want to find. For example, type District to locate that word. By default, Word 97 searches from the top of the document and does not worry about exactly matching your find text with the document's.

**5**

3. When Word 97 locates the first occurrence of the search word, Word 97 highlights the word (as shown in Figure 5.7). When Word 97 highlights a character, word, or phrase, Word 97 inverts the video to make the found text stand out. (As you'll see in the section titled "Selecting Text," this highlighted text is said to be *selected*.)

**Figure 5.7.**
*Word 97 found a match.*

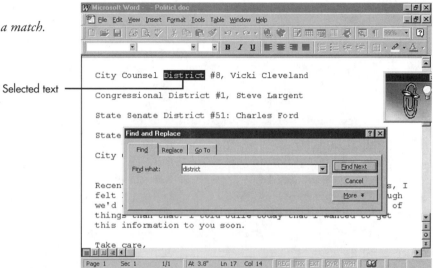

4. If the selected text is the text you wanted to find, click the Cancel button or press Escape to return to your document. Word 97 keeps the selected text highlighted so you can identify the found text. To remove the selection, press an arrow key or click anywhere in the editing area. If the selected text is not the text you want, click the Find and Replace dialog box's Find Next button to search for the next occurrence of the text.

## Replace Text

As you can probably guess from the name of the Find and Replace dialog box, Word 97 not only finds but also replaces text. Perhaps you wrote a lengthy business proposal to an associate you thought was named Paul McDonald. Luckily, before you sent the proposal over your corporate network (using Microsoft Outlook), you realized that Paul's last name is spelled *Mac*Donald.

Tell Word 97 to change all *McDonald*s to *MacDonald*s by following these steps:

1. Select Edit|Replace. Word 97 displays Figure 5.8's Find and Replace dialog box. Instead of the tabbed Find property sheet that you saw in the previous section, you'll see the Replace property sheet.

**Figure 5.8.**

*Tell Word 97 to find
and replace text for you.*

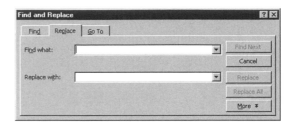

2. Type the word or phrase you want to find in the Find what field. Unless you change the default (you'll learn how to do this in the next section), you don't need to worry about distinguishing between uppercase and lowercase letters.

3. Press Tab to move the text cursor to the Replace with field.

4. Type the replacement text: in this case, MacDonald. Use the correct case because Word 97 replaces the find text with your exact replacement text.

5. If you want Word 97 to replace all occurrences of the text, click the Replace All button. When Word 97 finishes replacing all the occurrences, it tells you how many replacements were made. If you want to replace only one or a few of the occurrences (for example, there might be another person with the name McDonald in the business plan whose name is spelled that way), click the Find Next button, and Word 97 locates the next occurrence of the text. Upon finding a match, Word 97 selects the original text and gives you a chance to replace the text by clicking Replace.

6. Press the Find Next button if you think there are additional replacements to be made and press Escape or click Cancel if you're finished.

 **TIP**

If you want to delete all occurrences of a word or phrase, leave the Replace with field blank when you click Replace All.

## Advanced Find and Replace

Both the Find and Replace property sheets inside the Find and Replace dialog box (see the previous two sections) contain More buttons. As with most editing tasks, Word 97 makes the most common tasks the simplest. If you want more control over your text searches and replacements, click the More buttons when you want to find or replace text. The dialog box expands to show more options, as Figure 5.9 shows.

**5**

**NOTE**

As you can see, the More button becomes a Less button that you can click to return to the simpler Find or Replace property sheets.

**Figure 5.9.**

*Advanced options let you control your find-and-replace operations.*

Table 5.1 explains what each of the advanced find-and-replace options do.

## Table 5.1. The advanced Find and Replace dialog box options.

| Option | Description |
| --- | --- |
| Search | Determines the scope of the find and replace. Select All to search the entire document, Down to search from the text cursor's current position down in the document, and Up to search from the text cursor's current position up through the document. |
| Match case | Finds text only when the text exactly matches your search text's uppercase and lowercase letters. |
| Find whole words only | Matches only when complete text words match your search phrase. For example, if this box is checked, Word 97 does not consider *McD* a match for *McDonald*. If unchecked, *McD* matches *McDonald*, *McDonald's*, and *McDonalds*. |
| Use wildcards | Uses an asterisk (*) to indicate zero or more characters, or a question mark (?) to indicate single characters in your search. For example, if you search for *Mc\** and click this option, Word 97 matches on *Mc*, *McDonald*, and *McDonald's*. If you search for *M?cDonald*, Word 97 considers *MacDonald* a match but not *McDonald*. |

*continues*

**Table 5.1. continued**

| Option | Description |
| --- | --- |
| Sounds like | Bases the match on words or phrases that phonetically match the search phrase but are not necessarily spelled the same way as the search phrase. Therefore, Word 97 would consider both *to* and *too* matches for the search phrase *too*. |
| Find all word forms | Matches on similar parts of speech that match the search phrase. Therefore, Word 97 would not consider the verb *color* to be a match for the noun *color* when you check this option. |

**WARNING**

Word 97 cannot conduct a word-form search if you've checked either the Use wildcards or Sounds like options.

## Selecting Text

Word 97 is more of a document processor than a word processor, as you'll learn when you work with Word 97. Word 97 works with multiple words, paragraphs, pages, and complete documents when you need the power. Earlier in this hour, you learned how to insert and delete individual characters; you'll now learn how to insert and delete entire sections of selected text.

When you or Word 97 highlights (*selects*) text, you can perform text edits on that selection. Word 97 lets you select as much text as you need, including the entire document, to do whatever task you need done.

**NEW TERM**   Highlighted text that you want to work on as a single block is called a *selection*.

**TIP**

The skills you learn here also apply to the other Office 97 products. Therefore, when you master these skills in Word 97, you will already know them for the other Office 97 products.

You can select text with your keyboard or mouse. Table 5.2 shows the mouse-selection operations.

**5**

**Table 5.2. Word 97's advanced Find and Replace dialog box options.**

| To select this | Do this |
| --- | --- |
| Any text | Click the mouse at the start of the text and drag the mouse to the end of the text. Figure 5.10 shows a partial paragraph selection. |
| Word | Double-click the word. |
| Sentence | Press Ctrl and click the sentence. |
| Line | Click to the left of the line. |
| Paragraph | Double-click to the left of the paragraph or triple-click anywhere inside the paragraph's text. |
| Whole document | Press Ctrl and click to the left of the document. |

**Figure 5.10.**
*A partial text selection.*

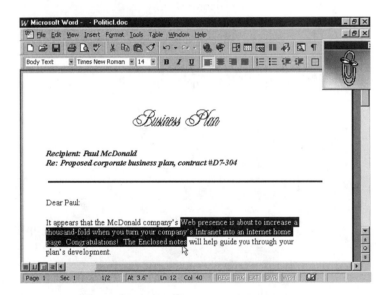

To select with your keyboard, move the text cursor to the beginning of the selection, press the Shift key, and move the text cursor (with the arrow keys or other cursor-movement keys you learned in the section titled "Entering Text") to the final selection character. When you release the Shift key, the selected text appears.

**TIP**

Ctrl+A selects your entire document. When you want to apply global formatting or clipboard-related (you'll learn about the clipboard in the next section) tasks to the entire document, Ctrl+A makes quick work out of selecting the whole document.

**NOTE**

Some people call a selected text section a *block* of text.

## Copying, Cutting, and Pasting

After you select text, you can *copy*, or move that text to a different location. One of the most beneficial features that propelled word processors into the spotlight in the 1980s was their capability to copy and move text. In the medieval days (before 1980), people had to use scissors and glue to cut and paste. Now, your hands stay clean.

**NEW TERM** To *copy* is to make a copy of selected document text and send a copy of that selected text to the clipboard.

Use the Windows *clipboard* during the copy, cut, and paste processes. The clipboard is an area of memory reserved for text, graphics, and whatever other kind of data you need to place there.

**NEW TERM** The *clipboard* is an area of Windows where you temporarily store data.

**WARNING**

The clipboard contents are temporary! Windows replaces the clipboard contents as soon as you send new contents to the clipboard. Also, when you exit Windows, Windows erases the clipboard.

To copy text from one place to another, select the text, copy the selected text to the clipboard by selecting Edit|Copy (or by pressing Ctrl+C or clicking the Copy toolbar button), and *paste* (that's computer lingo for *insert from the clipboard*) the clipboard contents in their new location. To paste, select Edit|Paste, press Ctrl+V, or click the Paste toolbar button. You can keep pasting the text again and again wherever you want it to appear.

**NEW TERM** To *paste* is to send the clipboard contents to a location inside your document.

When you *cut* text from your document (with Edit|Cut or by clicking the Cut toolbar tool), Word 97 erases the text but sends the text to the clipboard where you can paste the clipboard contents elsewhere. In effect, cutting and pasting moves the text. Ctrl+X also works as the standard Windows keyboard shortcut for the cut operation.

**NEW TERM** To *cut* text means to delete the selected text and send that text to the Windows clipboard where you later can paste the text elsewhere.

**TIP**

> You can move and copy with your mouse. After you select text, click the selection and drag the text to its new location. To copy with your mouse, press Ctrl before you click and drag the selected text. Word 97 indicates that you are copying by adding a small plus sign to the mouse cursor during the copy.

# AutoCorrecting and AutoFormatting

Word 97 is smart. Often, Word 97 fixes problems without you ever being aware of them, thanks to Word 97's *AutoCorrect* feature. AutoCorrect uses a Microsoft-created technology called *Intellisense* to hunt constantly for errors. As you type, Word 97 analyzes the errors and makes corrections or suggested improvements along the way.

The Office Assistant is always there to guide you, but AutoCorrect is more integral to Word 97 as well as to the other Office 97 products. If AutoCorrect recognizes a typing mistake, AutoCorrect immediately corrects the mistake.

Here are just a few of the mistakes AutoCorrect recognizes and corrects as you type:

- ☐ AutoCorrect corrects two initial capital letters at the beginning of sentences. `LAtely, we've been gone` becomes `Lately, we've been gone`.
- ☐ AutoCorrect corrects sentences that don't begin with an uppercase letter by fixing the first letter for you.
- ☐ AutoCorrect capitalizes the names of days and months that you forget to capitalize.
- ☐ AutoCorrect corrects a sentence that you type with the wrong Caps Lock key mode. For example, `lATELY, WE'VE BEEN GONE` becomes `Lately, we've been gone`.
- ☐ AutoCorrect replaces common symbols' predefined characters. For example, when you type `(c)`, Word 97 converts the characters to a single copyright symbol.
- ☐ AutoCorrect replaces common spelling transpositions, such as *teh* with *the*.

If AutoCorrect corrects something that you don't want corrected, press Alt+Backspace and AutoCorrect reverses itself.

All of the AutoCorrections in this list are preset. You can add your own, as you'll want to do when you run across common words and phrases that you often type. For example, you'll most certainly want to add your initials to the AutoCorrect table so you only need to type your initials when you want to enter your full name in a document.

**5**

To add your own AutoCorrect entries, perform these steps:

1. Select Tools|AutoCorrect. Word 97 displays the AutoCorrect dialog box shown in Figure 5.11.

2. Type the AutoCorrect shortcut, such as an abbreviation.

3. Press Tab.

4. Type the AutoCorrect replacement text.

5. Press Enter.

**Figure 5.11.**

*Add your own AutoCorrect entries.*

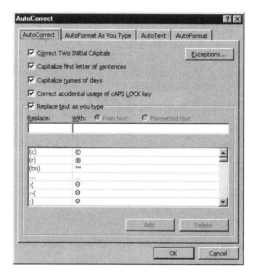

After you enter a new AutoCorrect entry, you can begin using the AutoCorrect feature immediately.

---

**Step-Up**

The Tools|AutoCorrect menu presents four property sheets that let you control on-the-fly AutoCorrecting, on-the-fly AutoFormatting, regular AutoFormatting, and AutoText entries. These were available on separate menus in previous Word versions.

---

In addition to AutoCorrect entries, Word 97 also automatically formats your document as you type. Word 97 will convert common typed fractions, such as 1/2, to their single character equivalent. You can control exactly which AutoFormat features Word 97 uses by selecting Tools|AutoCorrect and clicking the AutoFormat As You Type tab. Figure 5.12 shows you what options you can control.

**5**

**Figure 5.12.**
*Word 97 will format*
*your text as you type.*

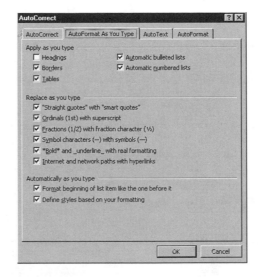

# If You Have Problems...

At any point you can *undo*, or reverse, your most recent edit or edits. Click the toolbar's Undo button (this performs the same action as Edit | Undo, and is easier to use in most cases). Therefore, if you delete a character, or even an entire paragraph, click Undo and Word 97 puts the deleted text right back where it was originally!

**NEW TERM**   An *undo* is the reversal of an edit.

**TIP**   As you edit documents, Word 97 changes its Edit | Undo menu option to reflect the next undo; that is, if you delete text, the Edit menu's first option becomes Undo Clear, indicating that you can undo the clearing of text that you previously performed.

Word 97 keeps track of multiple edits. Therefore, if you realize that you've been making wrong changes for the last three edits, click Undo three times and Word 97 reverses those three edits no matter what the edits were. If you go too far, press the Redo toolbar button, and Word 97 replaces the undo (in effect, undoing the undo! It gets confusing...). If you click the arrows next to either the toolbar's Undo or Redo buttons, Word 97 displays a list of up to 100 recent changes, which you can choose to undo or redo.

The reversal of an undo is a *redo*.

**NOTE**

> Word 97 can reverse any and all replacements you make with the Find and Replace dialog box.

In addition to undoing wrong edits, Word 97 works in the background to keep your documents as safe as possible. Table 5.3 describes Word 97's automatic file-saving features. (You can control these feature through the Tools|Options dialog box. You'll learn all about the Options dialog box in Hour 7.)

## Table 5.3. Word 97's file-saving features.

| Feature | Description |
| --- | --- |
| Automatic backup | When you begin editing an existing document, Word 97 saves a copy of the original document with the original name and the .bak extension (for *backup*). No matter how much you change (or mess up) your document, the original version is always safely stored until your next editing session on that document. |
| AutoRecovery | Automatically saves enough of your document to restore the complete document at that point. Subsequently, if your power goes out or your computer system crashes, you would normally lose your last edits and possibly your entire document. As long as you've turned on the AutoRecovery option, Word 97 will recover the document the next time you start Word 97. Of course, if you previously saved and exited Word 97, Word 97 will have no reason to recover the file because your saved changes will be kept. The more frequently you set AutoRecover's timer, the more likely you will be able to recover your most recent edits if a power failure or system crash occurs. |

**Step-Up**

The AutoRecovery feature replaces the AutoSave feature found in previous versions of Word.

5

# Summary

This hour introduces Word 97, Office 97's word-processing product. As you saw in this hour, Word 97 makes entering text simple, and Word 97 even corrects mistakes *as you type*.

One of Office 97's many productivity factors is that the products in the Office 97 suite often work in a similar manner. Therefore, many of the skills you learned this hour in Word 97 will carry over to the other products. If you have used Word in the past, you've already seen some of the improvements Microsoft made with Word 97.

The next hour delves further into Word 97 and shows you how to format your document's text. In addition, you will see how the Word 97 templates and wizards practically create your documents for you.

# Q&A

**Q What is the primary difference between a document and a file?**

**A** There is no real difference. All Office 97 products call data files *documents*. Although the term *documents* seems to make the most sense for Word 97 users because Word 97 creates and edits data files you typically think of as documents, an Office 97 Access database is also considered a document even though it is, technically, a database file.

The document concept lets all your file opens, closes, and saves operate uniformly. In addition, the uniform document-centric nature of Office 97 lets you transfer and share data between the Office 97 products more easily.

**Q How can I eliminate the wavy lines beneath some of the text I type?**

**A** The red and gray wavy lines indicate that Word 97 found a spelling or grammatical error. Word 97 is not perfect, just helpful, and sometimes Word 97 incorrectly flags such errors when they are not errors. You'll learn in Hour 7 how to handle the errors and teach Word 97 what is correct when needed.

**Q Does it matter if I press Tab or several spaces when I want to move text to the right?**

**A** In some cases, you'll see that pressing Tab and the spacebar several times produces the same results, but you should reserve Tab presses for those times when you want to indent or align several lines of text. You can more easily adjust tab spacing later if you want to change the indention. Use spaces only when you never need to align or change the spacing of your text.

5

**Q** **I create special charts and tables with Word 97, and I don't always want AutoCorrect to do its thing. How can I keep AutoCorrect from making certain corrections?**

**A** Select the AutoCorrect corrections you need from the Tools|Options menu. If you want AutoCorrect to make a particular correction *most* but not all of the time, you can always reverse a single AutoCorrect correction by pressing the toolbar's Undo button as soon as Word 97 makes the AutoCorrect change.

**5**

# Hour **6**

# Format with Word 97

This hour demonstrates Word 97's formatting features, which add style and flair to your writing. Not only can Word 97 help your writing read better, Word 97 can help your writing *look* better as well.

Word 97 supports character, paragraph, and even document formatting. You can control every aspect of your document. If you don't want to take the time to format individual elements, Word 97 can format your entire document automatically for you. When you begin learning Word 97, type your text before formatting it so that you get your thoughts in the document while they're still fresh. After you type your document, you can format its text.

The highlights of this hour include

☐ Which character formats Word 97 supports

☐ Why you should not get too fancy with most document formats

☐ What fonts are all about

☐ How to apply paragraph formats

☐ When different views are helpful

☐ Where to see a preview of your printed document

☐ How to format an entire document with a predefined style

# Simple Character Formatting

When you want to emphasize text to make a point, you can underline, boldface, or italicize your text. Figure 6.1 shows a document with boldfaced and italicized text on the top half, and with underlined text on the bottom half.

**NOTE**

These special formatting styles are called *character formats* even though you can apply them to multiple characters, paragraphs, and complete documents as easily as you can apply them to single characters. The character formatting styles attach themselves to whatever text you select for the formatting.

**NEW TERM**  A *character format* is a format that you can apply to characters and selected text.

**Figure 6.1.**

*Character formatting improves your documents.*

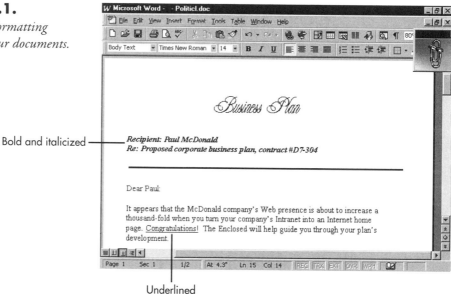

Bold and italicized

Underlined

6

**WARNING**

*Express but don't impress.* You'll learn how to add lots of fancy styles in this hour. Too many styles make your documents look busy and take away from your writing goals. Add only enough fanciness to add appeal to your writing.

To apply either of the three styles, select the text that you want to format and click either the Bold, Italic, or Underline toolbar button. To format only a single word, you only have to click within the word to select it.

**TIP**

The shortcut keys Ctrl+B, Ctrl+I, and Ctrl+U apply character formatting, and your hands don't have to leave your keyboard to click the mouse. Press one of the shortcuts before you type the text you want to format. When you want to stop formatting, press the same shortcut key to turn off the formatting.

# Special Character Formatting

In addition to the three standard character formatting styles, Word 97 supports several additional formats that make your writing stand out. One special character format that you can apply almost as easily as the three from the previous section is color. When you click the drop-down arrow next to the Font Color toolbar button, Word 97 displays the small Font Color dialog box shown in Figure 6.2. (You'll learn what a font is later in this section. For now, consider *font* to be synonymous to *character*.) Click a color, and Word 97 changes your selected text to that color.

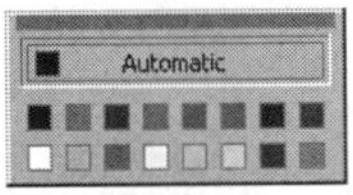

**Figure 6.2.**
*You can change the color of text.*

6

**Step-Up**

The Font Color toolbar button did not appear on previous versions of Word's formatting toolbar. In addition to text, you can colorize the document's background with Format|Background.

**TIP**  Remember that Office 97 now easily links with the Internet and the Internet's fancy colorful Wide World Web pages. You can use Word 97 to create a colorful Web page, so the Font Color button comes in handy.

One of the most helpful formatting changes you can make is to change your font's name and size. A *font* determines the way your character looks from its size to its curliness to its elegance. Different fonts have different names, such as *Courier New* and *Schoolbook*.

**NEW TERM**  The *font* is the character style that determines the look and size of your characters.

Think your of daily newspaper. The banner across the top of the page probably looks like old Gothic letters, while the headlines are more standard type. Either might or might not be boldfaced, underlined, or italicized (although a newspaper rarely applies underlining styles). Throughout your paper, the articles might contain the same font as the headline, but the font size is smaller in the articles.

The size of a font is measured in *points*. One point is 1/72nd of an inch. As a standard rule of thumb, a 10- or 12-point size is standard and readable for most word-processed writing. As you type and move your text cursor throughout a document, Word 97 displays the current font name and size on the formatting toolbar. To change any selected text's font name or size, click the drop-down arrow to the right of the Font Name button, or use the Font Size drop-down lists to select a new value.

**NEW TERM**  A *point* is a font character measurement that equals 1/72nd of an inch.

Instead of the toolbar, you can set multiple character formats with the Font dialog box. When you select Format | Font, Word 97 displays Figure 6.3's Font dialog box. (You can also display the Font dialog box by right-clicking selected text and choosing Font from the pop-up menu.)

Not only can you set multiple character formats from one location (the Font dialog box), but Word 97 displays a preview of the font in the dialog box's Preview area. Therefore, you can select various font names, sizes, and styles and see the results without actually closing the dialog box to apply those changes. When the previewed text looks the way you want, select OK and apply those changes to your selected text.

**Figure 6.3.**

*Set many character formats with the Font dialog box.*

---

**Step-Up**

Notice that Word 97's Font dialog box supports character formats that previous Word versions did not support: double strike-through, shadow, outline, emboss, and engrave.

---

**TIP**

If you select the Hidden character format, the hidden text can appear on your screen but will not print. Hidden text is great for notes to yourself and explanatory information that supports the surrounding text that you want to print. If you use hidden text, be sure to check the Hidden text option in the Tools | Options View page. Otherwise, the hidden text won't show up on your screen.

Although the Highlight tool does not actually format text, it is great for marking important text that you want to reference later or make stand out to the next reader. When you select text and click the Highlight tool (click the Highlight tool's drop-down arrow to change the highlighting color), Word 97 highlights the text as though you marked your screen with a yellow highlighter pen.

6

# Paragraph Formatting

Some formats work on characters, while others are better suited for paragraphs. This section describes the essentials for formatting your paragraphs so your documents look the way you want them to look.

## Justifying Text

Perhaps the most common paragraph formats are the justification formats. When you justify text, you determine the text's alignment. Word 97 supports these justification options:

- Left-justification aligns (makes even) text with the left side of the page.
- Center-justification centers text within the left and right margins.
- Right-justification aligns text with the right side of the page.
- Full-justification aligns both ends of text.

The simplest way to justify text is to click anywhere inside the paragraph that you want to justify (or select multiple paragraphs if you want to justify several) and click the toolbar's Left Align, Center, Right Align, or Justify (for full justification) buttons.

 **TIP**    Newspaper, magazine, and newsletter columns are usually fully justified. Both edges of both columns align evenly.

 **NOTE**    Although you can justify multiple paragraphs and even complete documents, a single paragraph is the smallest amount of text you can justify—hence, the term *paragraph format*.

**NEW TERM**    *Paragraph format* is a format that you can apply to paragraphs and selected text.

## Indentation and Spacing

If you need to change the *indentation* (the space between a paragraph's edges and the page margin) or *spacing* (the amount of blank space between lines), select Format | Paragraph to display Figure 6.4's Paragraph dialog box.

**NEW TERM**   *Indentation* is the space between a paragraph's edges and the page margin.

 **NEW TERM**   *Spacing* is the blank space between lines (sometimes called the *line spacing*).

**Figure 6.4.**

*The Paragraph dialog box holds indentation and spacing values.*

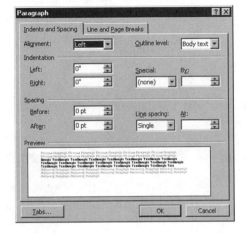

As you change the indentation, the Word 97 updates the preview at the bottom of the Paragraph dialog box to show your setting results. You can type a Left or Right indentation value or click the arrows to change the current values.

The drop-down Special values—(none), First Line, and Hanging Indent—determine how indentation applies itself to the paragraph. If you leave (none) selected, Word 97 indents the complete paragraph by the left and right indentation values you supply. If you select First Line, Word 97 uses the value in the By field to indent only the first line of the selected paragraph. A *hanging indent* paragraph is an indent of the entire paragraph *except* the first line.

 **NEW TERM**   A *hanging indent* is an indentation of all of a paragraph except the first line.

**WARNING**

If you indent the first line or apply a hanging indent, your Left and Right indentation values still apply to the entire paragraph. The first line and hanging indent values specify the *additional indenting* you want Word 97 to perform on the first or subsequent paragraph lines.

6

The Spacing section lets you specify exactly how many points you want Word 97 to skip before or after each paragraph. You can also select multiple line spacing by selecting from the Line spacing field.

 **TIP**

> Increase or decrease a paragraph's indentation by clicking the toolbar's Decrease Indent and Increase Indent buttons.

## Line and Page Breaks

When you click the Paragraph dialog box's Line and Page Breaks tab, Word 97 displays Figure 6.5's dialog box.

**Figure 6.5.**

*Control the way your paragraph lines break.*

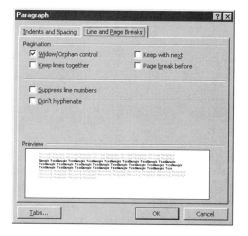

A *widow* is a paragraph's last line that prints at the top of the next page, and an *orphan* is a paragraph's first line that prints at the bottom of a page. Most of the time, widowed and orphaned lines look incomplete. If you click the Widow/Orphan control option, Word 97 adjusts page breaks, if necessary, so that two or more paragraph lines always begin a page and so that two or more paragraph lines always end a page.

The Keep lines together check box ensures that a page break never breaks the selected paragraph. The Keep with next check box ensures that a page break never appears between the current paragraph and the next. The Page break before check box forces a page break before the selected paragraph even if a page break would not normally appear for several more lines.

By enabling the Suppress line numbers check box, law pleadings and other documents with line numbers will not print the lines on the selected paragraph lines. If you've set up automatic hyphenation (described later in this hour), the Don't hyphenate option eliminates automatic hyphenation from the selected paragraph.

**TIP**  As with all of Word 97's formatting commands, you can apply a paragraph format *before* typing to apply the formatting to all subsequent paragraphs that you type.

## Tab Settings

Click the Paragraph dialog box's Tabs command button to display Figure 6.6's Tabs dialog box. A *tab* controls the vertical spacing for certain items in your text. The bottom line is that a tab keeps you from having to press your spacebar many times when you want to insert multiple spaces in your text.

**TIP**  Word 97's tabs ease your burden when you want to align certain columns of text. Not only do tabs help you create column alignment, but they help you *keep* that alignment if you change paragraph indentation, spacing, or width.

**Figure 6.6.**

*The Tabs dialog box.*

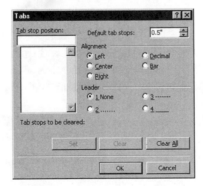

Table 6.1 describes each of the options in the Tabs dialog box. After you set tabs, press your Tab key as you enter paragraph text to move the cursor to the next tab stop.

## Table 6.1. The Tabs dialog box options.

| Option | Description |
| --- | --- |
| Tab stop position | Lets you enter individual measurement values, such as .25" to represent one-fourth of an inch. After you type a value, press Set to add that value to the list of tab settings. To clear a tab stop, select the value and click Clear. Click Clear All to clear the entire tab list. |
| Left | Left-aligns text at the tab stop (the default). |
| Center | Centers text at the tab stop. |
| Right | Right-aligns text at the tab stop. |
| Decimal | Aligns lists of numbers by ensuring that their decimal points align with each other. |
| Bar | Inserts a vertical bar at the tab stop. |
| Leader: None | Sets up blank leaders. A *leader* is a character that Word 97 displays in a tab's blank area. By default, Word 97 displays nothing (blanks only) for tab areas. |
| ....... | Displays a series of periods inside the tabs (often used for connecting goods to their corresponding prices in a price list). |
| ------- | Displays a series of hyphens inside the tabs. |
| _____ | Displays a series of underlines inside the tabs. |

## Margins and More

Figure 6.7's Page Setup dialog box, displayed from the File|Page Setup command or by double-clicking the top of the ruler, lets you control your paragraph and page margins. Enter values for your top, bottom, left, and right margins so your text does not span past the limits.

**Figure 6.7.**

*The Page Setup dialog box.*

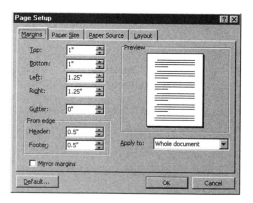

**WARNING**

Many printers, especially laser printers, cannot print right at the margin edge. Generally, one-half inch is the minimum margin size these printers allow.

The *gutter* is an area of the page where you might want to hole-punch the page or insert the page in a binder. The gutter value, if you indicate one, shifts all other measurements to the right on your page. (The Header and Footer values determine how far from the top and bottom of your pages the header and footer will appear if you supply a header or a footer. Hour 8, "Advanced Word 97," describes headers and footers.)

**NEW TERM**   The *gutter* is the left side of a page where you might punch holes or attach to a binder.

## Make the Ruler Work for You

As you specify indentation and tab information, Word 97's ruler updates to indicate your settings. Not only does the ruler show settings, but you can make indentation and tab changes directly to the ruler to eliminate the display of dialog boxes every time you want to change an indentation or tab value.

Figure 6.8 shows the ruler's various tab stops and indentation handles. From the text beneath the ruler, you can determine the kind of tab-stop character the ruler displays at each stop. Click anywhere on the ruler to add a tab stop after you select the appropriate tab from the tab selection area. To remove a tab, drag the tab stop down off the ruler. By dragging an indentation handle, you can change a paragraph's indentation on-the-fly.

**TIP**

Double-click the bottom of the ruler to display the Tabs dialog box, and double-click the top of the ruler to display the Page Setup dialog box.

6

**Figure 6.8.**

*The Page Setup dialog box.*

First line indent
Hanging indent
Ruler
Right indent

Click here to select a tab
Left indent
Left tab stop
Center tab stop
Right tab stop
Decimal tab stop

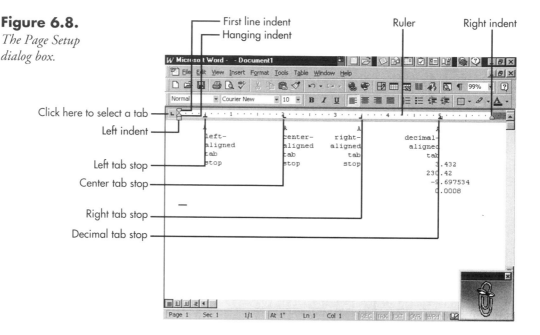

## Sneak a Peek at Formatting

Try this: Type and format some text. Press Shift+F1. Word 97's mouse cursor changes to a question mark. When you click over text, Word 97 displays all the information about that selected text, including the character and paragraph formatting applied. This is neat! Figure 6.9 shows an example. To get rid of the formatting description, press Shift+F1 once again.

**Figure 6.9.**

*You can find out a lot about formats!*

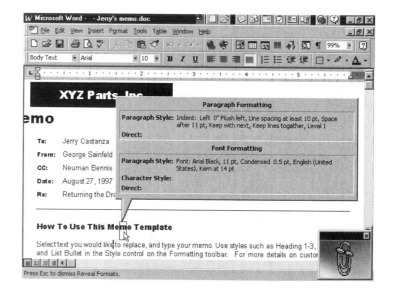

6

# Format with Styles

A *style* is a collection of character and paragraph formats grouped together. Each style has a name. Word 97 comes with several styles, and you can create your own.

 A *style* is a named collection of formatting styles for selected text.

Click the drop-down arrow on the Style toolbar field to see the names of Word 97's styles. When you select a style, Word 97 applies it to the current paragraph and subsequent paragraphs that you type. If you want to change a style's formatting or create a new style, select Format|Style to show the Style dialog box. If you want to modify the current style, click Modify; if you want to create a new style, click New.

Suppose you routinely write resumes for other people. You might have created three separate sets of character and paragraph formats that work well for a resume's title, applicant's personal information, and work history. Instead of setting up each of these formats every time you create a resume, format a paragraph with each style and store the styles under their own names (such as Resume Title, Resume Personal, and Resume Work). The next time you write a resume, you'll only need to click the Style toolbar button and select Resume Title from the style list. When you then type the title, the title will look the way you want it to look without you having to designate any character or paragraph format.

# Your Document's Views

Now that you can format your document, you need to know how to display your document on the screen to make the best use of the formatting during the editing process. Word 97 supports several display views that show your document in different formats. Use the View menu to select a view, or click one of the view buttons on the horizontal scrollbar above the status bar (you must be displaying the scrollbars to see the view buttons).

## The Normal View

For routine document creation and editing, the Normal view presents the cleanest screen approach and shows all character and paragraph formatting. If you choose to display special formatting characters, you'll see those in the Normal view as well. All screen shots in this and the previous chapters show the Normal view.

6

## The Outline Layout View

If you've prepared your document for outlining by using Word 97's built-in styles (such as Heading 1 and Heading 2), the Outline Layout view lets you quickly traverse your document. As Figure 6.10 shows, the Outline Layout view shows your document's headings on the left and the detail on the right. Jump to any document text simply by clicking the appropriate heading.

**Figure 6.10.**

*Traverse a document quickly with the Outline Layout view.*

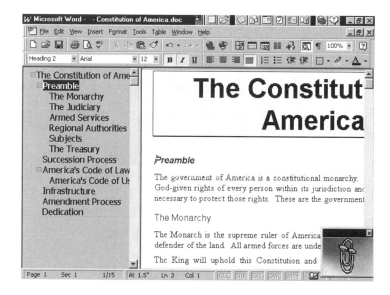

**TIP**

Drag the screen's dividing line right or left if you want to see more of the headings or more of the detail. If you cannot read all the headings, point to a heading and Word 97 will show you that full heading's title without requiring you to resize the window.

## The Page Layout

If you want to view your document exactly that way the document will print, select the Page Layout view. The Page Layout view shows any details, such as headers and footers, and shows you where page breaks occur.

## The Outline View

The Outline view gives you true expandable and collapsible views of your document in outline form. If you prefer to write from an outline, you can. Use Word 97's predefined heading styles to create your document's outline, then expand on the outline when you're ready to add detail. Figure 6.11 shows a document's Outline view.

**Figure 6.11.**

*If you work with outlines, the Outline view is for you.*

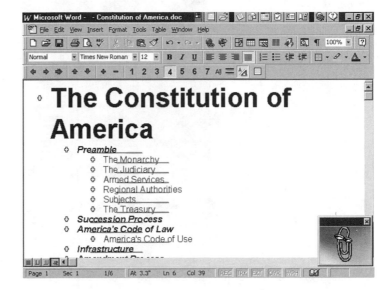

The Outline view shows the structure of the document, and shows exactly as much detail as you want to see. By clicking the heading numbers (corresponding to the styles Heading 1, Heading 2, and so on) or the plus and minus signs on the Outlining toolbar, you can see more or less detail. All the detail stays with your document, but all the detail does not appear at one time.

## Print Preview

Word 97's Print Preview shows how your document will look on paper. As Figure 6.12 shows, you can click Print Preview's Multiple Pages button to display several pages. You get a bird's-eye view of your printed document, which allows you to predict print format problems without wasting time or paper.

**6**

**TIP**

Click the Close button or press Esc to exit the preview.

**Figure 6.12.**
*View your printed document's pages.*

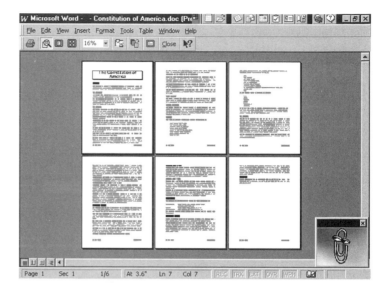

If you want a closer view of your Print Preview, click the magnifying glass mouse cursor anywhere on the preview to see the preview in more detail.

## Full Screen View

When you need to see as much of your document as possible, select View | Full Screen. Word 97 hides the toolbars, status bars, and menus to give more screen real estate to your document. Click the Restore window or press Esc to return to the previous viewing state.

## Determine Your Own View

When you display Figure 6.13's Zoom dialog box (by selecting View | Zoom), you can adjust the display size of your screen's characters to display a smaller percentage of their size, allowing you to see more text on individual screen lines. If your margins and font size make your document's text wider than your screen size but you want to see whole lines, shrink the percentage shown in the Zoom dialog box to squeeze more text on your screen.

6

**Figure 6.13.**

*Display as much of your text as you need to.*

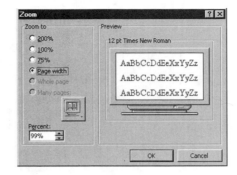

# Numbers and Bullets

Word 97 makes numbered and bulleted lists easy to produce. If you've set the proper AutoFormat options (see Hour 5, "Welcome to Word 97"), follow these steps to create a properly formatted and indented numbered list:

1. Press Tab to start the first numbered item.
2. Type the number, such as 1. (follow the number with a period).
3. Press Tab.
4. Type the text that goes with the first numbered item.
5. Press Enter. The Office Assistant (if you've turned it on) tells you that Word 97 converted your previous text to a numbered list. You can change it back to regular text, turn off the numbering, or click OK to continue the list.
6. Press OK if Office Assistant is present. Word 97 automatically formats the first item and types the second number for you to prepare you for the next item.
7. Keep entering numbered items. When you finish, press Enter after a number, and Word 97 converts that final numbered line to regular text.

In other words, to create a well-formatted numbered list, just start typing the list! Word 97 formats and numbers your list after you enter the first item. If you want to convert a series of paragraphs or lines to a numbered list, select the text and click the Numbering toolbar button.

Here's another numbering trick: Before typing the bulleted list, click Word 97's Bullets toolbar button. Word 97 starts the list, types the first number for you, inserts a tab, and you only have to complete the numbered item. Word 97 continues to add the numbers as you complete the list.

6

**TIP**

One of the best features of Word 97 is that you can delete and insert numbered items from and to numbered lists, and Word 97 automatically renumbers the other items!

If you want to create a bulleted list, type the items to be bulleted, select those lines, and click the Bullets button. Again, when you add and delete items, Word 97 automatically adds or removes the bullets and formats new items.

**NOTE**

Control the size of the bullets as well as the number styles in your bulleted and numbered lists by selecting Format | Bullets and Numbering.

# Format Like Magic

Instead of messing with all these character and paragraph formatting options, just let Word 97 do all the work! Type your document using no special format (except press Enter to end each paragraph and add blank lines), then select Format | Style Gallery to display Figure 6.14's Style Gallery dialog box.

**Figure 6.14.**

*Let Word 97 format everything in style.*

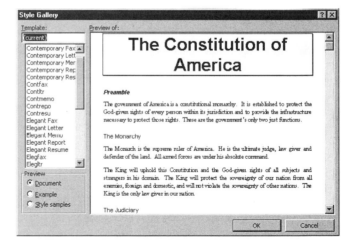

As you select from the style templates, Word 97 updates the preview window to show what your document would look like if you let Word 97 automatically format the entire document in that style. The styles range from contemporary to elegant to formal.

# A Word About Word 97's Wizards

This hour has discussed formatting your text and document as you type text or after you've entered the text. Word 97's wizards set up your document's format *before* you create your document. When you select File | New, Word 97 displays a list of wizards and templates from which you can select.

**NOTE**

> Templates contain formatting that you can use, as well as automated buttons that you can click to format certain text elements. Wizards are more interactive and produce more customized documents than do templates.

For example, select File | New, click the Publications tab, and double-click the Newsletter Wizard icon. Word 97 walks you through a step-by-step procedure to create a newsletter.

# Summary

This hour explains the various format options available to Word 97 users. Keep your audience in mind; don't overdo formats or your documents will look cluttered. Word 97 is powerful, but with that power comes responsibility. Keep your documents readable and remember your presentation as you format.

You can apply the character formats to individual characters as well as to selected text and the entire document. Paragraph formats control the spacing and justification of paragraphs. The views let you see your document from various perspectives so that you can determine whether your formats work well together. Perhaps the best indicator of style is the print preview, which shows how your document will look when you print it.

The next hour moves into document management and Word 97 customization. Depending on how you use Word 97, you might want to change the way Word 97 behaves in certain situations.

6

# Q&A

**Q  How can I type an italicized paragraph?**

**A**  Before typing any text that you want formatted in any way, set up the formatting. If you want to italicize a word, phrase, or an entire document that you're about to type, press Ctrl+I (or click the toolbar's Italic button) before you type, and Word 97 will italicize the text.

**Q  How can I see hidden text on both the screen and printer?**

**A**  Select Tools|Options Hidden Text to display hidden text on your screen. The hidden text still does not display on your printer... That's why it's called *hidden*! Nevertheless, you can print hidden text if you click the Hidden Text option on the Option dialog box's Print page.

**Q  How can I see my entire page on the screen at once?**

**A**  If you have an extremely high-resolution monitor and graphics adapter card, you can probably see an entire document page when you select the full-screen view (with View|Full Screen). If you want to see the toolbars, menu, and status bar, however, you'll probably have to adjust the zoom factor when you select View|Zoom. The only other way to see an entire page is to select the Print Preview mode; in preview mode, you can only make simple margin adjustments but no text changes.

**Q  How can I make margin adjustments in Print Preview mode?**

**A**  You should adjust the margins only when displaying a single page. Therefore, if you see multiple page previews, click the One Page button to show a single page. Then click the View Ruler bar to add a ruler to the top of the page. Use your mouse to drag and adjust the left, right, top, and bottom margins. Although such margin adjustment is not as accurate as you can set from within the Page Setup dialog box, you can visually see the results as you make margin adjustments on-the-fly.

**6**

# Hour 7

# Managing Documents and Customizing Word 97

This hour works more globally with your documents than the previous two hours do. Instead of concentrating on specific editing skills, you will see how to manage your document properties. Word 97 can keep track of several document-related items, and that tracking really comes in handy if you work in a group environment.

Word 97's proofing tools are powerful and work as you type. Word 97's spell checker acts as a mentor looking over your shoulder with a dictionary, supplying you with suggested spellings for mistyped words. Additionally, Word 97 helps with grammar, hyphenation, and synonyms.

The highlights of this hour include

☐ What document properties are

☐ Where to locate and change a document's properties

☐ How to request the spell and grammar checker

☐  Why you need to proof documents manually despite Word 97's proofing tools

☐  How to customize Word 97 to behave the way you want

# Document Properties

Each Word 97 document (as well as the other Office 97 documents) has properties. A *property* is information related to a particular document, such as the author's name and creation date. If you do not specify properties, Word 97 adds its own to your document. You'll see Figure 7.1's Properties dialog box when you select File | Properties.

 Information related to a certain document, such as the number of paragraphs inside the document, is called a *property*.

**Figure 7.1.**

*Track your document's properties.*

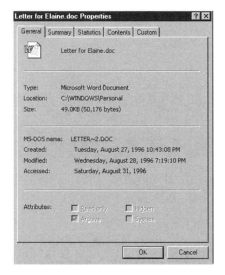

The Properties dialog box's tabbed sheets provide the following information:

☐  General—Contains the document's file information, including the date and time you created, last modified, and last accessed the document.

☐  Summary—Tracks a document title, author (your name by default), keywords, and comment notes.

☐  Statistics—Tracks the document's numeric statistics, such as character, word, and page counts, and total amount of editing time consumed for the document.

**7**

- ☐ Contents—Describes the parts of your document, such as the header, body, and footer.

- ☐ Custom—Keeps track of information you want in the order you specify. You can keep track of customized properties, such as the department responsible for creating or maintaining the document, a project group name that works on the document, and the person responsible for typing the document's information. As you add items to the Properties list box, indicate the item's data type (such as text or date) so Word 97 can properly format the property value you want to track. The Custom sheet is great for departments where many people see and edit the same set of documents.

Some properties are available elsewhere in Word 97. For example, you can find a document's statistics, such as word and paragraph counts, by selecting Tools | Word Count. Often, you can select from the menu option more quickly than displaying the document properties.

**TIP**

If you create numerous documents and continually search through your disk files for particular ones, be sure to add search keywords on the Properties Summary page so you can later find that document using Word 97's Open dialog box's Advanced Search option.

# Word 97's Advanced Proofreaders

Word 97 offers these proofreading services for your writing:

- ☐ Spell checker—Checks your spelling either as you type or for your entire document at once.

- ☐ Grammar checker—Checks your grammar either as you type or for your entire document at once.

- ☐ Thesaurus—Provides synonyms when you need them.

**NEW TERM**  A *thesaurus* is a list of synonyms.

- ☐ Hyphenation—Automatically hyphenates words, when appropriate, at the end of lines either as you type or for your entire document at once.

7

**Step-Up**

Previous versions of Word did not check grammar as you typed your documents. You could only request a manual grammar check after you typed the document.

**WARNING**

Word 97's built-in proofreading tools do not eliminate your proofing responsibilities! No matter how good Word 97 is, Word 97 cannot match human skills when deciphering the written language. For example, Word 97's spell check will have no problem with this sentence:

*Wee road two the see too sea the waives.*

The proofreading tools work only as guides to find those problems you might have missed during your own extensive proofing.

## Using the Spell Checker

Word 97 automatically checks your spelling and your grammar as you type your document. Any time you see red wavy underlines and gray wavy underlines as you type, Word 97 is letting you know about a suspicious spelling problem (the red line) or grammar problem (the gray line).

Depending on the options you (or someone else) have set, your version of Word 97 might not check both spelling and grammar as you type. Therefore, if you don't see any wavy lines, you should check your document's spelling and grammar after you've typed the document so you don't miss anything.

**NOTE**

You'll learn how to turn on and off options (including the spelling and grammar checkers) later in this chapter in the section titled "Customize Word 97 to Work for You."

When you see a red wavy line, you can correct the problem in these ways:

- [ ] Edit the misspelling.
- [ ] Right-click the misspelling to display Figure 7.2's pop-up menu. You can select one of Word 97's suggestions at the top of the pop-up menu, ignore all subsequent similar misspellings (in case you want to type foreign words or formal names but you don't want to add those words to Word 97's spelling dictionaries), add the

word to Word 97's dictionary so that Word 97 no longer flags the word as mis-spelled, select AutoCorrect and choose a correct word to add the misspelling to the AutoCorrect entries so that Word 97 subsequently corrects the word for you on-the-fly, or display Word 97's more comprehensive Spelling dialog box (shown in Figure 7.3).

☐ Ignore the misspelling and leave the red wavy line.

☐ Ignore the misspelling, but check the entire document's spelling when you finish typing the document.

**Figure 7.2.**

*Select your spell-correction choice when Word 97 finds a misspelling.*

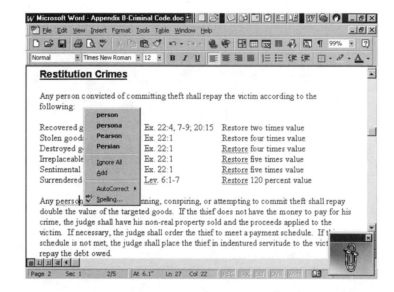

---

**Step-Up**

Previous versions of Word 97 did not let you add AutoCorrect entries from the pop-up spelling menu as you can do in Word 97 when you right-click a spelling problem.

7

**Figure 7.3.**

*The Spelling dialog box
offers more options than
the pop-up menu.*

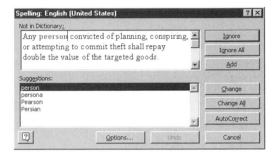

The Spelling dialog box appears when you click a misspelled word's pop-up menu Spelling
option or when you select Spelling & Grammar from the Tools menu. Table 7.1 lists the
Spelling dialog box's options.

**WARNING**

When you check the spelling of your document from Tools | Spelling &
Grammar, Word 97 checks from the cursor's current position down to the
end of your document. If you want Word 97 to check your entire
document's spelling in one step (assuming you've turned off the automatic
spell checking that occurs as you type), move your cursor to the top of
your document (Ctrl+Home) before requesting the spell check.

## Table 7.1. The Spelling dialog box options.

| Option | Description |
| --- | --- |
| Ignore | Tells Word 97 to ignore only this single occurrence of the misspelling. |
| Ignore All | Tells Word 97 to ignore *all* occurrences of this misspelling in this document. |
| Add | Adds the word to Word 97's spelling dictionary so that Word 97 subsequently knows the word's spelling. |
| Change | Changes this single misspelling to the selected correction. |
| Change All | Changes all of the document's misspellings of the current word to the selected correction. |

| Option | Description |
| --- | --- |
| AutoCorrect | Adds the misspelling and selected correction to your collection of AutoText entries. |
| Check Grammar | Lets you turn the automatic grammar checker on or off for this document despite the settings in effect. |
| Options | Displays Figure 7.4's Spelling & Grammar Options sheet on which you can modify the behavior of the spelling and grammar checker. |
| Undo | Undoes your most recent spell correction. |

**Figure 7.4.**

*Change the spell checker's behavior from this Spelling & Grammar options dialog box.*

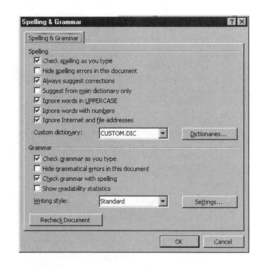

## Using the Grammar Checker

When you see a gray wavy line beneath a word, Word 97 is letting you know about a suspicious grammar problem. Figure 7.5 shows the pop-up menu Word 97 displays when you right-click a gray wavy-lined word.

**Figure 7.5.**

*Word 97 displays a pop-up menu when you right-click a word with a gray wavy underline.*

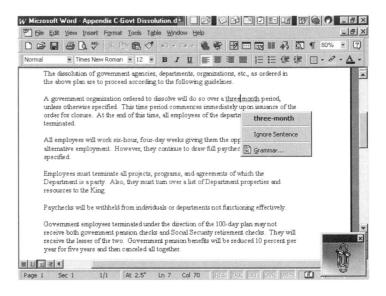

  **TIP**

Wait until you finish your document before you check the grammar. The grammar correction process takes a few minutes to complete. In most cases, you should turn off the automatic grammar checker to speed Word 97's response time as you type your document. When you finish typing the document, select Tools | Spelling & Grammar to check the grammar on the whole document. You can click the toolbar's Spelling and Grammar button to start the process as well.

Keep Office Assistant turned on when you check grammar. Microsoft added lots of plain-spoken grammar-correcting advice to the Office Assistant's repertoire of helpful topics.

As with the spelling pop-up menu, you can replace the grammar problem with the suggested word or words, ignore the suspected problem (just because Word 97 suspects a problem does not necessarily mean that there is one), or you can start the full grammar-checking system to correct that problem as well as the rest of the document.

When you check a document's grammar from the Tools | Spelling & Grammar option (to check the entire document) or by selecting the full grammar check from the pop-up menu, Word 97 displays the same Spelling & Grammar dialog box you see when you check for spelling only. However, as Figure 7.6 shows, the Office Assistant chimes in with its advice as well. The Office Assistant advice often provides very clear descriptions and examples of why your grammar might have a problem at the flagged location.

**7**

**Figure 7.6.**

*Select your grammar-correction choice when Word 97 finds a problem.*

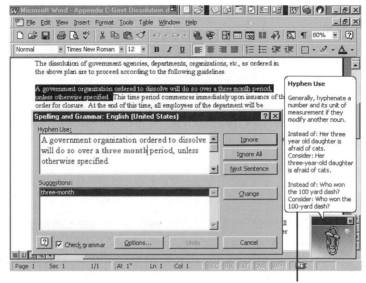

Office Assistant's
advice is good

## Using Automatic Hyphenation

Word 97 can hyphenate your text as you type, or you can manually hyphenate your entire document. Word 97 supports three kinds of hyphens:

☐ Regular hyphens, which Word 97 uses to break words at the end of lines (when needed) to maintain proper document formatting.

☐ Optional hyphens, which break special words (*AutoCorrect* becomes *Auto-Correct*, for example) only if those words appear at the end of lines (press Ctrl+- to indicate where you want the optional hyphen as you type the word).

**NEW TERM**    An *optional hyphen* breaks special terms and proper names only if those words appear at the end of a line.

☐ Nonbreaking hyphens, which keep certain hyphenated words together at all times; for example, if the hyphenated name *Brian-Kent* appears at the end of a line and you want to prevent Word 97 from breaking apart the names at the end of a line, press Ctrl+Shift+Hyphen to add that word's hyphen when you type the word.

**NEW TERM**    A *nonbreaking hyphen* keeps two hyphenated words together so they never break at the end of a line.

7

**NOTE**

You only need to indicate optional and nonbreaking hyphens when you type special words that Word 97 would not typically recognize, such as company names and special terms.

To automatically hyphenate your document as you type, select Tools | Language | Hyphenation to display Figure 7.7's Hyphenation dialog box. The Hyphenation zone field lets you determine the amount of space between the end of a line's last word and the right margin (a higher value reduces the number of hyphens that Word 97 adds). If you want to keep the hyphenation to a minimum, consider limiting the number of consecutive lines that Word 97 can hyphenate at one time by specifying a Limit consecutive hyphens to field value.

**Figure 7.7.**

*Specify automatic hyphenation.*

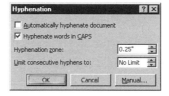

To manually hyphenate your document after you've created it, select Tools | Language | Hyphenation and click Manual. Word 97 prompts for your approval at each hyphen location.

If you want to stop Word 97 from hyphenating particular paragraphs, select those paragraphs, then select Format | Paragraph, click the Line and Page Breaks tab, and check the Don't Hyphenate option.

**WARNING**

If you export your document text to another program or computer system (such as a desktop publishing or typesetting system) for publication, do not let Word 97 hyphenate your document. The target system that produces the final output should control the hyphenation if possible. If you let Word 97 hyphenate your document, hyphens could appear in the middle of lines if the typesetter fails to eliminate all of Word 97's hyphens.

## Using the Thesaurus

When you just can't seem to think of a particular word, type a *synonym* (a different word whose meaning is similar) and ask Word 97's thesaurus for a suggestion. To see a list of synonyms, select a word (or click anywhere in the word) and select Tools | Language | Thesaurus (or press Shift+F7). Word 97 displays Figure 7.8's Thesaurus dialog box.

A *synonym* is a word whose meaning is similar to another.

**Figure 7.8.**
*Find synonyms fast.*

From the Thesaurus dialog box, you can select a replacement word (Word 97 automatically replaces the original word with the replacement), or use the replacement word list to look up additional synonyms. For example, if you cannot find a good synonym for *dissolve* but one of the replacement words for *dissolve* is *liquefy*, look up synonyms for *liquefy* by selecting the Thesaurus dialog box's *liquefy* entry and clicking Look Up. Through this link to related words, you might find the synonym you're looking for.

 **TIP**

Use the Thesaurus dialog box when you want to see *antonyms* (words with meanings that are opposite to the selected word). Word 97 supplies antonyms for some of the words as well. Click the Antonyms entry to see the antonyms.

 *Antonyms* are words that are opposite in meaning.

# Customize Word 97 to Work for You

If you don't like the way Word 97 does something, you can usually customize Word 97 to act the way you want. The Tools menu contains options that let you customize Word 97:

- ☐ Customize—lets you change the layout of Word 97's toolbars and menus.
- ☐ Options—lets you control the behavior of most of Word 97's automatic and manual editing features.

Figure 7.9 shows the Customize dialog box, which appears when you select Tools | Customize.

7

**Figure 7.9.**

*Customize toolbars and menus.*

The tabbed Toolbars sheet lets you specify exactly which toolbars you want to see, if any, during your editing sessions. Too many toolbars can clutter your screen and take away editing area, but different toolbars are useful at different times. For example, display the Tables and Borders toolbar any time you want to create or edit tables in your documents.

Most people modify the tabbed Commands sheet when they want to add or remove an item from Word 97's menus. Select the menu from the Categories list, and Word 97 displays that menu's items in the Commands list. You then can change a menu label or select one from the list that Word 97 doesn't already display for that menu item. Additionally, if you start automating Word 97 with *macros* (pre-defined keyboard shortcuts) or *Visual Basic for Applications* programs (which require some computer-programming skills), the tabbed Commands sheet lets you hook your own procedure commands to new menu items.

The tabbed Options sheet controls let you increase the size of the toolbar icons to read them more easily (at the expense of some editing area), to determine whether you want to see ToolTips, and to determine whether you want shortcut keys attached to those ToolTips.

 **TIP**

Select one of the Menu animations options to make the menu bar's drop-down menus appear more lively.

Tools | Options is the Library of Congress of Word 97 options. From this dialog box, you can modify the behavior of these Word 97 features:

☐ View—changes the way Word 97 displays documents and windows.

☐ General—Determines colors, animation, behavior, and the measurement standard (such as inches or centimeters).

**7**

   ☐  Edit—Changes the way Word 97 responds during your editing sessions.

   ☐  Print—Determines several printing options.

   ☐  Save—Specifies how you want Word 97 to save document changes.

   ☐  Spelling & Grammar—Lists several spell-checking and grammar-checking setting changes that you can make.

   ☐  File Locations—Lets you set disk-drive locations for common files.

   ☐  Compatibility—Lists a plethora of options you can change to make Word 97 look and feel like other word processors, including previous versions of Word.

   ☐  User Information—Holds your name, initials, and address for use with document summaries and automatic return addresses.

   ☐  Track Changes—Determines the format Word 97 uses when you make changes to documents in a group environment or when you want to track several revisions for the same document. (Word 97 can keep track of multiple versions of a document.)

# Summary

This hour explains how to manage your documents through the use of document properties. The document properties contain count statistics as well as other pertinent information that stays with your documents. If you work in an office environment, the properties help maintain order when many people edit the same document.

Part of managing your documents is proofing them to make them more readable and correct. Word 97's proofing tools include a spell checker, grammar checker, hyphenator, and thesaurus. Although these tools don't replace human proofreading, they can help you locate problems.

You can customize almost any part of Word 97. This hour gives you just a glimpse of the many modifications Word 97 allows. Take the time to peruse the Tools | Options tabbed property sheets. Even advanced Word 97 users forget some of the options that can make their editing lives simpler; check the options screens frequently as you learn Word 97 and you'll make Word 97 work the way you want it to.

Perhaps the most important reason to learn the spelling and grammar checker, as well as how to modify Word 97, is that the other Office 97 products use the same features. Therefore, you now know how to check the spelling for an Excel 97 worksheet or an Access 97 database.

The next hour wraps up Word 97 by teaching you its more advanced capabilities.

7

# Q&A

**Q  Does Word 97 update my document-property values for me?**

**A**  In some cases, Word 97 updates your document's property values. For example, as you type words into your document, Word 97 updates that document's word count. You must specify other user-specific properties, such as the document-search keywords and comments.

**Q  Why should I wait until after I create a document to proof it?**

**A**  Most Word 97 users prefer to turn on the automatic spell-checker, but wait until their document is finished before hyphenating and checking the grammar. During the editing process, edits frequently change hyphenation locations; depending on your computer's speed, Word 97 might slow down considerably to update changed hyphens when you change lines. Additionally, the grammar checker has to work constantly as you create your document, not only slowing down your edits but also indicating bad grammar in the places where you might be typing rough-draft material.

**Q  Should I modify Word 97 settings if several people use the same computer?**

**A**  If you share a computer with others, you should not customize Word 97 without telling the others what you've done. As a group, you might determine that certain Word 97 options are better defined than others, but be sure to make customization changes only with the consent of others. Otherwise, the next person who uses Word 97 might think Word 97 no longer can check spelling, when you've only turned off the spell checker temporarily.

7

# Hour 8

# Advanced Word 97

This hour wraps up Word 97 by giving you an idea of Word 97's uncommon features and advanced capabilities. Despite their advanced nature, Word 97's esoteric features are not difficult to use.

You'll find lots of tidbits throughout this chapter that you will use as you write. From inserting special characters to creating multiple column newsletters, Word 97 offers something for everybody's writing needs.

The highlights of this hour include

- ☐ How to type special characters that don't appear on your keyboard
- ☐ Where to go to insert the date, time, and page numbers in your documents
- ☐ When to add AutoText and when to add AutoCorrect entries
- ☐ How to prepare tables for your documents
- ☐ How to convert a single-column document to multiple columns
- ☐ What headers, footers, footnotes, and endnotes are all about

# Special Characters When You Need Them

*Symbols* are special characters that don't always appear on your keyboard. If you want to type special symbols, select Insert | Symbol to display Figure 8.1's Symbol dialog box.

 A *symbol* is a special character that doesn't appear on your keyboard.

**Figure 8.1.**

*Find a symbol you want to insert.*

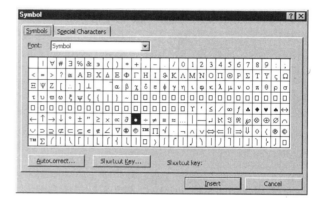

If you don't see the symbol you want to insert, select a different font from the Font drop-down list. Many fonts, such as *WingDings*, supply special symbols from which you can choose. If you find yourself inserting the same symbol over and over again, consider adding that symbol to your AutoCorrect table. Click the AutoCorrect button to see the AutoCorrect dialog box (in which Word 97 has already inserted the symbol); type the AutoCorrect entry that you'll use to produce the special symbol, press Enter, and you've created the AutoCorrect entry for that symbol.

 **NOTE**

> The status bar indicates the ASCII code number for whatever symbol you click.

In addition to adding a symbol-based AutoCorrect entry, you can assign a shortcut key to any symbol. Click the Shortcut Key button, type a shortcut keystroke (such as Alt+Shift+S), press Enter, and Word 97 assigns that shortcut keystroke to the special symbol. Subsequently, you won't have to display the Symbol dialog box to insert special symbols.

Many special characters already have AutoCorrect and shortcut-key entries. If you want to see these pre-defined symbols, click the Symbol dialog box's Special Characters tab to show Figure 8.2's Special Characters sheet. Scroll through the list to see the pre-defined characters currently set.

**Figure 8.2.**
*Word 97 comes pre-defined with many symbols.*

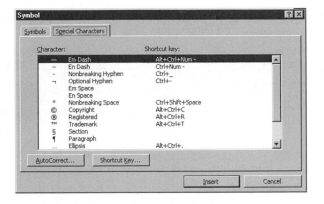

8

# Additional Inserts

In addition to special characters, you can insert the date and time at the cursor's current position. Select Insert | Date and Time, and select the date and time format from Word 97's selection list. If you click the Update automatically option, Word 97 constantly updates the date and time; if you leave the Update automatically option unchecked, Word 97 keeps the original date and time in the document.

If you want Word 97 to insert page numbers at the top or bottom of the document's pages, select Insert | Page Numbers. Word 97 displays the Page Numbers dialog box. Tell Word 97 whether you want the page numbers to appear at the top or bottom of the document pages as well as the portion of the page (left, center, right, inside on facing pages, or outside on facing pages) where you want the page numbers to appear.

**TIP**

Word 97 can format page numbers in several formats, such as 1, Page 1, -1-, Roman numerals, and even letters of the alphabet. Click Format to select from the various page number format options.

One of the most interesting items that you can insert in a Word 97 document is a comment. A *comment* does not print, but does show up on your screen highlighted in yellow so you're sure to see it.

Suppose you want to remind yourself to do something later when you edit the document, such as format the title with information you'll research. Just write yourself a comment! The comment acts like one of those yellow sticky notes. The comment stays attached to your text, but you can read or remove the comment whenever you want.

To insert a comment in your text, select Insert | Comment. Word 97 displays the comment's annotation window (shown in Figure 8.3).

**Figure 8.3.**

*Add comments to your writing.*

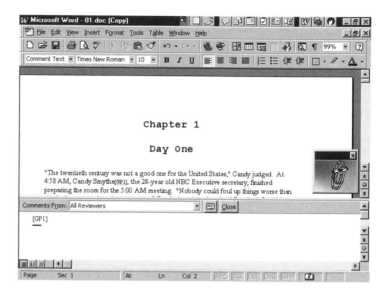

Word 97 names each of your comments using your initials (found in the document property settings). When you type your comment and click Close, Word 97 attaches the comment to your text and indicates the comment by highlighting the anchor text in bright yellow and inserting the comment name inside square brackets.

Subsequently, when you edit your document, you'll see the yellow comments. If you right-click the comment, Word 97's pop-up menu lets you edit (or read) the comment, or delete the comment from the text.

---

**Step-Up**

Microsoft substituted comments for the annotations you used in previous versions of Word.

---

# AutoText Entries

Whereas AutoCorrect is great for quickly inserting formal names and common phrases, *AutoText* lets you quickly insert completely formatted multi-lined text. AutoText is often called boilerplate text; *boilerplate text* is a publishing term used for text that appears frequently.

**NEW TERM**   *Boilerplate text* is text that you often type, such as your company name.

For example, suppose you often place your bold-faced, 16-point, name and address centered across the top of your personal letters. Instead of typing and formatting this text each time you need it, follow these steps to add the text as an AutoText entry:

1. Type and format the text you want to add to the AutoText entries.
2. Select the text.
3. Select Insert | AutoText | AutoText. Word 97 displays Figure 8.4's AutoCorrect page, which shows the AutoText entries currently in effect.

**Figure 8.4.**

*Adding an AutoText entry makes subsequent typing easier.*

4. Type an abbreviation for the AutoText entry in the field labeled Enter AutoText entries here.
5. Press Enter.

When you subsequently type the AutoText entry's abbreviation and press F3, Word 97 replaces the abbreviation with your expanded formatted AutoText entry. AutoText entries require the F3 keystrokes and AutoCorrect entries automatically appear when you type their abbreviations; nevertheless, AutoText entries can be more complex and span multiple lines, whereas AutoCorrect entries are more limiting.

**Step-Up**

Word 97 contains an assortment of pre-defined AutoText entries that previous versions of Word did not support. For example, if you type Created on and press F3, Word 97 adds the current date and time to the end of the Created on text in your document.

**TIP**

If you use the pre-defined AutoText entries often, you can add better shortcuts. For example, rename the Created on AutoText entry to cron so you don't have to type as much to enter the AutoText in your document.

# Adding Tables to Your Documents

Word 97's report-creation power shines when you see how easily you can create customized tables of information inside Word 97. *Tables* are collections of information organized in rows and columns. Tables might contain numbers, text, or combinations of both. Each row and column intersection is called a *cell*. When you use both Word 97 and Excel 97, you might want to embed some of an Excel 97's worksheet into a Word 97 table. Embedded worksheets let you report financial data from within Word 97. (The next hour introduces Excel 97.)

 A *table* is a collection of data organized in rows and columns.

 A *cell* is the value at a table's row and column intersection.

To create a new table, perform these steps:

1. Select Table | Insert Table. Word 97 displays Figure 8.5's Insert Table dialog box.

**Figure 8.5.**

*Use the Insert Table dialog box to prepare the new table.*

2. Specify the number of columns and rows your table will need. You can change these values later if your table needs change.

3. Enter a column width, or leave the Column width field set to Auto if you want Word 97 to guess the table's width. You can change a table's column width at any time (even after you enter data).

4. When creating your first table, press Enter. Once you get used to creating tables, you can click the AutoFormat button to select from a list of pre-defined table formats shown in Figure 8.6.

**Figure 8.6.**

*Word 97 can format
your table automatically.*

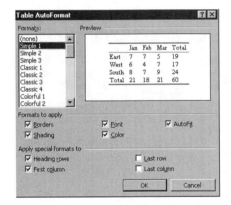

5. Click OK (or press Enter) to close the dialog box. Word 97 creates your table and outlines the table's cells in a grid format.

**TIP**  Word 97 contains two tools that help you build more customized tables. You can create a document with one of the table wizards when you select File | New. Also, you can draw your own tables by clicking the Insert Table toolbar button and dragging the resulting table of cells down and to the right until you've outlined the table size you prefer.

One of the easiest ways to enter data in a table's cell is to click the cell (which moves the text cursor to the cell) and type. As you type past the cell's right margin, Word 97 wraps the cell and increases the row height (if needed) to display the complete cell contents.

When you begin typing data, notice that Word 97's automatic formatting might not match the table's data; perhaps one of the columns is too narrow or too wide. Use your mouse to adjust the size of a row or column's width by clicking and dragging one of the table's four edges in or out. You can also expand or shrink individual columns and rows by dragging their edges.

**NOTE**

When you move your point to a table's row or column edge, Word 97 changes the mouse pointer to a table-adjuster cursor. When the mouse cursor changes, you can drag your mouse to resize the column or row.

Although you can click a cell with your mouse every time you want to enter or edit the contents of that cell, the table cursor-movement keystrokes come in more handy because you can traverse the table without ever removing your hands from the keyboard. Table 8.1 describes how to traverse a table's rows and columns.

### Table 8.1. Moving around a table.

| Press this... | To move the table's cursor here |
| --- | --- |
| Tab | The next cell |
| Shift+Tab | The previous cell |
| Alt+PageUp | The column's top cell |
| Alt+PageDown | The column's bottom cell |
| Alt+Home | The current row's first cell |
| Alt+End | The current row's last cell |

One of the first table problems you'll encounter is that you failed to create enough rows or columns for your table. That's okay. To insert or delete rows or columns, select a row or column and right-click your mouse.

Suppose you need to insert a column. Select the column that will appear *after* the new column by pointing above the column until the mouse pointer changes to a down arrow. Select multiple columns by dragging your mouse to the right after you've selected one column. Right-click your mouse to display a pop-up menu. The menu will be different depending on whether you've selected a row or column first. Select Insert Columns, and Word 97 inserts a new column before the selected column. The right-click menu also contains a Delete Columns command in case you want to delete several columns.

To highlight a row, point to the margin left of the row; Word 97 highlights the entire row. Drag your mouse down or up to select multiple rows. When you right-click your mouse, the pop-up menu will contain an Insert Rows and a Delete Rows command.

**8**

**TIP**

After you create a simple table, select Table | Table AutoFormat to select a style (such as Figure 8.7's 3D style). Figure 8.7's table is only a 2-column table, but Word 97 turned it into a professional-looking chiseled data storehouse.

**Figure 8.7.**
*Make elegant tables out of simple ones.*

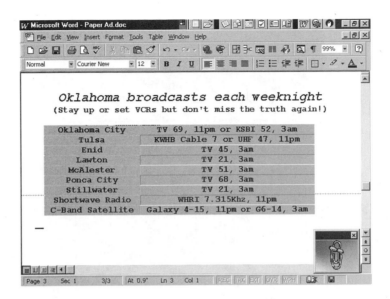

## Multiple Columns on a Page

When you want to create newspaper-style columns, such as those that appear in newsletters and brochures, configure Word 97 to format your text with multiple columns. You can assign multiple columns to all or to only a selected part of your document. Figure 8.8 shows a document with three columns and a single column for the title area. Generally, you should type your document's text before breaking the document into multiple columns.

**Figure 8.8.**
*Multiple columns often produce professional-looking documents.*

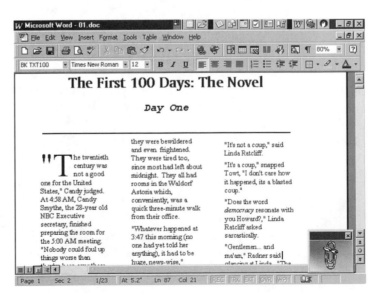

**TIP**   Do you like the way Figure 8.8's opening paragraph begins with the large letter *T*? Such opening characters are called *drop-cap* or *drop-capital characters* because they are capital letters that extend into the next line or two. To add a drop cap, select the text you want dropped, then select Format | Drop Cap.

When you want to set multiple columns, follow these steps:

1. Select the text you want to convert to multiple columns.
2. Select Format | Columns to display the Columns dialog box shown in Figure 8.9.
3. Click the preset column format and enter the number of columns you want to produce.
4. In the dialog box's Width and spacing area, adjust the column width and spacing between columns if you want to adjust the values that Word 97 sets by default. Generally, the default measurements work well. As you adjust the columns, Word 97 updates the Preview area to give you an idea of the final result.
5. If you want a line between the columns, click the Line between option.
6. When you click OK, Word 97 formats your document into multiple columns.

 **TIP**   To add multiple columns quickly and let Word 97 handle the spacing (which Word 97 can generally do well), select the text that you want to format into multiple columns, then click the toolbar button's Columns button. Drag your mouse to the left to select the number of columns (from one to four). When you release the mouse, Word 97 will format the multiple columns.

**Figure 8.9.**

*Set up multiple columns with the Columns dialog box.*

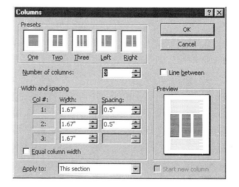

If you format your document into multiple columns that are right-justified, you'll probably need to hyphenate the document. Thin, justified columns often contain lots of extra spaces that Word 97 inserts to maintain the right-justification.

**WARNING**

# Headers and Footers

A *header* is text that appears at the top of each page (or the pages you select, such as all even pages) in your document. A *footer* appears at the bottom of your pages. The nice thing about headers and footers is that you don't have to add them to your document pages; Word 97 adds them for you.

**NEW TERM** A *header* contains text that appears at the top of your document pages.

**NEW TERM** A *footer* contains text that appears at the bottom of your document pages.

To add a header or footer, follow these steps:

1. Select View | Header and Footer to display both the header and footer toolbar as well as outline boxes where you can type the header and footer text. Figure 8.10 shows a document that displays the toolbar, as well as the header-entry box.

**Figure 8.10.**

*Use the header and footer toolbar to adjust your document's header and footer.*

Header entry box

Header and Footer toolbar

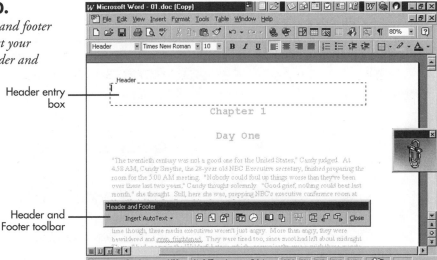

2. Type your header text. If you want to type footer text, click the toolbar's Switch Between Header and Footer button to display the footer text box and type your footer text. If you want to add page numbers, the date, or time to your header or footer text, click the appropriate toolbar buttons.

3. Click the Close button to anchor the header or footer in your document.

Word 97 normally dims header and footer text so that you can easily distinguish between the header, footer, and the rest of your document text when editing your document within the Page Layout view. If you want to specify that the header (or footer) appears only on certain pages, select the File | Page Setup option and adjust the Headers and Footers options.

**TIP**

> If you want to edit a header or footer, double-click the dimmed header or footer text while editing your document. Word 97 opens the header and footer toolbar and lets you edit the header or footer text.

A *footnote* differs from a footer in that a footnote appears only at the bottom of the page on which you include it. Word 97 inserts a footnote reference in the text where you choose to insert the footnote; if you later add text to the page that pushes the footnote reference to the next document page, Word 97 automatically moves the footnote as well so the footnote always appears on the same page as its reference.

*Footnotes* contain text that appears at the bottom of the page on which its corresponding footnote reference appears.

To insert a footnote, follow these steps:

1. Select Insert | Footnote. Word 97 displays the Footnote and Endnote dialog box shown in Figure 8.11. *Endnotes* are footnotes that appear at the *end* of your document in one location. Click the option you want to add—Footnote or Endnote.

*Endnotes* are notes that appear at the end of your document, each with its own endnote reference number that appears in the document.

**Figure 8.11.**

*Add footnotes and endnotes with this dialog box.*

2. If you want Word 97 to number the footnote (or endnote) sequentially starting with 1, click OK. If you want to use a different symbol for the number, click Custom mark and type the reference you want to use.

3. Click OK. Word 97 adds a separating line between your document and the note, adds the reference number to your document text where you inserted the footnote, and places the cursor at the bottom of the page next to the footnote reference number.

4. Type the footnote (or endnote) and click your mouse on the body of the document to resume editing.

You must display the page layout view to see headers, footers, footnotes, and endnotes in their proper places on the page. If you display your document in normal view, Word 97 displays the supplemental notes in a separate window.

## Summary

This hour wraps up this book's discussion of Word 97. You learned how to add the document extras that often turn simple writing into powerful cross-referenced published works. When you add tables and multiple columns, you add document flair that used to be available only to typesetters and printers.

To speed up your writing, use as many AutoCorrect and AutoText entries as you can. If you repeatedly type a phrase, sentence, or block of information, that text is a good candidate for AutoCorrect or AutoText.

If you need to display tabular information, let Word 97 create and format your tables so your data presentation looks clean. In addition, multiple columns work well for newsletters and brochures when you want to keep the reader's attention.

The next hour introduces you to Excel 97. As you'll see, Excel 97 lets you present numeric data as professionally as Word 97 presents your documents.

## Q&A

**Q Should I use AutoText or AutoCorrect?**

**A** You must decide how much formatting and effort the boilerplate text requires. If you need to type the same text often but the text consists of only a word or two and requires no special formatting, use AutoCorrect (Tools | AutoCorrect). With AutoCorrect, Word 97 makes changes for you as you type the AutoCorrect abbreviations. If, however, the text is lengthy or requires special formatting that spans multiple lines, add the text as an AutoText entry. When you type the

AutoText abbreviation, press the F3 key to expand the abbreviation into the formatted full text.

**Q  Why can I not see my headers and footers while editing my document?**

**A**  Perhaps you are displaying your document in normal view. Select View | Page Layout to see headers and footers in their correct positions on the page.

**Q  What is the difference between a table and a document formatted with multiple columns?**

**A**  Both tables and multi-column documents have multiple columns. The multi-column document, however, is useful when you want to create a newspaper-style document with flowing columns of text and graphics. A multi-column document might contain a table in one of its columns.

Use tables when you want side-by-side columns of information. Use multiple columns when you want your text to snake from the bottom of one column to the top of another.

**8**

# PART

# III

## Computing with Excel 97

## Hour

# Hour 9

# Excel 97 Workbooks

This hour introduces you to Excel 97. Excel 97 is to numbers what Word 97 is to text; Excel 97 has been called a *word processor for numbers*. With Excel 97, you'll create numerically based proposals, business plans, business forms, accounting worksheets, and virtually any other document that contains calculated numbers.

You'll probably have to take more time to learn Excel 97's environment than you had to do with Word 97's. Excel 97 starts with a grid of cells in which you place Excel 97's information. This hour takes things slowly to acquaint you with Excel 97 and explains the background necessary for understanding how an Excel 97 working area operates.

The highlights of this hour include

- ☐ How to start Excel 97
- ☐ How to stop Excel 97
- ☐ What workbooks are
- ☐ When you use a workbook and when you use a worksheet
- ☐ Which keys to use to navigate through Excel 97 data
- ☐ How to enter various kinds of Excel 97 data

# Getting Acquainted with Excel 97

You start Excel 97 when you do one of these things:

- ☐ Click the Office 97 Shortcut bar's New Office Document button and double-click the Blank Workbook icon to create a new Excel 97 document. (Click the General tab to see the Blank Workbook icon.)

- ☐ Click the Office 97 Shortcut bar's New Office Document button and click one of the Excel 97–based tabs to open an Excel 97 template or start a wizard. (A *template* is a preset document layout that you can edit to create a particular kind of document.)

- ☐ Click the Office 97 Shortcut bar's Open Office Document button and select an existing Excel 97 workbook you want to edit.

- ☐ Use the Windows Start menu to start Excel 97 by clicking Microsoft Excel on the Program menu.

- ☐ Select an Excel 97 document from the Windows Start menu's Documents option. Windows will recognize that Excel 97 created the document workbook and will start Excel 97, loading the workbook automatically. (The Start menu's Document option contains a list of your most recent work.)

- ☐ Click the Office 97 Shortcut bar's Excel 97 button to create a blank workbook. (Depending on your Office 97 Shortcut bar's setup, you might not see the Excel 97 button there.)

Figure 9.1 shows the opening Excel 97 screen. Your screen might differ slightly depending on the options that the installer set.

When you're finished with Excel 97, quit by performing any of the following:

- ☐ Select File|Exit.
- ☐ Press Alt+F4.
- ☐ Double-click the Control icon.
- ☐ Click Excel 97's Close Window button.

**WARNING**

Always quit Excel 97 and shut down Windows before turning off your computer so you don't lose your work.

**Figure 9.1.**
*Excel 97's opening screen.*

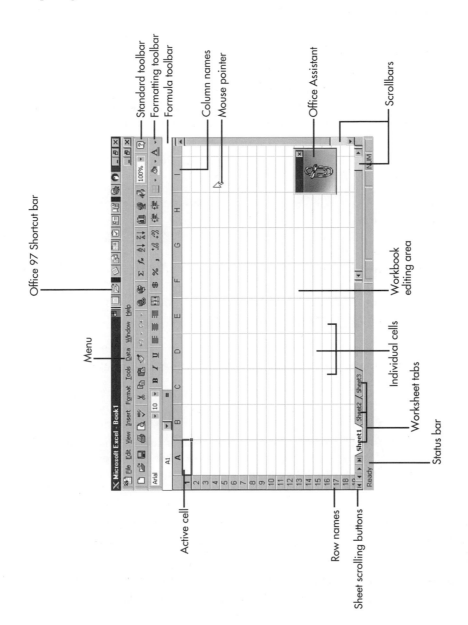

Office 97 Shortcut bar

Menu

Standard toolbar
Formatting toolbar
Formula toolbar

Column names
Mouse pointer

Office Assistant

Scrollbars

Workbook editing area

Individual cells

Worksheet tabs

Status bar

Active cell

Row names

Sheet scrolling buttons

# Workbooks and Worksheets

Excel 97 lets you create and edit workbooks. A *workbook* holds one or more worksheets (sometimes called *spreadsheets* or simply *sheets*). A *worksheet* is a collection of rows and columns that hold text and numbers.

 A *workbook* is a collection of worksheets.

 A *worksheet* is an Excel 97 table-like document that contains rows and columns that hold data.

> ### Step-Up
>
> Excel 97 is not limited to sixteen worksheets per workbook as were previous versions of Excel.

A worksheet acts a lot like a Word 97 table, except that Excel 97 worksheets can do much more numerical processing than Word 97 tables can. Just as Word 97 lets you edit multiple documents in memory at the same time, Excel 97 lets you edit multiple worksheets at once (but those worksheets must all appear in the same workbook).

 **TIP**

A workbook is useful for grouping a single project's worksheets together.

 **NOTE**

You can keep multiple work*books* open at once and move between them by pressing Ctrl+F6 (the same keystroke that moves between multiple Word 97 documents in memory). Multiple workbooks are often difficult to keep track of until you become familiar with Excel 97 and its worksheets. Display your Window menu to see a list of open workbooks if you want to review the ones you've opened.

Blank Excel 97 workbooks contain three worksheets named Sheet1, Sheet2, and Sheet3 (as shown at the bottom of Figure 9.1). When you click a sheet's tab, Excel 97 brings that sheet into view. If a workbook contains several worksheets, you might have to click one of the sheet-scrolling buttons to view additional worksheet tabs.

**9**

Each column has a heading; heading names start with A, B, and so on. Each row has a heading, starting with 1, 2, and so on. The intersection of a row and column, the *cell*, also has a name that comes from combining the row name and column number, such as C4 or A1. A1 is always the top-left cell on any worksheet. The gridlines help you distinguish between cells, but you can turn off gridlines at any time.

 **NEW TERM**    A *cell* is the intersection of a row and column.

**NOTE**    No matter how large your monitor is, you'll see only a small amount of the worksheet area. Use the scrollbars to see or edit information in the off-screen cells, such as cell M17.

Every cell in your workbook contains a unique name or address to which you can refer when you are working in one sheet but want to reference another sheet in the workbook. Preface a cell with its workbook name, followed by an exclamation point (!), to refer to a specific worksheet's cell. For example, Sheet3!G7 refers to the seventh row of column G inside the worksheet named Sheet3.

When you move your mouse over Excel 97's screen, notice that the mouse pointer becomes a cross when you point to a cell area. The pointer returns to its pointy shape when you point to another part of the Excel 97 work area.

# Basic Worksheet Skills

Although Excel 97 *excels* when it comes to numerical data, Excel 97 can work with the following kinds of data:

- ☐ Labels—Text values such as names and addresses
- ☐ Numbers—Numeric values such as 34, –291, 545.67874, and 0
- ☐ Formulas—Expressions that compute numeric results (some formulas work with text values as well)
- ☐ Special formats—Date and time values

As you'll see Part VII, "Putting Things Together," Excel 97 works with data from other Office 97 products. Additionally, you can *import* (transfer) data from other products, such as Lotus 1-2-3.

**NEW TERM**    To *import* is to load data from another program into Excel 97.

## Navigating in Excel 97

Your mouse and arrow keys are the primary navigation keys to move from cell to cell. Unlike Word 97, which uses a text cursor, Excel 97 uses a cell pointer to show you the currently active cell. The active cell accepts whatever data you enter next. As you press an arrow key, Excel 97 moves the active cell pointer in the direction of the arrow.

Table 9.1 lists the most commonly used navigational keystrokes that operate within a worksheet. Use your mouse to scroll with the scrollbars when you want to navigate your worksheet with the mouse. To *really* scroll long distances, press Shift while you scroll with the mouse.

**Table 9.1. Using the keyboard to navigate Excel 97.**

| This key... | Moves to here |
| --- | --- |
| Arrow keys | The direction of the arrow. |
| Ctrl+Up Arrow, Ctrl+Down Arrow | The top-most or bottom-most row with data in the worksheet. |
| Ctrl+Left Arrow, Ctrl+Right Arrow | The left-most or right-most column with data in the worksheet. |
| PageUp, PageDown | The previous or next screen of the worksheet. |
| Ctrl+Home | The upper-left corner of the worksheet (cell A1). |
| End, Arrow | The last blank cell in the arrow's direction. |

## Working with Workbooks

Any time you create, open, or save an Excel 97 file, you're working with a workbook. The workbook approach prevents you from having several worksheet files relating to a specific project. Therefore, your workbook name is the Excel 97 name you assign when you save a file.

**NOTE**

As with Word 97, Excel 97 often uses the term *document* to refer to a workbook file.

**9**

Although you can click a worksheet tab to display any worksheet inside the workbook, most Excel 97 users press Ctrl+PageUp and Ctrl+PageDown to bring a different worksheet from the workbook into the editing area.

To specify the maximum number of worksheets that a workbook will hold, select Options|Tools, click the General tab, and enter a number in the Sheets in new workbook field. When you create a new workbook, that workbook will contain the number of sheets you requested. As you can see from Figure 9.2, Excel 97's Options dialog box resembles Word 97's. Many of the options are identical in both products, as well as throughout the Office 97 suite.

**Figure 9.2.**

*The Options dialog box lets you decide how many worksheets to include in your workbooks.*

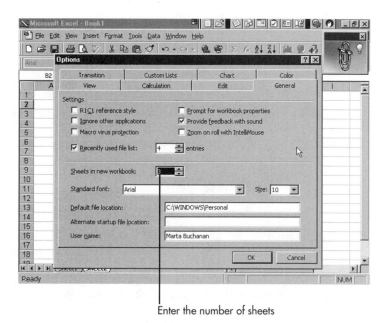

Enter the number of sheets

Situations arise when you only need a single worksheet in a workbook. For example, you might want to track your monthly household budget; such a budget rarely requires multiple worksheets. For your budget, the workbook is basically the same as the worksheet, but you should pare down excess worksheets instead of wasting memory on them. Excel 97 makes it easy to delete excess sheets: Simply right-click the tab of the sheet you want to delete and select Delete from the pop-up menu.

To insert a new worksheet into your workbook, right-click the worksheet tab that will fall *after* the new worksheet. Select Insert. Excel 97 displays Figure 9.3's Insert dialog box, on which you can double-click the Worksheet icon and press OK. The Insert dialog box contains several kinds of items you can add to a workbook, but worksheets will be the most common items you add. Insert|Worksheet also inserts a new worksheet.

**Figure 9.3.**

*Add a new worksheet to your workbook.*

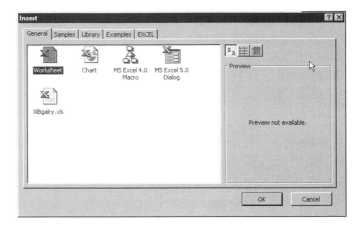

---

**NOTE**

If you don't like the default worksheet names (Sheet1, Sheet2, and so on), rename them by right-clicking the sheet name and selecting Rename. Type the new name. When you press Enter, the worksheet tab will display the new name.

One interesting workbook feature is the capability to rearrange worksheets within a workbook, and even to move worksheets between two or more different workbooks.

If you don't like the current order of the worksheets in your workbook (the worksheet tabs indicate the worksheet ordering), click and drag a worksheet's tag (the mouse cursor changes to let you know you've grabbed the worksheet) to fall before another sheet's tab. If you work with two or three particular worksheets the majority of the time, move those worksheets together so you can move between them easily.

**TIP**

Make a copy of a worksheet by pressing Ctrl before you click and drag a worksheet from one location to another. Excel 97 creates a new worksheet and uses the original worksheet for the new worksheet's data. Before you make extensive changes to a worksheet, you might want to copy it so you can revert to the old version if anything goes wrong.

**Step-Up**

Excel 97 contains a tracking system to track worksheet revisions. Use Tools | Track Changes to get to the tracking information.

If you need to move a worksheet from one workbook to another, open both workbooks and select Window | Tile to display both worksheets (as shown in Figure 9.4). Drag one of the worksheet tabs to the other workbook to move the sheet. To copy instead of move, hold Ctrl while you drag the sheet name.

**Figure 9.4.**

*Display both workbooks if you want to move or copy worksheets between them.*

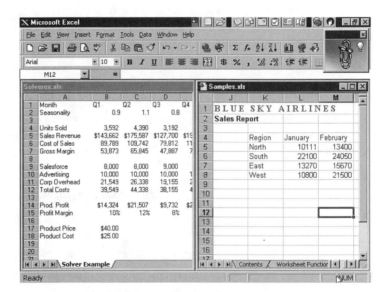

# Entering Worksheet Data

Often, entering worksheet data requires nothing more than moving the cell pointer to the correct cell and typing the data. However, different kinds of data behave differently when entered, so you should understand how Excel 97 accepts different kinds of data.

## Typing Text

If you want to put text (such as a title or a name) in a cell, simply type the text. Excel 97 left-justifies the text in the cell. As you type, the text appears both in the cell and in the formula bar. The Name box to the left of the formula bar displays the name of the cell into which you're entering data. When you press Enter, Excel 97 moves the cell pointer down one row.

**TIP**   Press the Tab or arrow keys instead of Enter to move the cell pointer in a different direction after you enter data.

If you press Esc at any point during your text entry, Excel 97 erases the text you typed in the cell and restores the original cell contents.

If your text is wider than the cell, Excel 97 does one of two things depending on the contents of the adjacent cell to the right:

☐ If the adjacent cell is empty, Excel 97 displays the entire contents of the wide cell.

☐ If the adjacent cell contains data, Excel 97 *truncates* (does not display) the wide cell to show only as much text as will fit in the cell's width. Excel 97 does *not* remove the unseen data from the cell; however, the adjacent cell, if that cell contains data, will always display instead.

Figure 9.5 shows two long labels (remember that *label* is another name for text data) in cells C5 and C10. The same label, which is longer than standard cell width, appears in both cells. Because no data resides in D5, Excel 97 displays all of C5's contents. The data in D10, however, overwrites the trail end of C10. C10 still contains the complete label, but only part of it is visible.

**NEW TERM**   A *label* is text data inside an Excel 97 cell.

**Figure 9.5.**

*Excel 97 may or may not display all of a cell's contents.*

No data in cell D5 to overwrite C5

Cell D10 contains data that overwrites C10

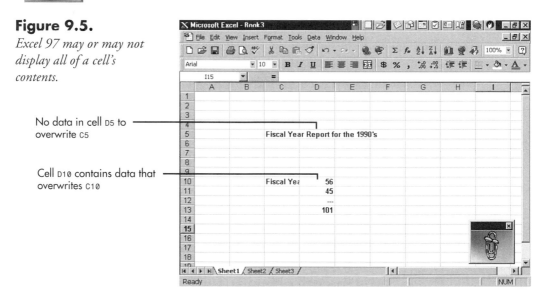

**9**

Some text data, such as price codes, telephone numbers, and zip codes, fool Excel 97. As you'll see in the next section, Excel 97 treats numeric data differently from text data when you type the data into cells. If you want Excel 97 to treat a number (such as a zip code) as a text entry (calculations are not performed on the cell), precede the contents with a single apostrophe ('). For example, to type the zip code 74137, you would type '74137; the apostrophe lets Excel 97 know to format the value as text.

## Typing Numbers

Excel 97 accepts numeric values of all kinds. You can type positive numbers, negative numbers, numbers with decimal points, zero-leading numbers, numbers with dollar signs, percent signs, and even *scientific notation* (a shortcut for writing extremely large and small numbers).

 The term *scientific notation* refers to a format scientists, mathematicians, and engineers often use to write extremely large and extremely small numbers.

**WARNING**

If you type a number but see something like `3.04959E+16` appear in the cell, Excel 97 converted your number to scientific notation to let you know that the cell is not wide enough to display the entire number in its regular form. Excel 97 does not extend long numbers into adjacent cells.

Excel 97 right-justifies numbers inside cells. You can change the justification for a single cell or for the entire worksheet, as you'll see during Hour 10, "Using Excel 97."

## Typing Dates and Times

Excel 97 supports almost every national and international date and time format. Excel 97 uses its AutoFormat feature to convert any date or time value that you type to a special internal number that represents the number of days since midnight, January 1, 1900. Although this strange internal representation might not make sense now, you'll use these values a lot to compute time between two or more dates. For example, you can easily determine how many days past due an account is.

**NOTE**

Excel 97 uses a 24-hour clock to represent time values unless you specify a.m. or p.m. To convert p.m. times to 24-hour times, add 12 to all time values after 12:59 p.m. Therefore, 7:54 p.m. is 19:54 on a 24-hour clock.

You can type any of the following date and time values to represent 6:15 p.m., July 4, 1976, or a combination of both 6:15 p.m. and July 4, 1976:

```
July 4, 1976
4-Jul-76 6:15 p.m.
6:15 p.m.
18:15
07/04/76 18:15
07-04-76 18:15
```

If you enter any of these date and time values, Excel 97 converts them to a shortened format (such as 4/4/76 18:15). You can enter only a date or only a time value if you want. As with most Office 97 formats, you can change this default format with the Format menu. The shorter format often helps worksheet columns align better.

## Summary

This hour introduces Excel 97, and covers Excel 97's screen and the concept of workbooks and worksheets. The workbook documents contain your worksheets, and your worksheets hold data, such as numbers and labels. As you'll see throughout this part of the book, Excel 97 supports a tremendous number of formatting options so that you can turn your numeric data into eye-catching, appealing output.

Although Excel 97 works best with numeric data, Excel 97 accepts text (called labels), date, and time values as well. Excel 97 is extremely lenient about how you type dates and times, but Excel 97 immediately converts such values into a special internal number so that you can calculate dates when you need to.

The next hour extends the concepts of this hour by showing you how to quickly add common data to an Excel 97 worksheet. In addition, you'll learn how to edit values that you type.

## Q&A

**Q  I'm not good at math; can I use Excel 97?**

**A**  If you were great at math, you wouldn't even *need* Excel 97! Seriously, Excel 97 will do all the calculating. Your job is to place the numerical data on the worksheets so that Excel 97 can do its thing. Many people use Excel 97 for uncommon applications, such as tracking exercise routines and grocery lists. Excel 97 is not just for accounting and mathematical applications.

**9**

**Q  Do I always enter the time along with the date?**

**A**  You can enter either a time value, a date value, or both when entering such
information. Excel 97 turns the information into an internal shortened format (you
can change the display format if you desire to make the data look better). If you
don't enter a date with a time value, Excel 97 accepts the time value only and
tracks just the time. If you enter a date, Excel 97 tracks only the date.

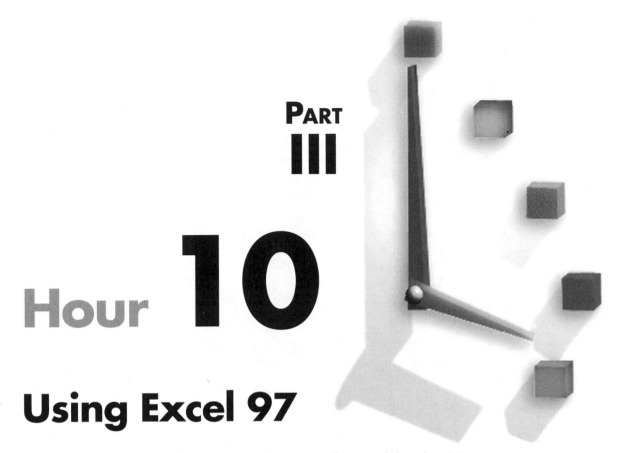

# Hour 10

# Using Excel 97

This hour teaches you ways to improve the accuracy of your worksheet data. Not only can you use AutoCorrect and the spell checker to check worksheets, but Excel 97 can actually enter values for you. When you ask Excel 97 to fill in a series of cell values, Excel 97 uses some intuitive guesswork to complete any series that you begin. If you often enter a special series of numbers or labels, you can teach Excel 97 that series to eliminate typing when you use the series again.

In addition to using Excel 97's automatic series and fill capabilities, this hour shows you how to edit the contents of one or more cells and how to decrease worksheet production time through copy, cut, and paste skills.

The highlights of this hour include

- ☐ How Excel 97 fills in a series of values for you
- ☐ When you must teach Excel 97 a new series
- ☐ How to use comments to describe a cell
- ☐ What you do to select multiple worksheet cells
- ☐ Why the spell checker and AutoCorrect are important to numeral-based worksheets
- ☐ How to find and replace worksheet data
- ☐ Why clearing a cell does not always equate to erasing the cell's contents

# Speed Data Entry

Excel 97 can often predict the data you want to enter into a worksheet. By spotting trends in your data, Excel 97 uses educated guesses to fill cell data in for you. Excel 97 uses *data fills* to copy and extend data from one cell to several additional cells.

One of the most common data fills you'll perform is to use Excel 97's capability to copy one cell's data to several other cells. For example, you might want to create a pro forma balance sheet for the previous five-year period. You can insert a two-line label across the top of each year's data. The first line would contain five occurrences of the label Year, and the second line would hold the numbers 1997 through 2000. To use Excel 97's data fill feature to create the five similar labels, perform these simple steps:

1. Type Year in the left-most cell. Don't press Enter or any cell-moving cursor keys after you type the label.

2. Locate the cell's fill handle. The *fill handle* is the small black box located in the lower-right-hand corner of the active cell.

**NEW TERM**   A *fill handle* is a cell pointer's box that you can drag to extend and copy the cell's contents.

3. Drag the fill handle to the right across the next four columns. As you drag the fill handle, Excel 97 displays the pop-up label Year indicating the value of the new cells.

4. Release the mouse button. Excel 97 fills all five cells with the label, as shown in Figure 10.1.

**Figure 10.1.**

*Excel 97 filled in the four extra labels.*

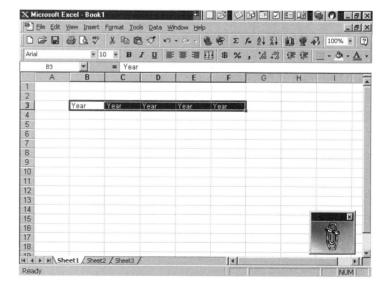

**10**

If you drag the fill handle down, Excel 97 copies the label down the column. Excel 97 will even fill a rectangular area if you drag the fill handle across and down the worksheet. Although the Edit | Fill command performs the same function as the fill handle, dragging the fill handle is much easier than selecting from the menu.

# Smarter Fills

Even if the only fill Excel 97 performed were the copying of data across rows and columns, the data fill would still be beneficial. Excel 97 goes an extra step, however: it performs smart fills with a feature known as AutoFill. *AutoFill* is perhaps the single reason why Excel took over the spreadsheet market a few years ago and has been the leader ever since. When you use AutoFill, Excel 97 examines and extends data you've entered.

**NEW TERM** *AutoFill* is the technique Excel 97 uses to extend data from a cell or cell selection.

For example, the five year pro forma period you were setting up in the previous section included the years 1997 through 2001 (we're close to that magic year number, aren't we?). You can type 1997 under the first Year title and type 1998 under the second title. Select *both cells* using the same dragging technique you learned in Word 97 selection, then drag the fill handle right three more cells. When you release the mouse button, you will see that Excel 97 properly fills in the remaining years (as Figure 10.2 shows).

**Figure 10.2.**

*Excel 97's AutoFill feature knew which years to fill.*

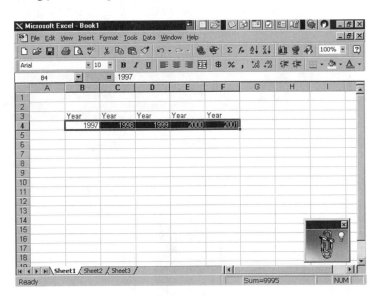

**WARNING**

> If you had only selected one cell, Excel 97 would have copied that cell across the worksheet. Excel 97 needed to see the two selected cells to notice the trend.

Figure 10.2's years don't exactly align under the first row, but you will learn how to format data in the next hour so that your titles align.

Excel 97 gets even better. If you want to use AutoFill to increment cells by a single number, as you are doing here with the years, you don't really need to select two cells first. If you select any cell that contains a number, press Ctrl, and drag the fill handle, Excel 97 adds a one to each cell that you extend to. Therefore, you could fill four years from 1998 through 2001 simply by pressing Ctrl before you dragged the first year's fill handle to the right.

As you know, Excel 97 works with text as well as with numeric values. AutoFill recognizes many common text trends, including

☐ Days of the week names

☐ Days of the week abbreviations (such as Mon, Tue, and so on)

☐ Month names

☐ Month abbreviations (such as Jan, Feb, and so on)

Suppose you want to list month names down the left of the pro forma sheet because you need to report each month's totals for those five years. All you need to do is type January for the first month name, and drag that cell's fill handle to the twelfth cell below. Figure 10.3 shows the result.

**Figure 10.3.**

*Let Excel 97 fill in the series of month names.*

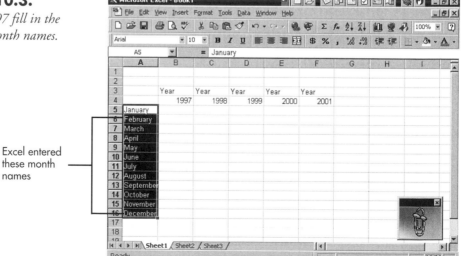

Excel entered these month names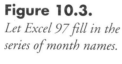

# Design Your Own Fills

In addition to the month and weekday names and abbreviations, Excel 97 can fill in *any* list of values. You can teach Excel 97 a new list to use with AutoFill. After you've shown Excel 97 the new list, any time you type the first value and drag that cell's fill handle in any direction, Excel 97 fills the remaining cells with your list.

To add your own AutoFill list to Excel 97's repertoire of lists, perform these steps:

1. Select Tools | Options.
2. Click the Custom Lists tab to display the current AutoFill lists in effect.
3. Click the Add button.
4. Type your list of values for AutoFill. If you have six departments, you might enter something like Dept 1, Dept 2, Dept 3, Dept 4, Dept 5, and Dept 6. Your screen would look like Figure 10.4.
5. Click OK to add your list to AutoFill's current list.

The next time you type the label Dept 1 in a cell and drag the fill handle to the right or down the worksheet, Excel 97 fills in the remaining departments. If you fill only four cells, Excel 97 uses the first four values. If you fill six or more cells, Excel 97 fills all six departments and starts repeating the department names for any number over six.

**Figure 10.4.**

*Teach Excel 97 new AutoFill entries.*

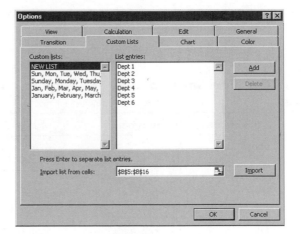

If you enter a series in a worksheet, then decide that the series would make a great AutoFill list (in case you want to add the list to another worksheet), Excel 97 doesn't make you re-enter the list. Simply select the entire list by dragging the mouse pointer through the list; when you open the Custom Lists dialog box, click Import to add the selected range to the AutoFill entries.

AutoFill is fine for a typical range of titles and for a series of a dozen or fewer entries, but some data series consume numerous entries. When you want to enter a larger number of values in a series, perform these steps:

1. Type the first value of the series in the first cell.
2. Select the cell and all subsequent cells that will receive the rest of the series.
3. Select Edit | Fill | Series to display the Series dialog box.
4. Select Rows if you've selected cells from a row or Columns if you've selected cells from a column.
5. Select the type of series you are entering. Table 10.1 describes each of the four types from which you can choose.
6. Select the subtype. For example, if the series is a series of months, check Month.
7. Enter the Step value, which describes how each value in the series increments or decrements.
8. Enter the Stop value if necessary (you rarely need to enter one). For example, if you want to enter a series that increases every three months, and you've checked the Month option and typed 3 for the Step value, Excel 97 will know the final month and you won't need to enter a month.

   Although you won't need to tell Excel 97 where to stop in most instances, a Stop value is useful if you use the Trend option. Excel 97 starts with your initial selected value (if numeric) and estimates the values between that starting value and the Stop value you supply.
9. Click OK to create and enter the series of values.

**Table 10.1. The Series dialog box requires one of these kinds of series.**

| Series name | If you type... | Excel 97 can complete with |
|---|---|---|
| Linear | 0 | 1, 2, 3, 4, 5 |
| | -50, 0, 50, 100 | 150, 200, 250 |
| Growth | 2, 4 | 8, 16, 32, 64 |
| | 10, 100 | 1000, 10000 |
| Date | 1-Jan, 1-Apr | 1-Jul, 1-Oct, 1-Jan |
| AutoFill | Acctg-101, Acctg-102 | Acctg-103, Acctg-104 |
| | Year '96 | Year '97, Year '98 |

**10**

# Adding Comments

As with Word 97, you can insert comments in a cell. The comments act like yellow sticky notes on the screen, except that Excel 97's notes don't get in the way when you don't want to see them. The comments don't appear in the cell; when you insert a comment, Excel 97 indicates that the comment resides within the cell by flagging the cell's upper-right corner with a red triangle. When you point to the cell, Excel 97 displays the attached comment.

**NEW TERM**   A *comment* is a note about a cell that doesn't appear as part of the cell's data.

To attach a comment to a selected cell, select Insert|Comment. Excel 97 opens the square shown in Figure 10.5. Type your comment here. Excel 97 automatically places your name at the beginning of the comment. The name tells who added the comment in case you work in a multi-user environment. You can erase the name if you don't want to see it.

**10**

**Figure 10.5.**

*Add comments to cells.*

Attached comment flags ——

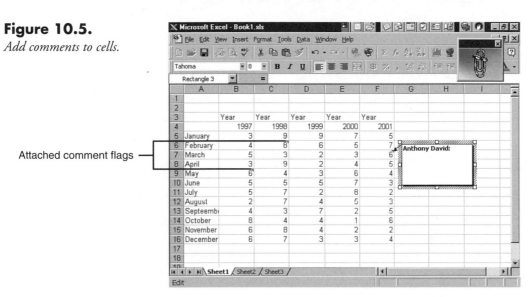

**WARNING**

If you select a group of cells and attach a comment, Excel 97 attaches the comment only to the upper-left cell in the selection. Excel 97 cannot attach a comment to an entire selection, only to individual cells.

The last section in this hour, "Clearing Data," tells you how to remove comments you no longer need.

# Selecting Cells

You can select a cell, a row of cells, or a column of cells just by clicking and dragging your mouse. As you drag your mouse, Excel 97 selects a rectangular region. You'll notice as you drag your mouse that Excel 97 displays how many rows and columns you've selected. For example, you'll see the message 10R X 4C appear in the toolbar's Name box if you've selected 10 rows and 4 columns. When you let up with your mouse, Excel 97 displays the selection's upper-left corner.

Not only can you select a rectangular region of cells, you can also select disjointed regions. Select the first area, then press Ctrl while you click another cell and drag the mouse. The selection highlight appears in both places on your screen.

Remove any selection by clicking your mouse on a cell or by pressing an arrow key.

# Worksheet Editing

Some of the most important Excel 97 skills you can learn are editing skills. Entering numerical data is error-prone at its best; the faster you edit cell values, the faster you'll complete accurate worksheets. The following sections show you the primary editing tools Excel 97 provides.

## Spell Checking

No worksheet program included a spell checker before Excel. After all, worksheets are for numbers, right? Of course, the primary purpose for worksheets is formatting, arranging, and calculating numbers. Numbers without titles, though, are worthless in most instances. You've got to present your numerical data in such a way that the worksheet user knows what he is looking at.

Given the amount of text you'll enter on your worksheets, a spell checker makes sense. You can only wonder why worksheet makers did not add spell checkers long before Microsoft added one to Excel.

Here are the ways you can check your worksheet's spelling:

☐ Click the Spelling toolbar button
☐ Select Tools|Spelling from the menu
☐ Press F7, the spelling shortcut key

**10**

**WARNING**

Unlike Word 97, Excel 97 does not include a grammar checker. Rarely will you include complete sentences on a worksheet, so the grammar checker would be wasted overhead in most cases.

Excel 97's spell checker works identically to Word 97's (see Hour 7, "Managing Documents and Customizing Word 97," for a quick review). Excel 97's spell checker will *not* check every worksheet in your workbook, but only the current worksheet active on your screen. If Excel 97 finds an error, you can choose to correct, ignore, or add the error to Excel 97's dictionary so the word no longer appears as an error (as might be the case for proper names).

## AutoCorrect Worksheets

Use AutoCorrect as you type Excel 97 entries just as you used AutoCorrect in Word 97. When you type an abbreviation for an AutoCorrect entry, Excel 97 converts that abbreviated form to the complete AutoCorrect entry for you when you press the spacebar or leave the cell.

**TIP**

Word 97, Excel 97, and all the other Office 97 products share the same AutoCorrect and spelling dictionaries! Therefore, when you make changes and additions in Word 97 or Excel 97's AutoCorrect and spelling dictionaries, the other products will recognize those changes.

To add AutoCorrect entries, perform the same steps as you do with Word 97:

1. Select Tools | AutoCorrect.
2. Type your abbreviated AutoCorrect entry in the Replace field.
3. Press Tab.
4. Type the replacement text in the With field.
5. Click OK to return to the worksheet editing area.

## Cell Editing

Much of your Excel 97 editing requires that you correct numeric data-entry. Of course, if you begin to type a number (or a formula, as you'll learn in the next hour) in a cell but realize you've made a mistake, press Backspace to erase your mistake or press the arrow keys to move the text cursor back over the entry to correct something.

10

If you've already moved to another cell when you recognize that you've entered an error, quickly correct the mistake like this:

1. Move the cell pointer to the cell you need to correct (click the cell to move the pointer there).

2. Press F2. F2 is the standard Windows editing shortcut key. (If you've still got your hand on the mouse, you can double-click the cell to edit the cell's contents also.) You'll know Excel 97 is ready for your edit when you see the text cursor appear in the cell.

3. Move the text cursor to the mistake.

4. Press the Insert key to change from overtype mode to insert mode or vice versa. As with Word 97, overtype mode lets you write over existing characters, while insert mode shifts all existing characters to the right as you type the correction.

5. Press Enter to anchor the correction in place.

If you want to undo an edit, click the Undo button. To redo an undo, click the Redo button. As you can see, once you've mastered one Office 97 product (as you have Word 97), you know a lot about the other products.

## Finding and Replacing

Like Word 97, Excel 97 contains a powerful search-and-replace operation that can search your worksheet for values and replace those values if needed.

**WARNING**

Excel 97's find-and-replace feature works a little differently from Word 97's. Excel 97's numeric nature requires a different type of find and replace. Therefore, read this section even if you've mastered Word 97's find-and-replace feature.

Figure 10.6 shows Excel 97's Find dialog box. You can request that Excel 97 search by rows or by columns. If your worksheet is generally longer than wide (as most are), select By Columns to speed your search. Indicate whether you want Excel 97 to match your uppercase and lowercase search text exactly (not applicable for numeric searches), and select the proper Look in option of Formulas, Values, or Comments.

Use Formulas if you're searching for part of a formula (you'll learn all about formulas in the next hour), use Values if you want Excel 97 to search only the calculated cells (not within formulas), and use Comments if you want Excel 97 to search through cell comments. Generally, you'll be searching through formulas, so Excel 97 makes Formulas the default search target.

**Figure 10.6.**

*Excel 97's Find dialog box looks for text or numbers.*

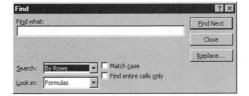

The Find entire cells only option tells Excel 97 that a cell must contain your entire Find value and nothing else before a proper match will be made.

If you want Excel 97 to replace the found value with another value, select the Edit | Replace command to display Figure 10.7's Replace dialog box.

**Figure 10.7.**

*Let Excel 97 replace values for you.*

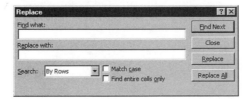

Click the Replace All button if you want Excel 97 to replace all occurrences of the found text. Otherwise, click Find Next to find the next matching value and, if that's a value you want to replace, click Replace.

**TIP**

If you only want to find or replace within a limited worksheet range, select the range before conducting the find or replace operation.

# Reviewing Excel 97's Copy, Cut, and Paste

If you mastered Word 97's copy, cut, and paste commands, Excel 97's will be a breeze. As with Word 97 and the other Office 97 products, Excel 97 uses the Windows clipboard to hold data that you're copying, cutting, and pasting from within your worksheet or between worksheets. If you open two workbooks at the same time and display both on your screen (by placing the workbook windows using Window | Arrange), you can easily copy, cut, and paste between the two workbooks.

To copy data from one location to another, select the cell or cells you want to copy and click the Copy toolbar button (or press Ctrl+C) to copy the worksheet contents to your clipboard. The contents stay in their original location because you elected to copy and not cut the cells. To paste the clipboard contents to another location, select the first cell in the target location (which may reside in another workbook) and click the Paste toolbar button (or press Ctrl+V). Excel 97 will overwrite the target cells with the pasted contents, so be sure of the paste target when you paste clipboard data.

---

**Step-Up**

The Office Assistant keeps a close eye on you at all times. If you attempt to paste over data, Office Assistant issues the warning shown in Figure 10.8. You can click OK to accept the overwrite or click Cancel to stop the paste.

---

**Figure 10.8.**

*Office Assistant lets you know if you are about to paste over data.*

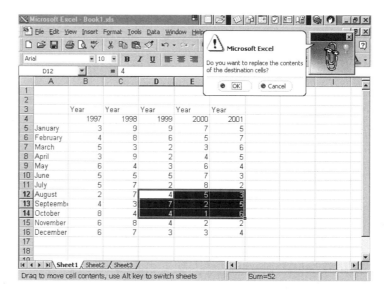

---

**NOTE**

Remember that the clipboard holds its contents until you replace them with other material. Therefore, you can continue pasting the clipboard to other worksheets as long as you keep selecting a target location and pressing Ctrl+V.

**10**

Excel 97 supports drag-and-drop editing, so after you select the cells to copy, press Ctrl and drag the selection to its new location. You *must* drag the selection by pointing to one of the selection edges; if you attempt to drag from the center of a selected cell set, Excel 97 changes the selection range. When you release your mouse button and the Ctrl key, Excel 97 pastes the contents to their target location. Of course, drag-and-drop editing works only when you can see both the source and the target copy and paste locations.

To cut contents and place them elsewhere, just select the cells that you want to cut and press Ctrl+X (or click the Cut toolbar button). Excel 97 removes the selection from its original location and places the selection on your clipboard. You then can paste the clipboard contents elsewhere. In effect, cutting and pasting performs a movement of the selected data. If you want to move the selection with your mouse, drag the selection without first pressing Ctrl as you did when copying the contents.

**TIP**　　If you want to drag and drop between two workbook's worksheets but you only have one worksheet displayed, press the Alt key before dragging your selection. When you drag the selection over the target worksheet's name tab, Excel 97 opens that worksheet, and you can drop the dragged contents to the open worksheet.

# Clearing Data

Due to the nature of worksheets, erasing worksheet data differs from erasing word-processed data. Other information on the worksheet can heavily depend on the erased data, as you'll see in the next hour's lesson. When you want to erase a cell's or a selection's contents, first decide which of the following kinds of erasure you want to perform:

☐　Erase the selection and send the contents to the clipboard (as you learned in the previous section)

☐　Clear only a portion of the selection, such as its formatting, comment, or data value

☐　Completely erase the selection and all formatting and notes attached to the selection

☐　Erase the selected cells and their position so that other cells in the row move left or cells below move up

A worksheet's cell contains lots more than just the numbers and text that you see on the worksheet screen. Not only can the cells also contain formulas and comments, but they often rely on other cells for information. Therefore, when you want to erase the selection, you must keep in mind how the selection affects other worksheet areas.

If you want to delete the selected cell's data, press Delete. Excel 97 retains any formatting and comments that you had applied before you deleted the data.

If you want to more selectively erase a cell, select the Edit | Clear command and select from one of the four options listed below.

- ☐ The All option deletes the entire selection, including the contents, format, and attached comments

- ☐ The Formats option erases only the selection's format; you can get rid of a cell's special formatting and revert to a general format without changing or erasing the contents of the cell

- ☐ The Contents option deletes the cell contents but leaves the formatting and comments intact

- ☐ The Comments option deletes any special comments that appear in the selected cells

- ☐ The Hyperlinks option removes any Internet-based references within the cell

**NOTE**

> Reverse an accidental deletion with Undo (Ctrl+Z).

Here's a quicker way to erase the values in cells: Select the cells and drag the fill handle up and to the left. As you drag the fill handle, Excel 97 grays out the cells that will be erased when you release the mouse button.

To remove the selected cells as well as their contents and close the gap left by the deleted selection, select Edit | Delete to display Figure 10.9's Delete dialog box. Select Shift cells left or Shift cells up so Excel 97 knows how to close the gap that the deletion leaves.

**Figure 10.9.**

*Remove cell contents and close the gap.*

# Summary

This hour teaches you how to speed up your data entry by using AutoFill and AutoCorrect. After you teach Excel 97 your own special series, Excel 97 fills in that series of values for you. Although accuracy is more important than speed, you'll welcome the speedy data-entry tools Excel 97 provides.

**10**

Excel 97's copy, cut, and paste operations work much the same as the corresponding operations in Word 97. This hour focuses more on the differences than similarities between the products. Worksheet data differs from a word processor's, and you must handle certain kinds of Excel 97 deletions differently than Word 97 deletions.

The next hour shows how to work with ranges, formulas, rows, and columns. Now that you've covered the groundwork, you're ready to learn about Excel 97's powerhouse tools for worksheets.

# Q&A

**Q How will I know if Excel 97 can fill a series I've started?**

**A** Enter the first couple of values, select the cells, and drag the selection's fill handle to the right or down, depending on your desired fill direction. As you drag the fill handle, Excel 97 shows in a ToolTips-like pop-up box which values will fill in the series. If Excel 97 does not recognize the series, the pop-up values won't be correct. You then can teach Excel 97 the new series as explained in this hour or enter the remaining values by hand. In many instances you'll be surprised at Excel 97's power; for example, if the first two values in your series are 10 and 20, Excel 97 guesses that you want to extend the series by 10s.

**Q Why does Excel 97 sometimes select additional cells when all I want to do is extend a series?**

**A** You are dragging the cell's contents, *not* the fill handle. Be sure that you drag the fill handle when you want Excel 97 to complete the series. If you drag with one of the cell's straight edges rather than its fill handle, Excel 97 attempts to move the cell contents from their original location to your dragging target, so be careful that you've grabbed the fill handle when you're ready for the fill.

**Q Why would I want to remove formatting, but not a cell's contents?**

**A** You'll learn in the next hour how to apply lots of formats to cells. For example, you can apply a date format to a cell so that Excel 97 displays a date based on the value and not a number. If you format a cell for a date and later, due to editing changes, that cell no longer holds a date but a value, you'll want to remove the date format. Excel 97 uses a general numerical format for all cells to which you don't specifically apply a different format.

10

# Hour 11

# Focus with Excel 97

This hour teaches you additional Excel 97 worksheet editing skills. You'll be surprised how Excel 97 helps you when you modify worksheets. For example, Excel 97 automatically adjusts cell range names and formulas when you rearrange your worksheet.

Understanding ranges becomes critical if you want to really master Excel 97. Therefore, be sure that you master this hour. You'll use range names and addresses in Excel 97 formulas and functions.

In addition to the editing tools, you'll also learn how to format worksheets to make them look better. This hour teaches the formatting essentials, so you'll be ready for the fancy stuff in the next hour.

The highlights of this hour include

☐ What Excel 97 does when you insert or delete rows and columns

☐ How ranges differ from selections

☐ Why range names are important

☐  What the fundamental math operators do

☐  How to organize formulas so they compute in the order you desire

☐  Which functions save you time and errors

☐  How to format cells to add eye-catching appeal to your worksheet

# Inserting and Deleting

As you saw in the previous hour, Excel 97's requirements are somewhat different from Word 97's, even though both programs perform tasks in a similar manner and with similar menu commands and dialog boxes. The nature of worksheets make them behave differently from word-processed documents. The next few sections explain how to insert and delete information from your worksheets.

## Deleting Entire Cells

When you deleted cells in the previous hour, you learned how to remove selected cells completely from the worksheet and close the gap with the Delete dialog box. The Delete dialog box not only deletes cells, but also deletes entire rows and columns.

To delete a row or column, perform these steps:

1. Select a cell that resides in the row or column you want to delete.

2. Select Edit | Delete to display the Delete dialog box.

3. Select either the Entire row or Entire column option.

4. Click OK to perform the deletion. Excel 97 shifts columns to the left or rows up to fill in the missing gap.

**TIP**

If you want to delete multiple rows or multiple columns, select cells from each column or row you want to delete before displaying the Delete dialog box.

## Inserting Entire Cells

Inserting cells, as opposed to inserting data inside a cell, requires that the existing worksheet cells move to the right and down to make room for the new cell. When you want to insert a cell, perform these steps:

11

1. Select the cell that should appear *after* the inserted cell.
2. Select Insert | Cells to display the Insert dialog box.
3. Click either the Shift cells right option or the Shift cells down option to determine the direction of the shift. The shift makes room for your new cell.
4. Click OK to begin the shift.

Some people prefer to use the mouse to shift cells right or down to make room for new data. Press Shift and drag the cell's fill handle (or the selection's fill handle if you've selected a group of cells) down or to the right. Excel 97 grays out the areas that will be left blank by the shifting.

# Inserting Rows and Columns

To insert a row or column (and thus move the other rows down or other columns to the right), perform these steps:

1. Select the row or column that will appear *after* the inserted rows or columns. Click the row or column header to select the entire row or column. If you want to insert more than one row or column, select that many existing rows or columns by dragging the row or column selection.

2. Select Insert | Rows or Insert | Columns. Excel 97 shifts the existing rows or columns to make room for the new empty row or column. Instead of selecting from the menu bar, you can point to the selected row or column and display Figure 11.1's pop-up menu by right-clicking the mouse and selecting Insert to insert the new row or column. (Excel 97 inserts multiple rows or columns if you first selected more than one row or column.)

**Figure 11.1.**

*You can insert rows or columns with the pop-up menu.*

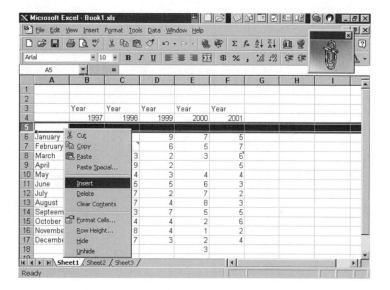

### Deleting Rows and Columns

Perform these steps when you want to delete a row or column (as opposed to erasing the row or column's contents):

1. Select the row or column to delete.
2. Right-click over the selected row or column to display the pop-up menu.
3. Select Delete. Excel 97 shifts the remaining part of the worksheet to close the gap.

## Worksheet Ranges

A *range* is a group of cells. A selected group of cells comprises a range, but ranges don't always have to be selected. A range is always rectangular. A range might be a single cell, a row, a column, or several adjacent rows and columns. The cells in ranges are always contiguous. Even though you can *select* noncontiguous cells, ranges *always* form rectangular worksheet regions.

**NEW TERM**   A *range* is a rectangular collection of cells.

Figure 11.2 shows three ranges on a worksheet. You can describe a range by the range's upper-left cell's address (the *anchor point*) and the range's lower-right cell's address. As you can see from Figure 11.2, you must designate multi-cell ranges by listing the anchor point, followed by a colon (:), followed by the range's lower-right cell address. Therefore, the range that begins at B3 and ends at F4 has the range of B3:F4.

**NEW TERM**   An *anchor point* is a range's upper-left cell address.

You'll work quite a bit with ranges. One of the ways to make your worksheets more manageable is to name your ranges. For example, you might assign the name Titles to your column titles, Months to your column of month names, and so on.

To name a range, perform these steps:

1. Select the cells that you want to include in the named range.
2. Click the Name box at the left of the formula bar (the text box that displays cell addresses).
3. Type the range name.

**11**

4.  Press Enter. When you subsequently select the range, you'll see that Excel 97 displays the range name instead of the range address in the Name box.

**Figure 11.2.**

*Ranges on a worksheet.*

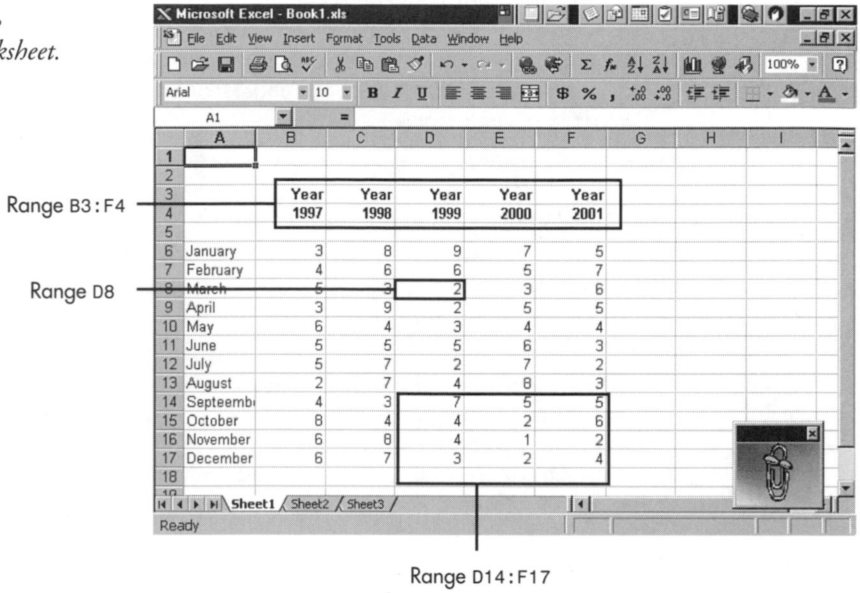

Range B3:F4 ——

Range D8 ——

Range D14:F17

Names are easier to remember than range addresses. For example, if you create a payroll worksheet and assign the names GrossPay, NetPay, HoursWorked, TaxRate, and PayRate to the ranges that hold that data, you never again have to type the range addresses. When you want to move or copy one of the ranges or use the range as a formula, just refer to the range name and let Excel 97 figure out the correct addresses.

NEW TERM    A *range name* is a name you assign to a range of cells.

**TIP**

> Here's an even better reason to name ranges: If you move a range, Excel 97 moves the name with the cells! If you tracked range addresses and not names, you would constantly have to track down the latest addresses when you referred to the range. By naming ranges, you never have to worry about keeping track of addresses because the names won't change even if the addresses do.

**NOTE**

Use meaningful names. Although AAA will work as a name for a column of net sales figures, NetSales makes a lot more sense and is easier to remember. Your range names can include between 1 and 255 characters, and can contain alphabetic letters, numbers, periods, and the underscore. Although you cannot include spaces, you can mix uppercase and lowercase letters and include the underscore to help distinguish between words in a single name.

If you create a large worksheet and you need to return to a named range to make some changes, click the Name box and type the name. Excel 97 instantly displays that range and selects the range for you.

**WARNING**

Fight the urge to ignore range names when you create your worksheets. The tendency is to put off naming ranges until later, and later often does not come. By naming key ranges as you create your worksheet, you'll more rapidly create the worksheet and the worksheet will contain fewer errors.

# Formulas

Without formulas, Excel 97 would be little more than a word processor for tables of information. When you use formulas, however, Excel 97 becomes an extremely powerful time-saving planning, budgeting, and general-purpose financial tool.

**NOTE**

Some people credit worksheet programs for the tremendous PC growth in the 1980s. Without formulas, worksheets would never have been able to create such a demand for personal computers.

On a calculator, you typically type a formula, then press the equal sign to see the result. All Excel 97 formulas *begin* with an equal sign. For example, here is a formula:

=4*2-3

The asterisk is an *operator* that means *multiply*. This formula requests that Excel 97 compute the value of 4 multiplied by 2 minus 3 to get the result. When you type a formula and press Enter or move to another cell, Excel 97 displays the *result*, not the formula, on the worksheet.

**11**

As Figure 11.3 shows, the answer 5 appears on the worksheet, and you can see the cell's formula contents right on the Formula bar area.

**Figure 11.3.**

*Excel 97 displays a formula's result on the worksheet.*

The cell's formula appears here

The formula's answer is here

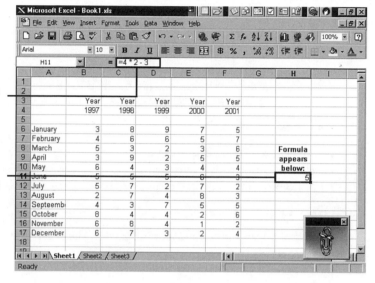

You can format a worksheet to show the actual formula instead of the answer, but you would do something like that only when printing worksheet content listings that you wanted to study.

Table 11.1 lists the primary math operators you can use in your worksheet formulas.

## Table 11.1. The primary math operators.

| Operator | Example | Description |
|---|---|---|
| ^ | =7 ^ 3 | Raises 7 to the power of 3 (called *exponentiation*) |
| / | =4 / 2 | Divides 4 by 2 |
| * | =3 * 4 * 5 | Multiplies 3 by 4 by 5 |
| + | =5 + 5 | Adds 5 and 5 |
| - | =5 - 5 | Subtracts 5 from 5 |

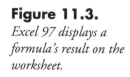 The *exponentiation* operator raises one number to a higher power.

You can combine any and all of the operators in a formula. When combining operators, Excel 97 follows the traditional computer (and algebraic) *operator hierarchy model*. Therefore, Excel

97 first computes exponentiation if you raise any value to another power. Excel 97 then calculates all multiplication and division in a left-to-right order (the first one to appear computes first) before addition and subtraction (also in left-to-right order).

**NEW TERM** The *operator hierarchy* dictates the order that operators compute in formulas.

The following formula computes 14 because Excel 97 calculates the exponentiation, then the division, then the multiplication, and finally the subtraction. Even though the subtraction appears first, the operator hierarchy forces the subtraction to wait until last to compute.

```
=18 - 2 ^ 3 / 4 * 2
```

If you want to override the operator hierarchy, put parentheses around the parts you want Excel 97 to compute first. For example, the following formula computes a greatly different result from the previous one, despite the same values and operators used:

```
=(18 - 2) ^ 3 / 4 * 2
```

Instead of 14, this formula computes 2,048! The subtraction produces 16, which is then raised to the 3rd power (producing 4,096) before dividing by 4 and multiplying the result by 2 to get 2,048.

Excel 97's true power shows itself when you use cell addresses and range names in formulas. All of the following are valid formulas. Cell addresses or range names appear throughout the formulas.

```
=(SalesTotals)/NumOfSales
```

```
=C4 * 2 - (Rate * .08)
```

```
=7 + LE51 - (Gross - Net)
```

When you enter formulas that contain range addresses, you can either type the full address or point to the cell address. If you want to include a complete named range in a formula (formulas can work on complete ranges, as you'll see later this hour), select the entire range and Excel 97 inserts the range name in your formula. Often, finding and pointing to a value is easier than locating the address and entering the exact address.

# The Magic of Copying Formulas

When you copy formulas that contain cell addresses, Excel 97 updates the cell addresses so they reference *relative addresses*. For example, suppose you enter this formula in cell A1:

```
=A2 + A3
```

**11**

**New Term** A *relative address* is an address that references cells based on the current cell's location.

This formula contains two addresses. The addresses are relative because the addresses A2 and A3 will change if you copy the formula elsewhere. For example, if you copy the formula to cell B5, B5 holds this:

```
=B6 + B7
```

The original relative addresses update to reflect the formula's copied location. Of course, A1 still holds its original contents, but the copied cell at B5 holds the same formula referencing B5 instead of A1.

An *absolute address* is an address that does not change if you copy the formula. A dollar sign, $, always precedes an absolute address. The address $B$5 is an absolute address. $B5 is a partial absolute address; if you copy a formula with $B5 inside the computation, the $B keeps the B column intact but the fifth row updates to the target cell's row location. If you type the following formula in cell A1:

```
=2 * $B5
```

and then copy the formula to cell F6, cell F6 will hold this formula:

```
=2 * $B10
```

The dollar sign keeps the row B absolute no matter where you copy the formula, but the relative row number can change as you copy the formula.

**New Term** An *absolute address* is an address that references cells using their specific addresses and does not change if you copy the cell holding the formula.

The bottom line is this: Most of the time, you'll use relative addressing. If you insert or delete rows, columns, or cells, your formulas remain accurate because the cells they reference change as your worksheet changes.

Consider Figure 11.4's worksheet. The bottom row needs to hold formulas that total each of the projected year's 12-month values.

How would you enter the total row? You could type the following formula in cell B19:

```
=B6+B7+B8+B9+B10+B11+B12+B13+B14+B15+B16+B17
```

Once you've typed the formula in B19, you then *could* type the following formula in cell C19:

```
=C6+C7+C8+C9+C10+C11+C12+C13+C14+C15+C16+C17
```

You then *could* type the values in the remaining total cells. Instead of doing all that typing, however, *copy* cell B19 to cell C19. Hold Ctrl while you drag B19's cell edge to C19. When you

11

release the mouse, cell C19 properly totals column C! Press Ctrl and copy C19 to D19 through F19 to place the totals in all the total cells. The totals are accurate, as Figure 11.5 shows.

**Figure 11.4.**

*A total row is needed for the project's yearly values.*

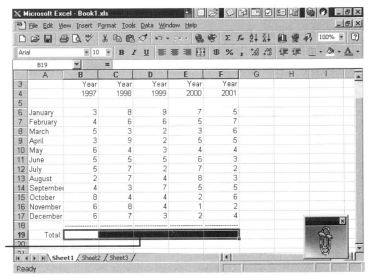

This row needs a total

---

**NOTE**

If cell B19 contained absolute addresses, cells C19 through F19 would all total column B!

---

**Figure 11.5.**

*Relative references make totaling these columns simple.*

Copied from B19

After you set up formulas, your job is done; Excel 97's, however, has just begun. If you change any value in the worksheet, Excel 97 recalculates all formulas automatically! Therefore, Excel 97 keeps your worksheet fresh and accurate as you modify values. You can use the same worksheet each month and change only the monthly data. If you leave the formulas intact, Excel 97 computes and displays the correct answers.

You can turn off the automatic recalculation and manually recalculate when ready if you use a slow computer and want to save time when editing a large worksheet. Select Tools | Options and press the Calculation tab. Click the Manual option to force manual recalculation. If you now change the data, Excel 97 will not recalculate your worksheet until you press F9 (the Calculate Now shortcut key).

# Functions Do Lots of Work

The previous section explains how to enter a formula once, using relative addresses, and copy that formula to other cells. Although you only had to type the formula one time, this kind of totaling formula is tedious to type:

```
=B6+B7+B8+B9+B10+B11+B12+B13+B14+B15+B16+B17
```

Fortunately, Microsoft included several built-in *functions* that perform many common mathematical calculations. For example, instead of summing a row or column of values, use the Sum() function.

 *Functions* are built-in calculations and data manipulations that perform work on formulas and values.

Function names always end with parentheses, such as Average(). A function accepts zero or more *arguments*. The arguments, if any, go inside the parentheses. Functions generally manipulate data (numbers or text), and the argument list inside the parentheses supplies the data to the function. For example, the Average() function computes an average of whatever list of values you pass in Average()'s argument list. Therefore, all of the following compute an average from the argument list:

```
=Average(18, 65, 299, $R$5, 10, -2, 102)

=Average(SalesTotals)

=Average(D4:D14)
```

 An *argument* is a value that a function operates with; arguments appear inside a function's parentheses.

As with many functions, Average() accepts as many arguments as needed to do its job. The first Average() function computes the average of seven values, one of which is an absolute cell address. The second Average() function computes the average of a range named SalesTotals. No matter how many cells comprise the range SalesTotals, Average() computes the average. The last Average() function computes the average of the values in the range D4 through D14 (a columnar list).

The Sum() function is perhaps the most common function due to the fact that you'll so often total table columns and rows. In the previous section, you entered a long formula to add the values in a column. Instead of adding each cell to total the range B6:B17, you could more easily enter the following function:

```
=Sum(B6:B17)
```

If you copy this Sum() function to the other cells at the bottom of the yearly projections, you'll achieve the same results as the added values, but the worksheet will be easier to maintain if you make modifications later.

**NOTE**

Suppose you want to track 24 bi-weekly totals instead of 12 monthly ones. Insert 12 additional blank rows, change the row titles (to something like JanWk12, JanWk34, FebWk12, and so on), and enter the bi-weekly values. You won't have to change the total calculations! When you insert rows within the Sum() range, Excel 97 updates the range inside the Sum() function to contain the 12 new values.

## Use AutoSum for Speed

Before looking at a table of common functions, Excel 97 helps you with summing functions by analyzing your selected range and automatically inserting a Sum() function if needed. Here's how to do that:

1. Select the range that you want to sum. For example, if you want to sum this hour's sample worksheet's months over the projected years, select the row with the January label, as shown in Figure 11.6.

2. Click the AutoSum toolbar button. Excel 97 guesses that you want to sum the selected row and inserts the Sum() function in the cell to the right of the row.

3. Make any edits to the summed value if Excel 97 included too many or not enough cells. You can click the cell and press F2 to edit the sum. Usually, no edits are required.

**11**

**Figure 11.6.**

*Getting ready to request a sum.*

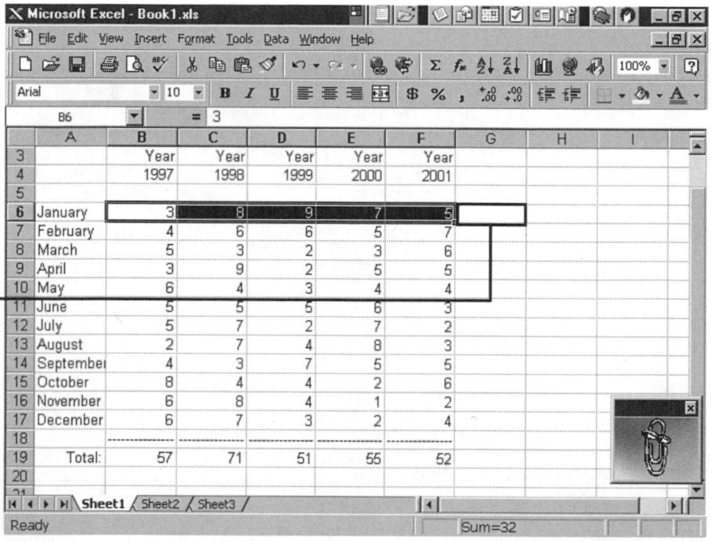

Excel 97 will place the Sum() function here

After Excel 97 generates the Sum() function, you can copy the cell down the rest of the column to add the month totals. However, can you see another way to perform the same month totals with one selection? Select the *entire set* of monthly values with one extra blank column at the right (the range B6:G17). Excel 97 sees the blank column and fills it in with each row's sum when you click AutoSum. (If you did not leave the blank column, Excel 97 would sum the bottom of the selection and that set of values is already totaled from an earlier section.) You now can select the new column of totals and let AutoSum compute the totals. Figure 11.7 shows the result of the new sums after you add underlines and a title.

## Common Functions

Functions will improve your accuracy. For example, if you want to average three cell values, you might type something like this:

```
=C2 + C4 + C6 / 3
```

This formula will *not* compute an average! Remember that the operator hierarchy forces the division calculation first. If you use the Average() function, as shown next, you don't have to worry as much about the calculation's hierarchy.

```
=Average(C2, C4, C6)
```

**Figure 11.7.**

*AutoSum in action.*

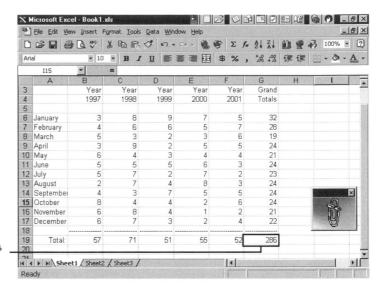

AutoSum summed this
entire column

 **TIP**

Another advantage of using functions is that you can modify them more
easily than you can long calculations. For example, if you want to throw
another cell value into the previous average, you only need to add the
extra cell to Average(); if you use a formula, you must remember to
change the 3 to 4.

Table 11.2 describes common Excel 97 built-in functions that you'll find lots of uses for as
you create worksheets.

## Table 11.2. Common Excel 97 functions.

| Function Name | Description |
| --- | --- |
| Abs() | Computes the absolute value of its cell argument (good for distance- and age-difference calculations). |
| Average() | Computes the average of its arguments. |
| Count() | Counts the number of numerical arguments in the argument list. |
| Counta() | Counts the number of all arguments in the argument list. |
| CountBlank() | Computes the number of blank cells, if any exist, in the argument range. |
| Max() | Returns the highest (maximum) value in the argument list. |

**11**

| Function Name | Description |
| --- | --- |
| Min() | Returns the lowest (minimum) value in the argument list. |
| Pi() | Computes the value of mathematical pi (requires no arguments) for use in math calculations. |
| Product() | Computes the product (multiplicative result) of the argument range. |
| Roman() | Converts its cell value to a Roman numeral. |
| Sqrt() | Computes the square root of the cell argument. |
| Stddev() | Computes the argument list's standard deviation. |
| Sum() | Computes the sum of its arguments. |
| Today() | Returns today's date (requires no arguments). |
| Var() | Computes the argument list's sample variance. |

**NOTE**

Excel 97 supports *many* more functions than Table 11.2 lists. Excel 97 even supports complex mathematical, date, time, financial, and engineering functions. As you learn more about Excel 97 and create more complex worksheets, you'll run across these functions as you read through the online help.

Some of the functions require more arguments than a simple cell or range. For example, Excel 97 contains many financial functions that compute loan values and investment rates of return. If you want to use one of the more advanced functions, click the Paste Function toolbar button to display Figure 11.8's Paste Function dialog box.

**Figure 11.8.**

*Let Excel 97's Paste Function dialog box type complex functions for you.*

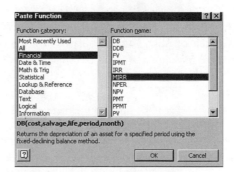

When you select the category in the left-hand column, the Paste Function displays a list of functions within that category. When you click one of the functions, the Paste Function dialog box gives you a helpful mini description. When you find the function you need, double-click it and Excel 97 displays an additional dialog box that requests each of the function arguments, such as the one shown in Figure 11.9. As you continue with the Paste Function dialog box, Excel 97 builds the function in the cell for you. As you get more proficient, you will no longer need the Paste Function dialog box's help.

**Figure 11.9.**

*The Paste Function dialog box walks you through each function argument.*

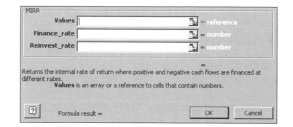

# Introduction to Worksheet Formatting

Until now, you've seen no fancy worksheets. I kept the fancy stuff out of the way so you could concentrate on the work at hand. It's now time to show you how to pretty things up. This hour is about to come to a close, but you still have time to learn some cell-formatting basics and you can continue with Excel 97's more advanced formatting features in next hour's session.

## Justification

Excel 97 right-justifies numbers (and formulas that result in numbers) and left-justifies text labels. You don't have to accept Excel 97's default justification, however. To left-, center-, or right-justify any cell's (or range's) contents, select the cell (or range) and click the Align Left, Center, or Align Right toolbar buttons. Center titles above columns and adjust your numbers to look just right.

**TIP**

Excel 97 offers a trick that even some Excel 97 gurus forget: if you want to center a title above several columns of data, type the title in a cell above the data. If you cannot center the title over the values by clicking the Center toolbar button, select all the cells around the title so that you've selected as many columns as there is data. Click the Merge and Center toolbar button. Excel 97 centers the title, even though the title resides in a single cell, across the entire column selection.

## Row and Column Height and Width

As you learn more formatting tricks, you'll need to adjust certain row and column widths and heights to hold the newly formatted values. To adjust a row's height, point to the line that separates the row number from previous or subsequent rows. When the mouse pointer changes to a double-pointing arrow, drag the row's top or bottom edge up or down. Excel 97 adjusts the entire row height as you drag your mouse. Sometimes large titles need the larger row heights. When you release the mouse, Excel 97 anchors the new row height where you left it.

In the same manner, to change a column's width, point to the column name's left or right edge and drag your mouse left or right. Excel 97 adjusts the column width to follow your mouse movement. When you release the mouse, Excel 97 anchors the new column width where you left it.

**WARNING**

> If you shrink a column width so that the column can no longer display all the data, Excel 97 displays pound signs (#####) to warn you that you need to widen the column.

**TIP**

> To adjust the column width so the column (or range of columns) is exactly large enough to hold the largest data value in the column, select the column (or columns) and double-click the column name's right edge. Excel 97 adjusts the column to hold the widest data value in the column.

## Font Changes

Feel free to change the worksheet's font to add appeal. Simple font changes, such as boldfacing, italicizing, and underlining, greatly improve the look of titles. The Bold, Italic, and Underline toolbar buttons add the proper formatting to your selected cell or range. If you select Format | Cells and click the Font tab, Excel 97 displays the Font dialog box (virtually identical to Word 97's), in which you can select a new font name and size. As Figure 11.10 shows, simple font changes can make a big improvement on otherwise dull worksheets.

**Figure 11.10.**

*Already this worksheet looks better.*

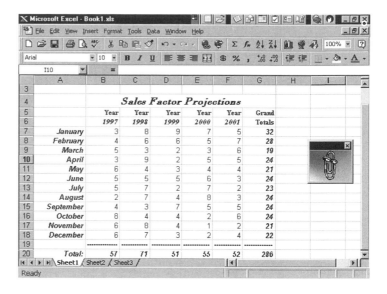

---

 **NOTE**

> If you format a row with a font that's larger than the current row size, Excel 97 adjusts the row height to make room for the new font.

Of course, you can use the Font and Font Size toolbar buttons to change a font name or size without displaying the Font dialog box.

# Format Changes

Now that you've mastered Excel 97 basics, it's time to learn the general format categories Excel 97 uses for worksheet data. Table 11.3 describes each of the format categories. Unless you change the default, Excel 97 uses the General format for data of all kinds.

**Table 11.3. Excel 97's fundamental formats.**

| Format Name | Description |
| --- | --- |
| General | The numeric data has no special formatting and generally appears exactly the way you enter the data. |
| Number | You can set the number of decimal places Excel 97 displays for all numerical values. |
| Currency | Displays a dollar sign and two decimal places for dollar amounts. |

**11**

| Format Name | Description |
| --- | --- |
| Accounting | Aligns currency and decimal points in a column. |
| Date | Displays date and time values as values whose formats you can change. |
| Time | Displays only the time portion of a date and time value. |
| Percentage | Divides the cell by 100 and displays a percent sign. |
| Fraction | Displays numbers as fractions (great for stock quotes). |
| Scientific | Uses scientific notation for all numerical values. |
| Text | Formats *all* data as text. Great for zip codes that are all numbers but that you'll never use for calculations. |
| Special | Formats zip codes, phone numbers, and Social Security numbers. |
| Custom | Lets you define your own cell format. You can decide if you want to see the plus or minus sign, and you can control the number of decimal places. |

Format a selection by selecting Format | Cells and clicking the Number tab to display a scrolling list of Table 11.3's formats. If you select the Time format from that list, you must select one of the Time format display variations so that Excel 97 knows how you want the time displayed.

You can also right-click the selection and select the pop-up menu's Format Cells command. When you do, you'll see a dialog box that lets you assign Table 11.3's formats directly to your data.

After you choose a format, use these toolbar buttons to adjust your selected numeric format: Currency Style, Percent Style, Comma Style, Increase Decimal (to increase the number of decimal places), and Decrease Decimal (to decrease the number of decimal places).

# Summary

This hour extends your worksheet knowledge by giving you more editing tools to insert and delete columns, rows, and cells. After you name important worksheet ranges, you won't have to track specific addresses in your worksheet; the name is easier to remember, and Excel 97 changes the range if you insert data in or delete it from the range.

One of the most powerful aspects of worksheets is their recalculation capability. If you change data or a formula, Excel 97 recalculates the entire worksheet as soon as you make the change. You're always looking at the computed worksheet with up-to-date formulas no matter what kind of data changes you make. When you add formulas to cell calculations, you'll not only improve your worksheet accuracy, but you'll finish your worksheets faster.

The next hour picks up where this one leaves off, going into formatting in more detail. Additionally, you'll see that graphics spruce up your worksheet and are easy to produce.

# Q&A

**Q  What is the difference between a selection and a range?**

**A**  Selections cannot be named, and can be comprised of several disjointed areas of your worksheet. A range, on the other hand, can be named, and can be any contiguous rectangular collection of cells, including one single cell or your whole worksheet data area. Often, you'll select an entire range, but all selections are not ranges.

**Q  Why would I ever use absolute addressing?**

**A**  Relative addressing seems to make the most sense for most worksheets. If you have to rearrange your worksheet, all your relative addresses update as well. Absolute addresses are great when a formula references a single cell, such as an age or pay value, that rarely changes. You could use dollar signs to anchor the single cell in the formula that uses that cell, but keep the other addresses relative in case you need to copy the formula around the worksheet.

**Q  What's the difference between the formatting you get by clicking the Center toolbar button and the formatting you get by clicking the Merge and Center button?**

**A**  If you need to center the contents of one cell, both centering formats perform the same task. If, however, you want to center data (such as a title) above a range of cell columns, select the range the centered cell is to go over and click Merge and Center; Excel 97 completes the centering across the multiple columns.

**11**

# Hour **12**

# Making Worksheets Look Great

This hour concludes your Excel 97 tutorial by explaining how to format your worksheet with professional styles. Excel 97's AutoFormat feature quickly formats your worksheet within the boundaries you select. If you want to format your worksheet by hand, the formatting commands you learn here will let you pinpoint important data and highlight that data so that others who look at and use your worksheets will find your highlighted information.

After you create and format your worksheets, use Excel 97's Chart Wizard to produce colorful graphs. Often, a worksheet's trends and comparisons get lost in the numeric details. The graphs that Excel 97's Chart Wizard generates look great, and Excel 97 does all the drawing work for you.

The highlights of this hour include

☐ What AutoFormat can do with your worksheets

☐ How to apply custom formats to selected cells

☐ When special orientation and wrapped text improve your worksheet appearance

☐ How to use the Chart Wizard to produce graphs that show data trends and comparisons

☐ How to modify your charts so they look exactly right

# AutoFormatting Worksheets

Before diving into additional formatting commands, you should know that Excel 97's AutoFormat feature converts an otherwise dull worksheet into a nice-looking professional one. If your worksheet needs sprucing up, try AutoFormat before messing with individual format commands because AutoFormat will give a good-looking, consistent dimension to your worksheet. Once AutoFormat finishes, you can modify the worksheet with more specific formats to highlight important cell information, such as special totals that you want to make more obvious.

To use AutoFormat, select the entire worksheet. Select Format | AutoFormat to display Figure 12.1's AutoFormat dialog box.

**Figure 12.1.**

*Let AutoFormat improve your worksheet.*

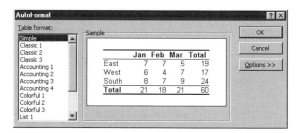

To omit certain AutoFormat format styles, click the AutoFormat's Options button to check or uncheck styles. For example, you can keep AutoFormat from changing your worksheet's font by unchecking the Font option.

Scroll through the AutoFormat samples until you find an interesting name. Click once on the name to see the style's sample in the Sample window. When you click OK, Excel 97 applies the format to your selected worksheet cells. Figure 12.2 shows that AutoFormat knows to highlight totals and also knows to separate headings from the data detail.

**12**

**Figure 12.2.**

*AutoFormat helped this worksheet.*

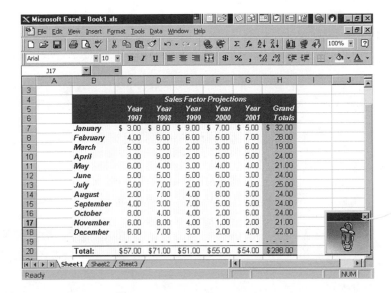

# Make Your Own Default Format

Suppose you often print worksheets to fax to others, and your fax requires boldfaced worksheets so the recipients can read the numbers. Instead of changing your worksheet text to boldface before faxing the worksheet, you can make boldface the default font style. Excel 97 lets you change several of the font defaults, so if you find yourself applying the same font style over and over, consider making that style part of Excel 97's default style.

To modify the default style, follow these steps:

1. Select Format | Style to display Figure 12.3's Style dialog box.

**Figure 12.3.**

*You can change any named style.*

**12**

2. Select the default style, Normal, from the Style name drop-down list box. (The Normal style will probably already be the style you see when you open the dialog box.) The style named Normal is the default style. Like Word 97, Excel 97 lets you create special sets of formatting commands and name them as a single style; when you apply that style by selecting Format | Style, Excel 97 applies the style set by the Style dialog box to the selected cells.

**NEW TERM** *Normal style* is the default style Excel 97 normally uses for all your worksheet cells.

3. To change the Normal style, click the Modify button. Excel 97 displays Figure 12.4's Format Cells dialog box, from which you can modify the named style.

**Figure 12.4.**

*The Format Cells dialog box modifies any format currently set.*

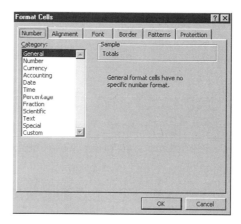

4. Click OK to close the Format Cells dialog box.
5. Click OK to close the Style dialog box. Excel 97 applies your style to the selected cells. If you made changes to the Normal style, Excel 97 will automatically use that format on future worksheets unless you modify the format or style.

# Additional Formatting Options

Many of Excel 97's formatting features are identical to Word 97's, such as the boldface, italics, underline, font color, and fill color (the cell's background color) features. In addition, you now know how to change a selection's alignment. Excel 97 supports several special formats that go further to improve the look of your worksheets. AutoFormat uses some of these special formats, and you can create your own styles that use these formats as well.

**12**

The following sections briefly introduce you to these Excel 97 formatting options so you'll see additional ways to add impact to your worksheets. You can change any of these formats from the Format Cells dialog box. Open the Format Cells dialog box by selecting Format | Cells, by changing one of the stored styles as you learned in the previous section, or by right-clicking a selection and choosing Format Cells.

## Special Alignment

Not only can you left-justify, center-justify, and right-justify, as well as justify across selected cells, you can also orient text vertically or to whatever slant you prefer. When you click the Format | Cells Alignment tab, Excel 97 displays the Alignment dialog box, on which you can adjust text orientation.

---

### Step-Up

Excel 97's vertical text orientation is easier to adjust than in previous versions because Excel 97 draws a line to show the text rotation angle as you change the angle.

---

When you click the Alignment dialog box's first orientation text box (the text box with the word Text dropping down the screen), Excel 97 changes all selected cells to vertical orientation. If you want to slant text, such as titles, select a different Degrees value or click the rotating text pointer to the slant you desire. When you click OK, Excel 97 rotates the selected text to your chosen angle. Figure 12.5 shows an example of slanted titles produced with a 45-degree angle in the Alignment dialog box.

**12**

**Figure 12.5.**

*You can change the vertical alignment of selected text.*

Slanted text alignment

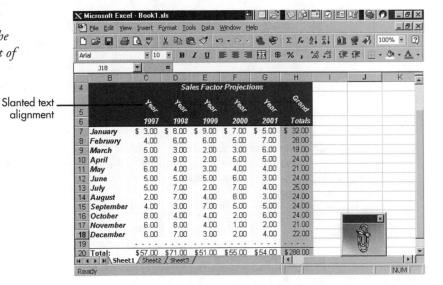

**NOTE**

> If you need to include lots of text in one or more cells, you already know (from Hour 9, "Excel 97 Workbooks") that Excel 97 either truncates the cell or pours the cell's contents into the next cell at the right. Excel 97 offers several other options, as well. When a cell requires lots of text, select the Alignment dialog box's Wrap Text option. Excel 97 wraps the text within the cell's width, increasing the cell (and, therefore, row) height to display all the wrapped text. If you click the Shrink to fit option, Excel 97 decreases the cell's font size (as much as feasible) to display the entire cell contents within the cell's current width and height. If you click Merge cells, Excel 97 combines adjacent cells into one single wide cell.

## Special Cell Borders

With Figure 12.6's Format | Cells Border dialog box, you can apply an outline, or *border*, around selected cells.

 **NEW TERM**    A *border* is a cell outline that you can apply to enclose selected cells.

**Figure 12.6.**

*Add borders around cells to highlight key data.*

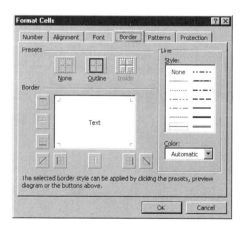

The Border dialog box lets you add a border to any side of the selected cells as well as diagonal lines inside the cells. As you select among the Outline and Inside options, the preview area shows what the resulting border will look like.

**TIP**  The Borders toolbar button is quicker to use than the Border dialog box, but you cannot control as many border details.

Select from the Border dialog box's Line Style options to change the pattern of the border that you choose. If you want to remove any selected cell's border, click None.

## Special Cell Shades

The Format | Cells Pattern dialog box lets you add coloring or a shading pattern to selected cells. Although the Fill Color toolbar button colors cell backgrounds more quickly than the Pattern dialog box, the Pattern dialog box lets you add a shading pattern to the background.

When you click the Pattern dialog box's Pattern drop-down box, Excel 97 displays Figure 12.7's pattern selection.

**Figure 12.7.**

*Choose a pattern for the selected cell.*

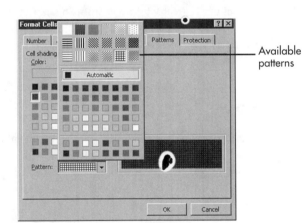

Available patterns

## Locked and Hidden Cells

A *locked cell* is a cell whose contents you cannot change, and a *hidden cell* is a cell whose contents you cannot see. When you create worksheets for others, you'll want to lock titles and formulas so that users can enter and change the data areas without harming the worksheet's integrity. A hidden cell is useful when you want to write a note to yourself, such as a description for the worksheet or for specific cells, but such notes should not appear on the resulting worksheet under normal working conditions.

A *locked cell* is a cell whose contents you cannot change if the worksheet is protected.

 A *hidden cell* is a cell whose contents you cannot see if the worksheet is protected.

The Format | Cells Protection dialog box controls the locked and hidden status of selected cells. You can enable and disable locking as well as control the hidden status by clicking the appropriate Protection dialog-box options.

**WARNING**

The locked and hidden cell status activates only when you turn on worksheet protection by selecting Tools | Protection and selecting one of the protection options.

Cell locking is great when you want to keep accidental worksheet changes from occurring. If the protection needs to go further than simple safety, add a password when you protect the selection. Only someone with the worksheet's (or workbook's) password will be able to unlock locked cells or show hidden cells.

# Custom Graphs

A picture is worth a thousand words and numbers, and Excel 97 produces professional looking graphs from your worksheet data. Although you can learn a lot about graphing and charting to create extremely sophisticated Excel 97 graphs, Excel 97's Chart Wizard performs very well in most cases to produce great-looking graphs quickly and easily. When you click the Chart Wizard toolbar button, Excel 97 displays Figure 12.8's opening Chart Wizard dialog box.

 The *Chart Wizard* is an Excel 97 wizard that analyzes your worksheet data and produces colorful graphs.

Table 12.1 describes each of the chart types that Excel 97 creates. You can select an appropriate chart type from the Chart Wizard's opening screen. To preview your worksheet when formatted with any chart, select a chart type, then a chart subtype, and click the button labeled Press and hold to view a sample. Excel 97 analyzes your worksheet data and displays a small sketch of the chart you selected.

**Figure 12.8.**

*Excel 97's Chart Wizard creates graphs for you.*

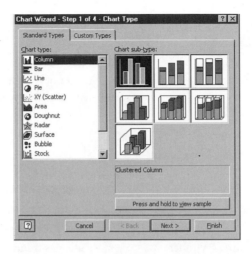

 **NOTE**

A data series is a single group of data that you might select from a column or row. Often, a series is comprised of a time period, such as a week, month, or year. One person's weekly sales totals (from a group of several salespeople's weekly totals) would also form a series. Some graphs, such as pie charts, graph only a single series, while other graphs show comparisons between two or more data series.

 **NEW TERM** A *data series* is a single column, row, or set of cell values that you group together, such as a week's, month's, year's, or a single salesperson's sales for a given region.

**12**

**Table 12.1. Excel 97 generates all these charts.**

| Chart type | Description |
| --- | --- |
| Column | Shows changes over time and compares values. |
| Bar | Compares data items. |
| Line | Shows trends and projections. |
| Pie | Illustrates the proportional size of items in the same series. |
| XY (scatter) | Shows relationships of several values in a series. |
| Area | Emphasizes the magnitude of changes over time. |
| Doughnut | Illustrates the proportional size of items in multiple series. |

*continues*

**Table 12.1. continued**

| Chart type | Description |
|---|---|
| Radar | Each category contains an axis that radiates from the center of the graph (useful for finding the data series with the most penetration, as needed in market research statistical studies). |
| Surface | Locates optimum combinations between two data series. |
| Bubble | Shows relationships between several series values, but also (with circles, or bubbles of varying sizes) shows the magnitude of data intersections. |
| Stock | Illustrates a stock's (or other investment's) high, low, and closing prices. |
| Cone, Cylinder, Pyramid | Indicates trends and comparisons with special 3D cone, cylinder, and pyramid symbols. |

 **TIP**

If you are new to graphing, you may not know which graph works best for a particular worksheet. Try one! If you see that a bar graph does not show a trend that you want to demonstrate, generate a line graph. Excel 97 makes it easy to select from among several graphs to find the best graph for your needs.

As you look through the graph samples, if one of the series looks extremely large in comparison to the others, Excel 97 is probably including a total column or row in the graph results. Generally, you'll want to graph a single series (such as monthly costs) or several series, but *not* the totals because the totals will throw off the data comparisons. Therefore, if you see extreme ranges at the beginning or end of your graph, select only the data areas (not the total cells) from the Chart Wizard's second dialog box shown in Figure 12.9.

You'll need to tell the Chart Wizard which direction the data series flows by clicking either Rows or Columns from the Chart Wizard's second dialog box.

When you click the Next button to see the third Chart Wizard dialog box (shown in Figure 12.10), Excel 97 lets you enter a chart title that will appear at the top of the resulting chart as well as *axis* titles that will appear on each edge of your chart. An *axis* is an edge of your graph that indicates a type of data series (such as time or dollar amounts).

**Figure 12.9.**

*Be sure to select only data areas for your graph.*

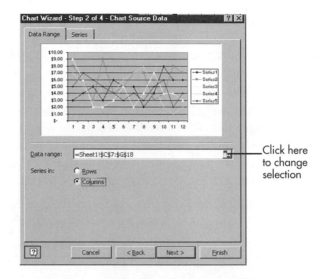

Click here to change selection

NEW TERM An *axis* is a graph edge that indicates a type of series, such as time or dollar amounts.

**Figure 12.10.**

*It's time to enter titles that you want to see on the chart.*

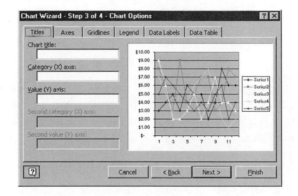

You'll find other tabs across the Chart Wizard's third dialog box that let you control the placement of the *legend* (the series and axis descriptions) and a *data table* (a miniature summarized worksheet that appears beneath graphs).

NEW TERM A *legend* is a description that describes the chart's data series or axis.

NEW TERM A *data table* is a miniature summarized worksheet that appears beneath graphs.

When you click Next to see the final Chart Wizard dialog box, you determine exactly where and how to place the generated graph. Excel 97 can create a new worksheet for the graph or embed the graph inside the current worksheet as an embedded object. You can, in turn, embed the object in other Office 97 products, as you'll learn in Part VII, "Putting Things Together."

Click the Finish button to see your resulting graph. If you've chosen to embed the graph inside your current worksheet, you may have to drag the graph's *sizing handles* (the eight black squares that appear around the graph's outline) to expand or shrink the graph. In addition, you can drag the graph anywhere you want it to appear on your worksheet. Excel 97 displays the Graph toolbar in case you want to change the graph.

 **NEW TERM**    *Sizing handles* are eight black handles that appear around certain objects, such as graphs, with which you can resize the object by dragging.

> **TIP**
>
> If your graph does not look exactly right, you can often click the Graph toolbar buttons to make the graph work. You can even change the graph type (from a line chart to a bar graph, for instance) from the Graph toolbar without re-running the Chart Wizard. The Graph toolbar ensures that all data selections and titles remain in place when you change your graph. If you need to make more extensive graph changes, re-run the Chart Wizard.

In addition to using the Graph toolbar, you can often change specific parts of your graph by right-clicking the graph. For example, if you point to your chart's title and right-click your mouse, Excel 97 displays a pop-up menu with which you can format the title's pattern, font, and alignment.

> **Step-Up**
>
> Excel 97 lets you move or resize the legend by clicking the legend and dragging the handles with your mouse.

# Summary

This hour completes your Excel 97 tutorial! You can now format your worksheets to look any way you want. Add color, patterns, shading, and borders to your worksheets. If you want to let Excel 97 give formatting a try, select your worksheet data and start Excel 97's AutoFormat feature.

The Excel 97 Chart Wizard makes graphical charts look great. By working through the Chart Wizard's dialog boxes, you'll give Excel 97 all the information needed to generate custom graphs. Graphs can analyze data, compare values, and show trends faster than the worksheet's details can often show.

Now that you've learned to create worksheets, you'll want to show those worksheets to someone. Why not use PowerPoint 97? The next hour introduces PowerPoint 97, Office 97's colorful presentation creator and editor.

# Q&A

**Q When would I want to create a style?**

**A** If you find yourself applying the same kinds of format commands on cells quite often, consider putting that set of format commands in a style with the Format | Style dialog box. After you create a style, you can apply that style by selecting it from the Style dialog box's list.

If you modify the style named *Normal*, you change the default style that Excel 97 applies when you enter data into worksheets.

**Q How can I change a locked cell?**

**A** If you lock a cell, your intent is to *not allow* changes. Locked cells are especially useful when you create worksheets for others to use. By locking the titles and formulas, you ensure that the user can only change data areas. Nevertheless, if you need to edit a locked cell, turn off the worksheet's protected status. After you edit the cell, turn on the protection so the worksheet is safe from inadvertent changes.

**Q I get confused with all the graph terms; how do I know which chart works best for my worksheet?**

**A** Often the best way to find the right chart type is to try a few. Excel 97's Chart Wizard is so simple and fast that you can generate several chart types before you find just the right one. As you produce more and more charts, you'll begin to better judge which graphs work best for certain kinds of worksheets.

**12**

# PART
# IV

## Presenting with PowerPoint 97

# Hour

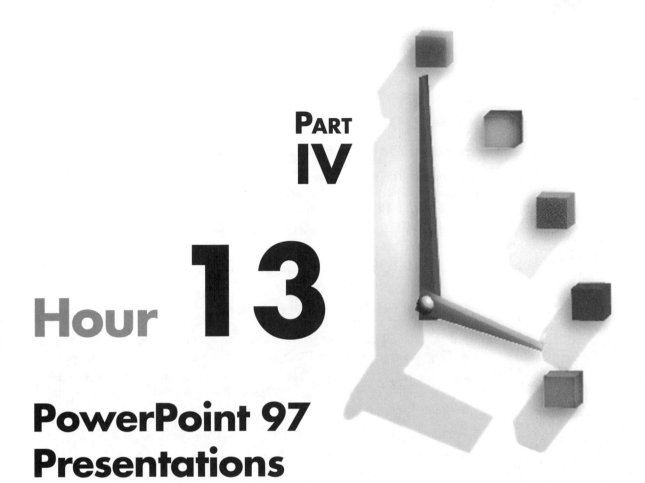

# Hour 13

# PowerPoint 97 Presentations

This hour introduces you to PowerPoint 97 and shows you how to get off to a good start: By using PowerPoint 97's predefined presentation tools, you'll generate good-looking presentations without needing to worry about design, format, and color specifics.

After PowerPoint 97 generates a sample presentation, you need only to follow a few simple procedures to turn the sample presentation into your own.

The highlights of this hour include

- ☐ How to start PowerPoint 97
- ☐ How to exit PowerPoint 97
- ☐ What the AutoContent Wizard does for you
- ☐ When to use the design templates
- ☐ What a blank presentation requires

# Getting Acquainted with PowerPoint 97

You start PowerPoint 97 when you do one of these things:

☐ Click the Office 97 Shortcut bar's New Office Document button and double-click the Blank Presentation icon to create a new PowerPoint 97 document. (Click the General tab to see the Blank Presentation icon.)

☐ Click the Office 97 Shortcut bar's Open Office Document button and select an existing PowerPoint 97 presentation you want to edit.

☐ Use the Windows Start menu to start PowerPoint 97 by clicking Microsoft PowerPoint on the Program menu.

☐ Select a PowerPoint 97 document from the Windows Start menu's Documents option. Windows will recognize that PowerPoint 97 created the presentation document and will start PowerPoint 97 and load the presentation file automatically. (The Start menu's Document option holds a list of your most recent work.)

☐ Click the Office 97 Shortcut bar's PowerPoint 97 button to create a blank presentation. Depending on your Office 97 Shortcut bar's setup, you might not see the PowerPoint 97 button there.

Figure 13.1 shows the opening PowerPoint 97 screen. Your screen might differ slightly depending on the options that the installer set.

**Figure 13.1.**

*PowerPoint 97's opening screen.*

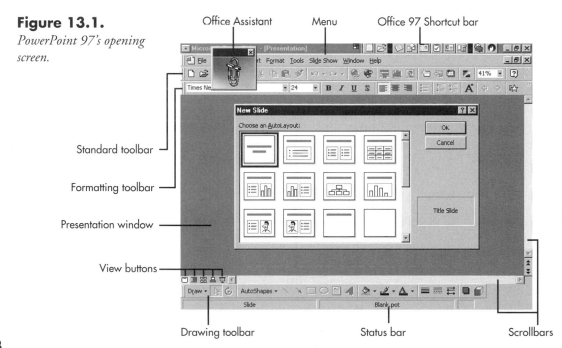

13

Unlike the other Office 97 products, PowerPoint 97 begins by starting a wizard-like template query that prompts you for the type of presentation you want to create.

When you're finished with PowerPoint 97, quit by performing any of the following:

- ☐ Selecting File | Exit.
- ☐ Pressing Alt+F4.
- ☐ Double-clicking the Control icon.
- ☐ Clicking PowerPoint 97's Close Window button.

**WARNING**

> Always quit PowerPoint 97 and shut down Windows before turning off your computer so you don't lose your work.

# PowerPoint 97's Purpose

The primary purpose of PowerPoint 97 is to help you design, create, and edit presentations. A *presentation* is a set of screens that you'll eventually present to people in a group or workbook tutorial. You don't have to be a design specialist to create good-looking presentations because of the wide variety of pre-defined PowerPoint 97 templates available to you.

**NEW TERM** A *presentation* is a set of screens that you'll share with a group of people.

PowerPoint 97 slides can contain information from:

- ☐ Data you type into PowerPoint 97
- ☐ Word 97 documents
- ☐ Word 97 document outlines
- ☐ Excel 97 worksheets
- ☐ Excel 97 graphs and charts
- ☐ Access 97 databases
- ☐ Graphics programs that you use to create and edit graphics
- ☐ Other software programs, such as desktop publishing programs, whose data you import into PowerPoint 97

After you create your presentation, present it to an audience in one or more of these ways:

- ☐ Transparency overheads
- ☐ Computer screens

**13**

- [ ] Internet Web page presentations
- [ ] Audience handouts
- [ ] Workbook contents
- [ ] 35mm slides
- [ ] Color printer documents
- [ ] Reference notes for a speaker

**NOTE**

> Not only can you create and edit presentations with PowerPoint 97, but PowerPoint 97 can show your presentation as well. PowerPoint 97 can move from screen to screen, as a slide show does, at whatever pace you request.

## Creating a New Presentation

Figure 13.1 shows the opening window that you see when you start PowerPoint 97 and begin a new presentation. The figure shows several design templates that contain layouts from which you can select for a new slide (templates are stored in files that contain the .pot extension). The design template works well for creating a PowerPoint 97 presentation one slide at a time, but the design template might not be the best place to begin in many instances.

**TIP**

> Plan your presentations! Think about your target audience. Presenting identical information to two different audiences might require two completely different approaches. For example, the same company's annual status presentation would be different for a stockholder's meeting than for the board of director's meeting. After you determine your target audience, think about the content of the presentation. In the next hour, "PowerPoint 97 Power," you will learn about PowerPoint 97's outlining feature, which you can use to outline a presentation before you create the presentation slides.

**NOTE**

> Throughout this book, the term *presentation* refers to the entire PowerPoint 97 collection of slides, while the term *slide* refers to an individual screen within a presentation.

**13**

A *slide* is a screen from a presentation.

## AutoContent Wizard and Presentation Design

Perhaps the best place to begin creating a new presentation is the *AutoContent Wizard*. This wizard contains a sample presentation with content and a selected design. Use the wizard's dialog boxes to select a design that best suits your needs.

 The *AutoContent Wizard* is a presentation design wizard that contains sample data from which you can select and edit to create your customized presentation.

To use AutoContent Wizard to create your presentation, follow these steps:

1. Start PowerPoint 97.
2. Cancel the design template screen (the one you saw in Figure 13.1).
3. Select File | New to display PowerPoint 97's Presentation dialog box.
4. Answer the AutoContent Wizard's questions to design a presentation shell that best fits your application's requirements.

The AutoContent Wizard's primary goal is to create a blank presentation in a format that best matches the goals of your presentation. As you follow the AutoContent Wizard, you'll have to determine the answers to these questions: What message do you want to convey to your audience? Who is your audience? Are you selling or offering something?

The AutoContent Wizard selects the best choice from among these 20 template styles after you complete the wizard:

- ☐ Brainstorming
- ☐ Business Plan
- ☐ Achieve Certificate
- ☐ Communicating Bad News
- ☐ Company Meeting
- ☐ Corporate Financial Overview
- ☐ Corporate Home Page
- ☐ Corporate Locations Directory
- ☐ Facilities Assistant
- ☐ Employee Orientation
- ☐ Flyer

13

☐  Human Resources Kiosk

☐  Marketing Plan

☐  Organization Overview

☐  Personal Home Page

☐  Recommending a Strategy

☐  Reporting Progress

☐  Selling a Product, Service, or Idea

☐  Training

☐  Who's Who

All of these AutoContent Wizard templates are available to you if you don't want to run the wizard first. PowerPoint 97 supplies two styles for each template: one for an online intranet or Internet PowerPoint 97 presentation, and one a standalone PowerPoint 97 presentation.

## Creating Presentations with Design Templates

As you saw in this hour's first section, PowerPoint 97 presents you with the New Slide dialog box when you open a new presentation. If you start PowerPoint 97 and select File | New, PowerPoint 97 presents you with the New Slide dialog box. The New Slide dialog box contains several templates that you can choose to start your presentation's first slide.

**WARNING**

If you click the toolbar's New button, PowerPoint 97 does not open the New Slide dialog box. Therefore, despite the similar icons, the File | New command does not perform the same command as the New toolbar button.

Display the New Slide dialog box whenever you need to create a new slide for a presentation. A presentation contains one or more slides, so you'll need to display the New Slide dialog box every time you are ready to add the next slide to the presentation. To display the New Slide dialog box at any time, click the New Slide option in the Common Tasks floating menu.

As you click through the templates, the New Slide dialog box's right side displays a description, such as Chart & Text, which describes the template's best use.

**NOTE**

After you use the AutoContent Wizard a few times, the templates will begin to look familiar. The AutoContent Wizard uses several of the templates for its individual slides.

**13**

When you double-click the template that best describes the slide you want to create next, PowerPoint 97 creates a new slide based on that template (as shown in Figure 13.2).

**Figure 13.2.**

*A template's generated slide.*

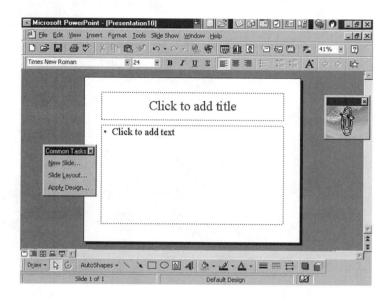

The instructions on the template's generated slide tell you what to do next. In most cases, you'll edit the text, possibly change colors, and perhaps add a graphic image to the slide to complete it. After you complete the slide, click the Insert New Slide toolbar button to display the New Slide dialog box and create your presentation's next slide.

## Opening a New and Blank Presentation

When you create a new presentation from scratch, you can still take advantage of the design templates. One of the design templates that you'll see in the New Slide dialog box selection list is the Blank template, shown in Figure 13.3.

**TIP**

> If you design your own slide from a blank template you can later apply one of the template styles to the slide! Therefore, if you don't like what you generate from scratch, PowerPoint 97 lets you redesign the slide without requiring you to re-enter the slide's text.

**13**

**Figure 13.3.**

*Use the Blank template
to create your own slide
layout.*

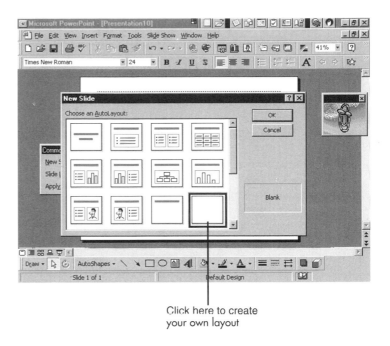

Click here to create
your own layout

**WARNING**

Blank presentations require that you lay out every slide element, including
the text, titles, and body. Most slides have a title, text, and an optional
graphic image. Why not let PowerPoint 97's AutoContent Wizard or
templates start things off right? The pre-defined slides work for so many
purposes. Resist the temptation to create your own slides from scratch until
you acquaint yourself with the pre-defined slides. In most cases, the
AutoContent Wizard and templates provide exactly what your presentation needs.

After PowerPoint 97 displays the new and empty slide, you must add text, graphics, and styles
to complete the slide.

## Summary

This hour introduced you to PowerPoint 97 by showing you how to start PowerPoint 97,
how to exit PowerPoint 97, and how to prepare for your initial slide presentation. PowerPoint
97 prepares all kinds of presentations, all of which have one or more slides (screens). Use
PowerPoint 97 to create, edit, and even present your presentations in a slide-projector
format.

**13**

The AutoContent Wizard is perhaps the best way to start using PowerPoint 97. By answering a few simple questions, AutoContent Wizard creates a presentation with sample text and formatting. To turn the generated presentation into your own, simply change the text and, optionally, change the slides' design elements.

The design templates also provide help when you want to add a new slide to a presentation. When you need to create a new slide, select the closest match from the list of design templates. After the design template creates a sample slide, simply edit and modify the text.

If you are bold or have a good eye for design, you can create a blank presentation from scratch. Blank presentations require the most work.

The next hour shows you how easy it is to turn the AutoContent Wizard or template-designed slides into your own.

# Q&A

**Q  Do I begin with a PowerPoint 97 template, the AutoContent Wizard, or a blank presentation when I want to create a presentation?**

**A**  Unlike the other Office 97 products, you'll almost always create a presentation with the AutoContent Wizard or with a template. A blank presentation requires you to lay out all your slide titles and text, which is too much work for most presentations. Unless your presentation requires unusual features, the AutoContent Wizard and templates produce presentations that end up being close to your desired presentation.

As you familiarize yourself with the AutoContent Wizard and templates, you'll begin to learn which will produce the presentation you need at the time. The AutoContent Wizard is perhaps the best for PowerPoint 97 newcomers because it presents a series of specific style choices and lays out sample text that you can easily change to fit your presentation needs.

Basically, all three presentation-generation techniques end up producing a new slide on which you must add text, modify colors, change formatting, and add optional graphics. You'll learn how to apply these slide edits and improvements in the next hour.

**Q  I'm still confused… What is the difference between the AutoContent Wizard and the design templates?**

**A**  The AutoContent Wizard uses the design templates for its slides. The biggest difference between the two presentation-design tools is that the AutoContent Wizard creates an entire sample presentation, whereas the design templates create individual slide samples.

**13**

# Hour 14

# PowerPoint 97 Power

This hour shows you what to do after you generate a sample slide or presentation. PowerPoint 97's AutoContent Wizard and template samples generate good-looking presentations, but it's up to you to turn those presentations into the specific presentation that you desire.

First, change the sample's text to your text. In the process, you might change or add slide titles and formatting, or maybe a graphic image for more impact. This hour teaches you a few shortcuts you can use to turn the sample presentations into the presentation you need.

The highlights of this hour include

☐ When the various views help streamline your PowerPoint 97 work

☐ Why you'll work most often with the Outline view

☐ How the Slide Sorter view arranges your slide show

☐ What editing tools PowerPoint 97 supplies for your slide's text

☐ How to select the presentation printing option you need

# The Views

PowerPoint 97 requires that you change views perhaps more than any of the other Office 97 products. Therefore, you'll produce presentations more quickly if you master views now and learn the advantages and disadvantages of each view.

 **TIP**

The following list not only describes PowerPoint 97's views, but also explains how to use them to convert the template and AutoContent Wizard text to your own. As you read this section, pay attention to the information that teaches how and when to edit text from the AutoContent Wizard and design template.

PowerPoint 97 supports the following views:

- ☐ Outline view—Lets you edit and display all your presentation text in one location instead of one slide at a time. Figure 14.1 shows a presentation's Outline view. The large titles start new slides, and the details below the titles provide each slide's bulleted text.
- ☐ Slide view—Lets you see each slide, one at a time, and modify each slide's format, color, graphics, style, or text.
- ☐ Notes Pages view—Lets you create and edit notes for the presentation's speaker.
- ☐ Slide Sorter view—Displays your entire presentation so you can add, delete, and move slides. The Slide Sorter view acts like a preview tool. You can review your presentation and use the Slide Sorter as an engine that presents your slides at a preset timing and a specific transitional effect when one slide changes to another.

Change views by clicking one of the view buttons to the left of the vertical scroll bar. You'll work in the Outline view most often when creating and editing your presentation's text, and you'll work in the Slide view most often when formatting individual slides.

**NEW TERM**  The *Outline view* is the view that holds all of your presentation's text.

**14**

**Figure 14.1.**

*A presentation's Outline view shows the presentation's text.*

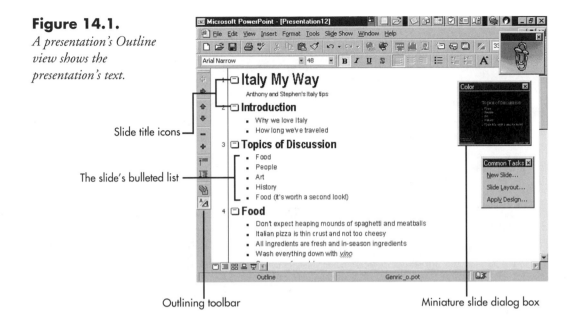

Slide title icons —

The slide's bulleted list —

Outlining toolbar

Miniature slide dialog box

## Using the Outline View

After you generate a sample presentation by using the AutoContent Wizard or by creating slides from the design templates, go to the Outline view to work on your presentation's text. Click the topic or detail you want to change and edit the text. As you enter and change Outline-view text, PowerPoint 97 updates the *miniature slide* dialog box with your new text so you can get a *thumbnail sketch* (a preview) of your finished slide.

 The *miniature slide* is the small slide preview window that shows when you work in Outline view.

 A *thumbnail sketch* is a miniature view of an object (such as a PowerPoint 97 slide).

 **NOTE**

This miniature slide dialog box shows what each individual slide currently looks like. As you change the Outline view text, PowerPoint 97 updates the miniature slide dialog box window to show your edits.

All the familiar copy, cut, and paste features work in the Outline view. For example, if inside the Outline view you drag a title's icon or a bulleted list's item down or up the screen, PowerPoint 97 moves that item to its new location. When you drag a title, all the points under the title move with it. When you drag a bulleted item, PowerPoint 97 moves only that item.

**14**

**WARNING**

> Unlike other Office 97 products, PowerPoint 97 does not copy an item if you press Ctrl before dragging the item elsewhere.

To add items to the Outline view text, click at the end or beginning of a bulleted item to insert a new entry. If you want to insert a completely new slide, click the Common Tasks dialog box's New Slide item, and PowerPoint 97 displays the New Slide dialog box from which you can select a design and then enter the text. You can also click at the end of an item and press Enter to enter a blank slide.

One of PowerPoint 97's most beneficial text features is its capability to read documents from other Office 97 products. If you create a Word 97 document that you want to include on a slide (or series of slides), select Insert | Slides from File and select the Office 97 file that you want to import to your presentation. The document's Heading 1 style text becomes slide titles, and the subsequent heading styles become text under the title.

**TIP**

> While in Word 97, click the Present It toolbar button to turn your document into a PowerPoint 97-ready presentation.

The Outlining toolbar appears to the left of the Outline view. The Outlining toolbar's most important feature may be its *promotion arrows*. If you type a detail item that you want to become a new slide's title, click the Outline toolbar's left arrow (the *promote button*). To convert a title to a bulleted item, click the Outline toolbar's right arrow (the *demote* toolbar button).

**NEW TERM** *Promotion arrows* are Outlining toolbar arrow buttons that promote Outline view items to slide titles or demote slide titles to Outline view bulleted detail items.

**NEW TERM** The *promote button* is the outlining toolbar button that converts detail text to title text.

**TIP**

> Click the up and down Outlining toolbar arrows to move an outline's item up or down in the outline.

**14**

## Using the Slide View

While in Outline view, you can look at any item's Slide view by double-clicking any slide title's icon that appears at the left of each Outline view slide title. As Figure 14.2 shows, the Slide view displays the same slide as your miniature slides dialog box, only you'll see the slide in a full-screen view. You can make edits to your slide text and see the results of those edits as they affect the final slide.

**NEW TERM** The *Slide view* displays each of the presentation's slides one at a time for editing and formatting.

**Figure 14.2.**

*A presentation's Slide view shows one of the presentation's slides.*

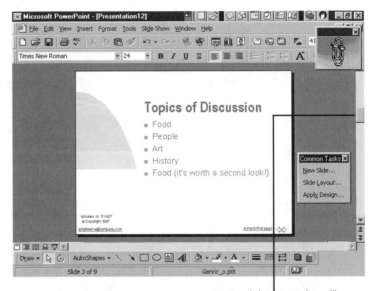

Next slide's vertical scrollbar

To move from slide to slide while in the Slide view, perform any of the following:

☐ Click the vertical scrollbar

☐ Press the PageUp or PageDown keys

☐ Click the vertical scrollbar's Preview slide's button or Next slide's button

When you want to edit a text (or graphic) object from the Slide view, click the object. PowerPoint 97 displays a sizing box surrounded by sizing handles. PowerPoint 97 treats a slide's title as a single object and the slide's bulleted set of items as another object.

**14**

To edit text, perform these steps:

1. Click the text you want to edit to display the sizing box.

2. To move the text, drag one edge of the text's resizing box in the direction you want to move the text.

3. To shrink or enlarge the selected text object, drag one of the sizing handles in or out to adjust the object's size. PowerPoint 97 does *not* shrink or enlarge text inside the sizing box as you resize the sizing box.

4. After you display the sizing box, click inside the box at the point where you want to edit text. PowerPoint 97 inserts the text cursor; using it, you can insert and delete text as well as change the font, color, and style. To increase or decrease the size of text, use the Format|Font dialog box.

 **TIP**   Select any text, then click the Increase Font Size toolbar button to quickly increase the size of the selected text's font. The Increase Font Size button works faster than opening the Font dialog box.

If graphics appear on the slide, double-click them to edit the images with graphic-editing tools.

**Step-Up**

Although the Internet-connection feature can be somewhat advanced, if you right-click an object (such as a graphic object) and select the Action Settings option, PowerPoint 97 displays Figure 14.3's Action Settings dialog box. By assigning an Internet hyperlink address, a Windows program, or a sound wave file to the mouse movement or click, PowerPoint 97 connects to that hyperlink location, runs the program, or plays the sound during the presentation. You can provide push-button access to programs and Internet Web pages while presenting your presentation!

**Figure 14.3.**

*Assign events to mouse clicks and movements.*

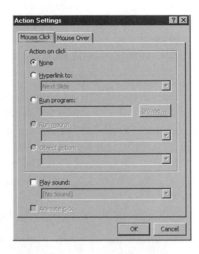

## Using the Slide Sorter View

Use the Slide Sorter view to rearrange slides, not to edit text or graphics on the slides. When you display the Slide Sorter view, PowerPoint 97 displays several of your presentation slides (as shown in Figure 14.4). The Slide Sorter view lets you quickly and easily drag and drop slides to reorder your presentation. Although you can rearrange slides from the Outline view, the Slide Sorter view lets you see the global results of your slide movements.

**NEW TERM**   The *Slide Sorter view* displays your slides as though they are in a projector.

**Figure 14.4.**

*Rearrange slides in the Slide Sorter view.*

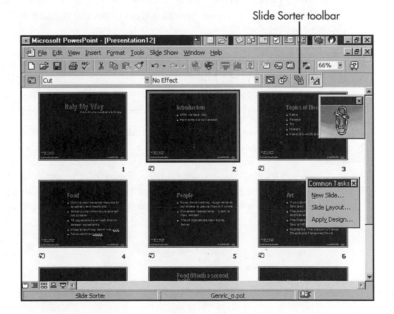

14

Use your mouse to drag slides from one location to another in the presentation. Remember that the Undo command (Ctrl+Z) reverses any action that you accidentally make. You may also use the Windows clipboard to copy, cut, and paste, although dragging with your mouse is easier. To delete a slide, click the slide once and press the Delete key.

One of the more advanced (but useful) Slide Sorter features involves the Slide Sorter toolbar, which appears at the top of the Slide Sorter view. The toolbar's Slide Transition Effects drop-down list determines how the PowerPoint 97 Slide Show feature will *transition* (dissolve) from one slide to the next when you use PowerPoint 97 to display your presentation. The next hour's session, "Advanced PowerPoint 97 Power," discusses PowerPoint 97's Slide Show in more detail. For now, click the Slide Transition Effects drop-down list to see how PowerPoint 97 can move from one slide to the next. The Text Preset Animation determines how the slide's transitional text appears during the slide show.

 A *transition* is the dissolving, or wiping, effect that PowerPoint 97 uses when one slide replaces the previous one during a slide show.

To set up slide-transition and text-animation effects, click a slide and select the desired effects from the Slide Sorter toolbar. Click the icon below each slide to see how the set transition effect will look during the slide show.

## Using the Notes Pages View

When you click the Notes Pages view, PowerPoint 97 displays your presentation's first slide (as Figure 14.5 shows). The Notes Pages view contains a small version of the slide and a location for a text description of that slide below. Therefore, the speaker's notes will contain the slides that the audience sees as well as notes the speaker wrote about each slide to tell the audience.

 Use the *Notes Pages view* to create and keep the notes for the presentation's speaker.

**NOTE**

> The Notes Pages are designed to be printed for the speaker. However, the speaker can also display the Notes Pages view during a presentation to eliminate paper shuffling. If the speaker's computer has two video cards and two monitors, PowerPoint 97 can send the slides to one monitor and the speaker's slide/note pages to the other. When the speaker moves to the next slide, the speaker's notes will change as well.

**14**

**Figure 14.5.**
*Prepare speaker's notes with the Notes Pages view.*

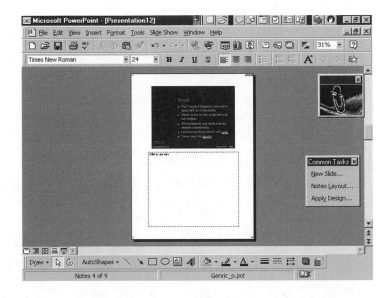

 **NOTE** Use the PageUp and PageDown keys to scroll through the slides and see the speaker's notes at the bottom of each slide. If the text area is not large enough to read the notes, expand the viewing area by using the Edit menu's Zoom command.

 **TIP** Use the IntelliPoint mouse (if you've installed it according to Appendix A's instructions) to view the text. The IntelliPoint mouse wheel lets you easily select a zoom factor that's readable, and lets you zoom several times during the course of a presentation in case room or screen changes make the speaker's screen less readable.

# Save and Print Your Work!

Be sure to save your presentation after creating and finalizing it. PowerPoint 97 saves your presentation with the .ppt document filename extension.

Of course, you will also need to print your presentation, either to paper, to a color printer, or to a printer that supports transparencies. PowerPoint 97's File|Print dialog box works differently from Word 97's and Excel 97's. Instead of globally printing the presentation, you must tell PowerPoint 97 exactly how and what you want to print.

**14**

**TIP**

Several companies convert PowerPoint 97 presentations to color slides, which you can use in slide projectors for presentations. Consult your PowerPoint 97 documentation for companies that can create slides for you.

When you display Figure 14.6's Print dialog box, open the Print what drop-down list to view the selection list.

**Figure 14.6.**

*Decide exactly what you want to print.*

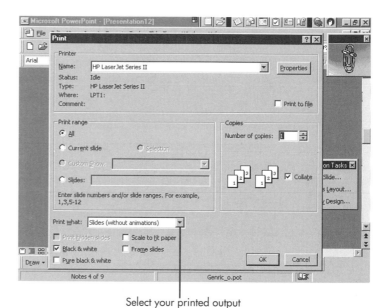

Select your printed output

PowerPoint prints your presentation in a black-and-white format. You'll need to change to color printing if you print on a color printer. Use the Print what drop-down list box to print your presentation in any of these styles:

☐ Slides only for the presentation

☐ Handouts (which can hold from two to six slides per page) so you can give comprehensive notes to the audience

☐ Notes for the speaker

☐ The outline for proofreading purposes

**14**

# Summary

This hour furthered your PowerPoint 97 knowledge by showing you how to turn a sample presentation into the presentation you desire. The views are more critical in PowerPoint 97 presentation development than in Word 97 or Excel 97. The views give you a completely different perspective of the presentation. Whereas one view is for the audience, another completely different view exists for the speaker.

As you might expect, you can change PowerPoint 97 slide text easily using the basic editing skills you've already mastered. The views let you keep your slides, outline, and speaker's notes separated but connected to each other.

The next hour concludes your PowerPoint 97 tutorial by showing you how to format your slides in more detail, how to test and start the PowerPoint 97 Slide Show, and how to spruce up your slides with graphics.

# Q&A

**Q What are the primary PowerPoint views and what does each view do?**

**A** The two primary working views are the Outline view and the Slide view. The Slide view is great for working on each slide's color and format. Use the Outline view to keep an overall presentation goal in mind as well as to see all your presentation's text in one location where you can better edit the text.

**Q I want to use PowerPoint 97 to present my slides, but I don't want to mess with the Slide Show feature's transition and timing requirements. Can I still use PowerPoint 97 to display my slides?**

**A** You'll learn about the PowerPoint 97 Slide Show's details in the next hour, but rest assured that PowerPoint 97 supports manual slide shows in which you control the appearance of the next slide. Actually, *most* presenters want complete control over the timing of the slides, and PowerPoint 97 supports such manual transitions. As a matter of fact, you'll probably *never* let PowerPoint 97 perform a completely hands-off presentation unless you use PowerPoint 97 for a moving, eye-catching, store display to promote a product as customers walk by.

**Q Can I print everything (all views) with a single File | Print command?**

**A** No, you can only print individual slide-show components, such as the speaker's notes, audience handouts, or slides, from the File|Print menu. If you want to print everything and every view, select File|Print multiple times and print a different component each time.

14

**Q I'm using a service to turn my presentation into individual color slides. Do I need the PowerPoint 97 Slide Show?**

**A** You'll learn about the Slide Show in next hour's session. Nevertheless, PowerPoint 97 is great for individual slides that you print or display inside PowerPoint 97, from the Web, or from any other source that displays PowerPoint 97 presentations.

**14**

# Hour 15

# Advanced PowerPoint 97 Power

This hour wraps up your PowerPoint 97 tutorial by explaining how to better format your presentations. You can format your entire presentation at one time or apply styles one slide at a time.

In addition to being able to apply global presentation and slide styles, you can edit text and other objects on specific slides. Generally, the AutoContent Wizard and the design templates create presentations that require little editing; however, if you want to touch up specific parts of your slides, PowerPoint 97 provides the tools you'll need.

After you complete your presentation, use the PowerPoint 97 Slide Show view to watch the presentation one screen at a time. PowerPoint 97 follows your slide-show instructions and moves the slides forward at the pace and in the style you request.

The highlights of this hour include

- How to modify your entire presentation's style
- Why you sometimes need to make minor edits to individual slides
- How to insert art into a slide
- What PowerPoint 97 tools you can use to work with text objects
- When to go to the Clip Gallery for the object you need
- How to set up the Slide Show view to produce special effects
- How to prepare your slide-show presentation

# Changing Your Entire Presentation's Design

PowerPoint 97 lets you apply a design template to your entire presentation. If you develop a presentation with the AutoContent Wizard, with individual design templates, or from scratch, you can change the format and look of your entire presentation easily.

**TIP**

One reason you might want to change your presentation's design is because your target audience changes. Suppose you give a seminar to your employees on ethics and morals in the workplace, then learn that your local Chamber of Commerce wants to see your presentation. You should formalize the style when you present the presentation to strangers, which might require a change in your presentation's design.

*Master layout* is the term applied to a presentation's overall design. Here's the process for changing the entire presentation's master layout:

1. Click the Common Tasks dialog box's Apply Design option to display Figure 15.1's Apply Design dialog box.
2. Search the Apply Design dialog box's folders for a design you like. Double-click the design's folder to open it. PowerPoint 97 shows a preview of that template in the Apply Design dialog box as you select different designs to study. You can look in the Presentation and Presentation Design folders for templates.
3. When you highlight the design template you want, click the Apply button. After PowerPoint 97 finishes changing your presentation, page through the slides to see whether you chose a good design.

**15**

NEW TERM    The *master layout* is a presentation's overall format and design.

**Figure 15.1.**
*Use the Apply Design dialog box to change the entire presentation's design.*

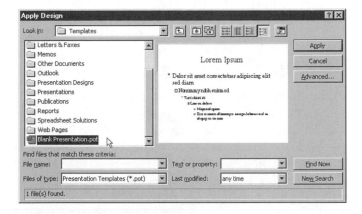

# Changing a Single Slide's Design

In the Slide view, you can change only that slide's design (called the *slide layout*) by clicking the Slide Layout option on the Common Tasks dialog box. PowerPoint 97 displays Figure 15.2's Slide Layout dialog box, which is the same dialog box that PowerPoint 97 displays when you create a new slide.

NEW TERM    The term *slide layout* refers to a single slide's format and design.

**NOTE** ▶    The Slide Layout dialog box's Apply button changes to Reapply if you click the slide's current layout.

**Figure 15.2.**
*Use the Slide Layout dialog box to change a single slide's design.*

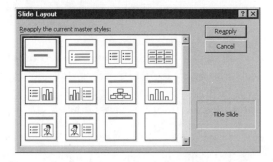

The previous section explained how to use a master layout to change the appearance of your overall presentation. If you use the Slide Layout dialog box to change an individual slide but apply a different master layout, the master layout takes precedence and changes your individual slide (if the master layout differs from the slide).

# Adding Art

Suppose you select a slide layout that contains a place for art. Presumably, you have an art image to place on the slide or you would have chosen a different slide layout. When you select a slide layout that includes a place for art, PowerPoint 97 lets you know exactly where the art should go. For example, Figure 15.3 shows an applied slide layout that includes a place for artwork. PowerPoint 97 makes it easy to add the art. Follow the slide's instructions, and double-click the area that will get the art.

**Figure 15.3.**

*PowerPoint 97 lets you know exactly where the art goes on the slide.*

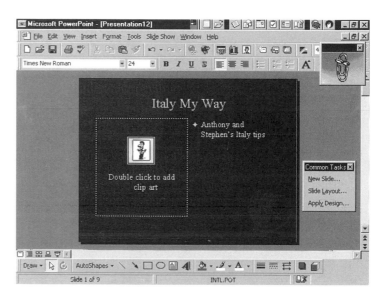

When you double-click the art area, PowerPoint 97 displays the Microsoft Clip Gallery dialog box shown in Figure 15.4. A *clip* (an abbreviation for *clip art*) is a graphic image, and the *Clip Gallery* is a collection of clip-art images. Microsoft arranges the Clip Gallery by subject, and you can see a preview of the selected image on your screen as you look through the Clip Gallery.

**NEW TERM**  The term *clip art* refers to a graphic image you can place on a slide.

**15**

The term *clip* is typically an abbreviation for a *clip-art* file. Sometimes a clip refers to other kinds of files as well, such as a sound or video file.

 A *Clip Gallery* is a collection of clip-art images arranged by subject.

 As you can see, the Microsoft Clip Gallery dialog box also lets you include picture, video, and sound clip files. PowerPoint 97 supports the insertion of these other kinds of objects, so if you want a sound to play when a slide appears, you can insert the sound file.

**Figure 15.4.**

*Select art from Microsoft's Clip Gallery.*

 If you click the button labeled Microsoft Clip Gallery's Connect to the Web for additional clips (the button that appears in the gallery dialog box's lower-right-hand corner), PowerPoint 97 accesses the Web (logging you on if necessary) and grabs files that you can point to from the Internet.

If you want to change the slide's clip art, double-click the art, and PowerPoint 97 displays the Microsoft Clip Gallery dialog box once again.

# Editing Individual Slides

In most instances, the master layout and the individual slide layouts provide ample variability and style. Rarely will you have to make substantial edits to your presentation slides. Unlike most PowerPoint 97 tutorials, this book will not go into great slide-editing detail because you just don't need to edit individual slides in most cases due to the layouts that PowerPoint 97 provides.

About the only major change you must make is to add text to the slides. All the spell-checking and AutoCorrect features that were so important in Word 97 and Excel 97 also work for text you place in a presentation; a red wavy line beneath a word indicates that Office 97's spell checker does not recognize the word. Correct the word, or add it to PowerPoint 97's dictionary by right-clicking the word.

If you're importing a Word 97 document that uses the standard styles (such as Heading 1 and Heading 2), it automatically inserts as a presentation for which you only need to select a style.

Nevertheless, the following section describes the kinds of edits that you might want to make on individual slides when you need to hone a presentation.

# Updating Text and Text Boxes

To add text to a slide, such as text that describes clip-art details, add a text box. A *text box* holds text that you can format. To add a text box, follow these steps:

1. Click the Drawing toolbar's Text Box button.
2. Drag your mouse from the text box's upper-left corner to the text box's lower-right corner. When you release the mouse, PowerPoint 97 draws the text box (as shown in Figure 15.5).
3. Type your text.
4. Use the Formatting toolbar and the Format|Font command to modify the text style and format.
5. Click anywhere on the slide to deselect the text box and return to the rest of your editing chores.

**NEW TERM**   A *text box* is a box that holds slide text.

**Figure 15.5.**

*Type and format text
inside a text box.*

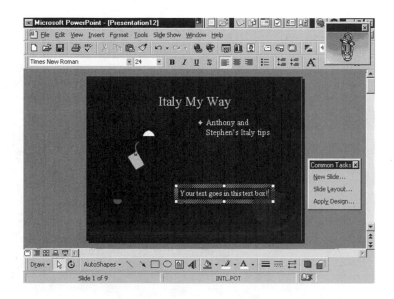

You can resize the text box, change the justification and font formatting, move the text box, add a border, and change the font and background colors by right-clicking the text box or by selecting the appropriate Formatting toolbar and Drawing toolbar buttons.

**TIP**

To change the text throughout your entire presentation, select View | Master | Slide Master to change the master layout. PowerPoint 97 displays Figure 15.6's Master Layout style slide, which you can change to update *every slide in your presentation*. For example, if you want to format a copyright message at the bottom of every slide, click the slide master's Footer area (to turn the footer area into a text box) and edit the text there (or delete the text to get rid of the footer throughout your presentation).

One of the neatest text-editing features is PowerPoint 97's *Free Rotate tool*. The Free Rotate tool lets you rotate text to any angle. For example, you might want to slant a title toward or away from text that falls below the title to add special effect or to call out a cautionary note on a slide.

**NEW TERM** A *Free Rotate tool* is a tool on the Drawing toolbar that rotates text, graphics, and any selected slide object in the degree and direction you want to rotate the object. The Free Rotate tool makes the creation of slanting titles and text as simple as dragging your mouse.

**Figure 15.6.**

*Change the slide master to update every slide's text properties.*

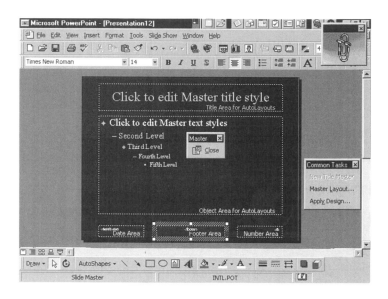

To rotate text, click the text to display the text box. Remember that a text box appears around any text, including bulleted lists and titles, when you click those objects. After you display the text box, click the toolbar's Free Rotate tool, and the mouse cursor changes to a spiral-shaped pointer. Drag any of the text box's four corners to rotate the text along a rotating axis. Figure 15.7 shows a rotated text box. When you press Escape or click anywhere on the slide, the text box outline disappears and you'll see the rotated text.

**Figure 15.7.**

*Use the Free Rotate tool to rotate any slide's object.*

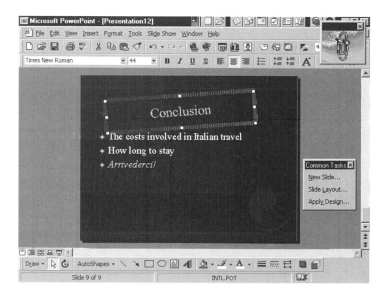

**15**

**TIP**

> The Free Rotate tool rotates selected bulleted lists and graphics as well as text boxes.

15

# Using PowerPoint 97's Slide Show

One of the best ways to see the overall effect of your presentation is to run *Slide Show*. Slide Show displays your slides in sequence, moving from one slide to another, *transitioning* (changing) with special effects that you have set up, and moving at a preset timing that you can control.

**NEW TERM**   *Slide Show* is the PowerPoint 97 slide projector that displays your presentation slides in sequence, with optional transitions between the slides.

**NEW TERM**   The term *transitioning* refers to the replacement of one slide with the next, often with a special effect that causes the second slide to cover the first in a unique way.

Follow these steps to start Slide Show:

1. Finish editing your presentation and save it to disk.
2. Select the Slide view.
3. Display the first slide in the presentation.
4. Click the Slide Show view button. PowerPoint 97 prepares the slides and displays each slide, full screen, one at a time, as you click the mouse or press PageUp and PageDown. PowerPoint 97 halts at the last slide in the presentation.
5. Press Escape to return to the Slide view.

As you watch the slide show, pay attention to the transition and timing between slides. Remember from last hour's session, "PowerPoint 97 Power," that you can control the way PowerPoint 97 transitions between each slide from within the Slide Sorter view.

If you want more control over the slide's transition, select the first slide (from within Slide view) whose exiting transition you want to change and select Slide Show|Slide Transition to display Figure 15.8's Slide Transition dialog box. From the dialog box, you can control the nature of the transition (choose a transition and watch the Effect window demonstrate the transition), the timing, and the action required to change to the next slide (such as a mouse click).

**Figure 15.8.**

*Select the transition effect.*

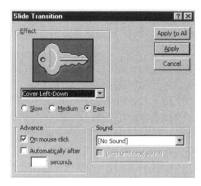

 **TIP**

To make sure the audience notices a new slide, add a sound effect to the transition. That way, when you move to the next slide, PowerPoint 97 plays the sound you associate with the transition.

If you want a uniform transition to all slides, click the Apply to All button. If you want the transition to affect only the current slide, click the Apply button to close the Slide Transition dialog box.

Of course, you'll want to automate your show as much as possible. If a speaker will control the presentation, the speaker will want to use the mouse to move from slide to slide. Otherwise, you might want to run the slide show continuously as a demo or informational display, as you might do at a trade-show booth.

To automate your slide show, select Slide Show | Set Up Show to display Figure 15.9's Set Up Show dialog box.

**Figure 15.9.**

*Fully automate your slide show with this Set Up Show dialog box.*

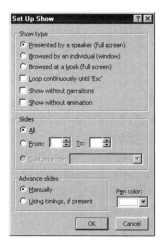

**15**

Select the option that your presentation requires. For example, if the speaker will control the show, click the first option. If you want the show to run continuously, click the Browsed at a kiosk option. In addition, you can limit the slides shown for a particular event.

When you subsequently click the Slide Show view button, PowerPoint 97 follows your Set Up Show dialog box instructions and displays the slides as you requested.

# Summary

This hour concludes the tutorial on PowerPoint 97. You can now make presentations look professional, and you can modify individual slides when needed. In addition to mastering PowerPoint 97's design and editing tools, you also understand how to set up and run the slide-show viewer.

When you use PowerPoint 97 to show your presentations, PowerPoint 97 acts like an intelligent slide projector and displays slides at the pace you select using the transition you request.

The next hour, "Outlook 97 Basics," introduces you Office 97's new organizing product called *Outlook 97*.

# Q&A

**Q  Why would I add a text box instead of using Outline view to add the text?**

**A**  The text on the Outline view is either a title or a bulleted item. If you want to place text outside these areas, you must draw a text box. You can draw a text box anywhere on a slide, and can even overwrite parts of a clip-art image with a text box. Text boxes are useful for describing figures and for placing extraneous notes on your slides.

**Q  What if I don't have extensive clip art to embed on my presentations?**

**A**  PowerPoint 97 comes armed with many images, so you may not need external graphic-art packages. In addition, PowerPoint 97 includes an Internet link, which allows you to search the Internet for clip-art (as well as picture, video, and sound) files.

   If you do not see the Clip Gallery when you request it, run the Office 97 setup program again, select the Clip Gallery, and rerun the install (your other files, including data and PowerPoint 97 programs already on your disk, will not be affected).

# Part V

# Organizing with Outlook 97

## Hour

# Hour 16

# Outlook 97 Basics

This hour introduces Outlook 97, a program that could change the way you organize your life! For several years, software developers have attempted to produce an all-in-one organizing and planning program. However, these programs were separate from your other programs, so if you used your word processor and needed an address, you had to open a separate organization program, look up the address, and type it into the word processor.

Previous versions of Office included the Schedule+ organizing program, but that program lacked common features, such as an integrated directory for e-mail and fax connections. Microsoft changed all that when they put Outlook 97 in Office 97. Your planning, scheduling, task lists, and mailing information are now in one location. You'll master Outlook 97 in this and the next hour.

Be careful! Outlook 97 is addictive ! Not only is Outlook 97 a true interactive planning and scheduling program, but it's fun to use.

The highlights of this hour include

☐ What Outlook 97 is all about

☐ Why Schedule+ users will feel right at home

☐ What screen elements reside on Outlook 97's screen

☐ How to navigate through Outlook 97's calendar views

☐ When to schedule events

☐ How to schedule meetings

☐ Which Outlook 97 tools help you manage tasks

☐ How to keep notes with Outlook 97

# An Outlook 97 Overview

Here are a few things you and Outlook 97 can do together:

☐ Organize your calendar

☐ Schedule meetings

☐ Keep an appointment book

☐ Track a prioritized to-do list

☐ Record your business and personal contacts

☐ Keep a journal

☐ Write notes to yourself that act like yellow sticky notes when you view them (like the Excel 97 comments you learned about during Hour 10, "Using Excel 97")

☐ Receive all your e-mail, faxes, and network documents in one location

**NOTE**

> Office 97 no longer contains a Schedule+ program, but if you've used Schedule+ before, you'll be fine. Outlook 97 reads all of Schedule+'s data files and adds much more functionality and integration to the Office 97 package.

**16**

# Getting Acquainted with Outlook 97

You start Outlook 97 when you do one of these things:

☐ Click one of the Office 97 Shortcut bar's Outlook 97-related buttons to send an e-mail message, enter a journal entry, or write a note.

☐ Use the Windows Start menu to start Outlook 97 by clicking Microsoft Outlook on the Program menu.

☐ Click the Office 97 Shortcut bar's Outlook 97 button to start Outlook 97. Depending on your Office 97 Shortcut bar's setup, you may not see the Outlook 97 button there.

Figure 16.1 shows the opening Outlook 97 screen. Your screen might differ slightly depending on the options that the installer set.

**Figure 16.1.**

*Outlook 97's opening screen.*

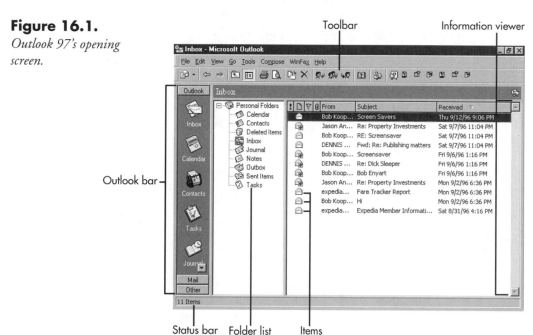

The Outlook 97 screen's format differs quite a bit from other Office 97 products' screens. You won't see the typical standard and formatting toolbars. And while Outlook 97's menu bar is similar to the other products', the rest of the screen is different due to the different nature of Outlook 97.

Therefore, take a moment to familiarize yourself with the following descriptions of Outlook 97's screen elements:

- Outlook bar—Contains shortcuts to Outlook 97 . You can rearrange the Outlook bar contents and resize the icons there. The Outlook bar lets you access all of Outlook 97's most frequently used areas.

- Folder list—Displays your Outlook 97 work folders. As you use Outlook 97, you'll subdivide your work into folder directories. For example, your inbox and outbox mail appear in folders within the Folder list. The number appearing after a folder (such as the Inbox folder) represents the number of unread items in that folder.

- Information viewer—Displays items from the selected folder. As you work with items, you'll often change the Information viewer's format. For example, when you look over your daily incoming mail, you will display summaries of your mail in the Information viewer. When you want to read something specific, you can display the entire item in the Information viewer and hide the summaries.

- Items—Contains the folder items such as contacts, appointments, and e-mail.

When you finish using with Outlook 97, quit by performing any of the following:

- Selecting File|Exit.
- Pressing Alt+F4.
- Double-clicking the Control icon.
- Clicking Outlook 97's Close Window button.

Always quit Outlook 97 and shut down Windows before turning off your computer or you might lose your work.

# Scheduling with Outlook 97

Outlook 97 includes a calendar that not only lets you organize and track dates, but also lets you track birthdays and anniversaries (and gives you automatic time-for-gift-buying reminders that might help your marriage), find open dates, keep a task list, schedule meetings, and remind you of appointments. The following sections show you how to use the Outlook 97 calendar to organize your life.

**TIP**

Not only will Outlook 97 remind you of specific appointments with an audible and visible reminder, but Outlook 97 easily sets up recurring appointments, such as weekly sales meetings.

**16**

# Working with Calendar

When you're ready to work with Outlook 97's calendar, display it by clicking the Outlook bar's Calendar icon, selecting Calendar from the Folder list, or by selecting Go | Calendar. To display more of your calendar, you can decrease the amount of screen space devoted to the Outlook bar and Folder list by dragging their edges towards the left side of the screen.

**NOTE**

You can adjust the screen columns to show more of any Outlook 97 feature. Most Outlook 97 users prefer to hide the Folder list, displaying it only when needed by selecting View | Folder List. Figure 16.2 shows the Outlook 97 screen with the calendar feature activated. Notice the Folder list is gone. To display a drop-down Folder list temporarily, click the active folder name pointed out in Figure 16.2.

**16**

**Figure 16.2.**
*Working with the calendar.*

Click here to see the drop-down list

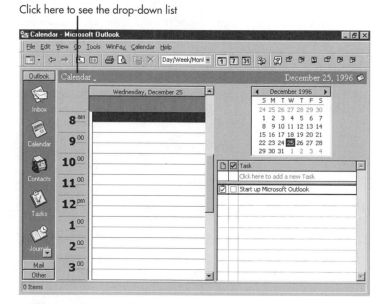

# Navigating Times and Dates

Notice that the calendar appears with these major sections:

☐ Monthly calendar

☐ Daily time planner

☐ Task list

The monthly calendar always highlights the current date (getting its information from the computer's internal clock and calendar). The calendar might show two months, depending on your screen settings. You can navigate the calendar through days and months by following these simple guides:

☐ Change days by pressing the left- or right-arrow keys or by clicking a date with your mouse.

☐ Change months by clicking to the left or right of the calendar's month name or by clicking the calendar's month name and selecting from the pop-up month list that appears.

Click through the calendar's days and notice that the daily time planner changes days accordingly. Although you probably won't have any appointments set yet, you'll quickly see how you can look at any day's appointments by clicking that day's date. The weekend day appointment pages are grayed to remind you that you're looking at Saturday or Sunday.

The calendar also provides a month-at-a-glance format when you click any of the seven day abbreviations above the calendar's day numbers. Figure 16.3 shows the month-at-a-glance calendar that appears when you select the entire month.

**Figure 16.3.**

*Looking at the
month-at-a-glance.*

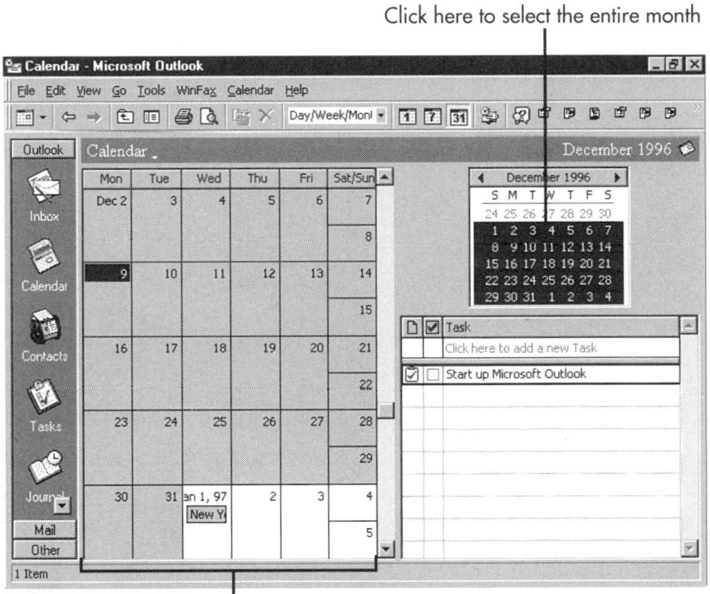

Click here to select the entire month

The entire month's appointments will appear here

16

> **TIP**
>
> If you select two or more days, Outlook 97 displays your selection's at-a-glance planning calendar.

As you acquaint yourself with Outlook 97's calendar, select from the View menu to customize the screen to your particular needs.

## Setting Appointments

To schedule an appointment, perform these steps:

1. Select the day on which you want to schedule the appointment.

2. Select the appointment time. You might have to click the time planner's scrollbar or use your up- and down-arrow keys to see the time you want.

3. Double-click the appointment time to display Figure 16.4's Appointment dialog box.

**Figure 16.4.**

*Scheduling an appointment is easy.*

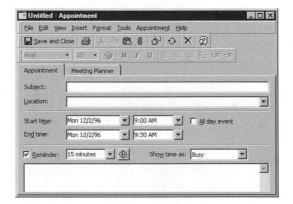

4. Enter the appointment's subject and location. Outlook 97 keeps track of your locations as you add them, so you don't have to re-enter them for subsequent appointments.

5. Set the start and stop times (use Tools|Options to change the default of 30-minute appointments if you often have different appointment lengths) or click the All day event option if necessary.

6. Set your reminder time if you want a reminder. Outlook 97 will audibly and visibly remind you of the appointment at the time you request.

7. Click the Recurrence toolbar button if the appointment will occur regularly. Outlook 97 displays the Appointment Recurrence dialog box shown in Figure 16.5. Set the recurrence options so that Outlook 97 knows how to schedule your recurring appointment.

**Figure 16.5.**

*Some appointments will*
*occur regularly.*

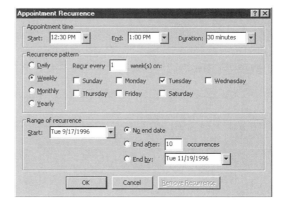

8. Click the Save and Close button. Outlook 97 displays your appointment in the time planner.

If you need to change a set appointment, double-click the appointment to display the Appointment dialog box, where you can change the appointment details. To change the appointment time, drag the appointment's top or bottom edges from the time planner to increase or decrease the appointment's duration. Drag the appointment's side edges to change the appointment's start time.

**TIP**

> Click the toolbar's New Appointment button to schedule a new appointment without first selecting the appointment's date and time.

## Scheduling Meetings

In Outlook 97 terminology, a meeting differs somewhat from an appointment. An *appointment* is for you; it does not involve other resources (such as people and equipment). A *meeting*, however, requires that you schedule more people than yourself, and perhaps requires that you schedule other resources (such as audio-visual equipment).

**NEW TERM**  An *appointment* is an activity for which you reserve time, but which does not require other people or resources.

**16**

**NEW TERM** A *meeting* is an appointment that involves other people and resources.

To schedule a meeting, create an appointment for that day and time as you would for an appointment. Click the Appointment dialog box's Meeting Planner tab to display the Meeting Planner dialog box shown in Figure 16.6. Click the Invite Others button and type names or select from the name list. The list might include people or resources, such as podiums. Outlook 97 gets the names from your contact manager's database, but you can enter new names as needed. Use the scrollbars to view the free and busy times for the people you invite. You must also select the meeting time. Outlook 97 shows you the invitees' available free time when you click AutoPick or you can use your mouse to schedule the attendees even if their free times all conflict.

**Figure 16.6.**

*Schedule meetings and plan people and resources.*

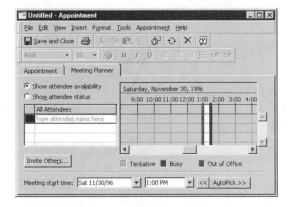

**NOTE**

Outlook 97 adjusts for time zones if you invite someone from another time zone. Obviously, you must be organized and know the invitees quite well to have access to their schedules. If you use Outlook 97 in a networked group setting, Outlook 97 can search the network for the contacts and their free times. The networked searching is the real reason Outlook 97 includes invitee free-time availabilities, because you would probably not otherwise know all free times of the people you invite.

When you complete the dialog box and click Send, all recipients (if networked or available by e-mail) get invited to your meeting using the notes you entered in the Meeting Planner dialog box.

## Scheduling Events

An *event* is a 24-hour activity, such as a holiday or birthday. When you want to record an event, such as your boss's birthday, select Calendar|New Event. Schedule the event as you would an appointment, but click the All day event button to show that the event lasts the entire day. Select the Show time as option if you want your calendar to show the time as Busy or Out of Office time.

 **NEW TERM** An *event* is a 24-hour activity, such as a birthday or holiday.

When you view the event, Outlook 97 shows it in a *banner*, or a highlighted heading for that day in the day planner's views.

**NEW TERM** A *banner* is a highlighted title that signals and describes a day's event.

## Managing a Task List

A *task* is any job that you need to track, perform, and monitor to completion. Outlook 97 tasks (like appointments and meetings) might be recurring, or they might happen only once. You can manage your Outlook 97 task list either from the Tasks folder in the Folder list or from the Calendar folder.

**NEW TERM** A *task* is any job that you need to track, perform, and monitor to completion.

> **WARNING**
>
> Unlike appointments, meetings, and events, tasks don't belong to any date or time.

To create a one-time task, perform these steps:

1. Click the New Task toolbar button or select File|New|Task. You can create a task even faster by clicking the task list's entry labeled Click here to add a task.

2. Enter a task description.

3. Type the due date (the date you must complete the task but not necessarily the day you will perform the task). If you click the Due Date drop-down list, you can select from a calendar that Outlook 97 displays. You can enter virtually any date in virtually any format, including Next Wednesday. Outlook 97 converts your format to a supported date format.

4. Further refine your task (if you need to) by double-clicking the task to display Figure 16.7's Task dialog box. You can specify recurring tasks as well as assign priority to the tasks. Click the Status tab to update the status of the task as you work on it. The Status page even tracks such task-related information as mileage, time involved, and billing information.

**Figure 16.7.**

*Modify the task's specifics and status.*

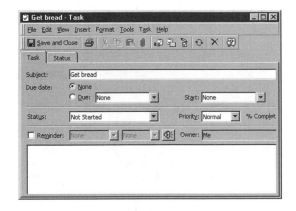

5. Click Save and Close to finalize the task.

When you complete a task, click the task's check box to cross the task from the list. Delete a task by selecting it and clicking the toolbar's Delete button.

# Writing Yourself Notes

Outlook 97 notes are equivalent to sticky yellow paper notes. You can post a note inside Outlook 97 and retrieve, edit, or delete the note later.

To see your notes, click the Notes icon in the Outlook bar or display the Notes item from the Folder list. Double-click any note to see its contents.

To create a new note, click the New Note toolbar button to display Figure 16.8's yellow note. Type your note and click the note's Close button to close the note. Resize the note by dragging its lower-right corner. Outlook 97 tracks the note's date and time. Change the note's font by selecting a new font from the Tools | Options Tasks/Notes tab. Select a different note color by right-clicking the note's icon.

**TIP**

Turn notes into appointments and tasks! Drag a note from the Notes work area to the Calendar or Tasks Outlook bar icons, and Outlook 97 opens an appropriate dialog box with the note's contents filling in the task or appointment's description. In the next hour, "Additional Outlook 97," you'll learn how to work with Outlook 97's e-mail and journal components; you can drag notes to those Outlook 97 programs as well.

**Figure 16.8.**

*Enter a note to yourself.*

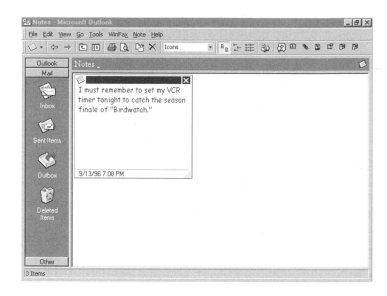

# Use Outlook 97 to Explore
# Your Computer

Although Outlook 97 is not a replacement for the Windows Explorer, it can function somewhat like Explorer to help you locate files and hardware. If you click the Outlook bar's Other button, the My Computer icon and two disk folders (you can change the folders displayed and add additional folders to the list) are displayed. When you double-click the My Computer icon, Outlook 97 opens the familiar (to Windows 95 and NT 4.0 users) My Computer details.

By double-clicking one of the disk folders, you can display your disk contents as shown in Figure 16.9. If you drag your favorite folder to the Outlook bar, Outlook 97 adds that folder to the Outlook bar permanently. That folder is then only a click or two away when you want to search through the document files inside the folder. Change your View menu options if you want to change the details of the window.

Microsoft did not replace the Windows Explorer with Outlook 97, but the Explorer-like access lets you quickly find files that you want to send to others or use in notes. You won't have to open both Explorer and Outlook 97 when you need to search your disk for information.

**16**

**Figure 16.9.**

*Explore your computer with Outlook 97.*

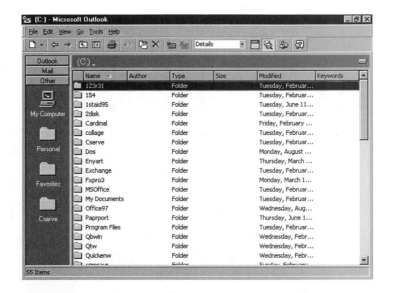

**TIP**
To launch a program from Outlook 97, double-click the program (or a document tied to an application, such as a Word 97 document) in the Outlook 97 listing, and Windows will keep Outlook 97 open while your selected program is opened. The right-click pop-up menu offers the same right-click functionality as you find in Explorer. Therefore, if you use Windows quick viewers, you'll find the familiar Quick View option on Outlook 97's right-click menus.

## Summary

This hour introduces Outlook 97 and explains some of the ways you can use Outlook 97 to check your calendar, manage appointments, meetings, and events, track tasks, keep notes, and explore your computer. If you've used any other personal information management program, you'll really like Outlook 97's integration into the Office 97 and Windows environment.

Office 97 references Outlook 97 when you send form letters to friends and keep track of contacts. (You'll learn more about Office 97's integration in the last part of this book.) The drag-and-drop capabilities between the Outlook 97 programs often make entering new items easy. If you write yourself a note that turns into a meeting or contact name, drag the note to the appropriate Outlook 97 program to generate an entry from the note.

The next hour shows you how to use Outlook 97's contact list to find your associates quickly and easily. Additionally, Outlook 97's journal tracks events as they happen, including tracking incoming mail and faxes that you receive inside Outlook 97's Inbox.

# Q&A

**Q  How can I assign a task to a specific day?**

**A**  You cannot assign tasks to days. Tasks transcend days because tasks are one-time or recurring items that you must accomplish within a certain time frame, but not on a particular day. Perhaps you are only confusing Outlook 97 terminology. If you want to assign a particular event to a time and day, assign an appointment or meeting. Tasks are items that you must accomplish and that you can track and assign to other people, but tasks are not tied to a specific time and date.

**Q  Once I set a reminder, how does Outlook 97 inform me of the appointment, meeting, or event?**

**A**  You must continually run Outlook 97 during your computing sessions for Outlook 97 to monitor and remind you of things you've got to do. Outlook 97 is one program that you'll probably want to add to your Windows Start-Up group so that it always starts when you start Windows.

Outlook 97 tracks incoming and outgoing events. Also, as you'll learn in the next hour, Outlook 97 monitors your electronic mail, faxes, and network transfers, and keeps an eye on your reminders to let you know when something is due. The only way Outlook 97 can perform these tasks is if you keep Outlook 97 running during your work sessions.

**16**

# Hour 17

# Additional Outlook 97

This hour concludes Outlook 97's coverage by showing you how to use Outlook 97's journal, contacts list, Inbox, and Outbox. Outlook 97's Inbox and Outbox components are central to using Outlook 97 as a repository for all your data throughput; these mail boxes constitute your computer's Grand Central Station.

Part of Outlook 97's effectiveness hinges on how well you keep your contact lists organized. Use Outlook 97 to keep track of clients, friends, employees, and anyone else you contact. Outlook 97 tracks not only routine name and address information, but e-mail addresses as well. After you set up your contacts list, other Outlook 97 programs (such as the Inbox) refer to the list when an address is needed. As you learned in the previous hour, you can even use Outlook 97 to schedule meetings with your contacts.

The highlights of this hour include

☐ What a contact is

☐ Why Outlook 97 works like a Web-page organizer

☐ When a journal will track items automatically

☐ How to enter items manually into the journal

☐ How to send and receive messages

☐ When to use the Outlook 97 Deleted Items folder

☐ How to read and reply to messages

## Recording Contacts

To record a new contact, click Contacts on the Outlook bar to select Contacts from the Folder list. An Outlook 97 *contact* is a person or organization that you correspond with, either by mail, e-mail, phone, or in person.

**NEW TERM** A *contact* is a person or organization that you correspond with, either by mail, e-mail, phone, or in person.

To record a new contact, perform these steps:

1. Click the Contacts screen's New Contact toolbar button to open Figure 17.1's Contact dialog box.

2. Type the contact's full name. If you click the Full Name button, Outlook 97 displays separate fields for the parts of the name (such as title, first name, and last name), so you can keep the parts properly separated when needed. The time you take to separate part names pays off when you use your contact information in form letters and database work later.

3. Enter the rest of the contact's information. Click the Address button to track separate parts of the contact's address. Open the drop-down lists to record separate pieces of related data. For example, you can record a business, a home, or another address by clicking the appropriate drop-down address type before entering the address. Open the phone-number drop-down lists as well to store different kinds of phone numbers for your contacts. You might find it useful to increase the dialog box's size to full screen to see all the fields.

4. Click the Save and Close buttons to save the contact information and display a blank dialog box for your next contact.

**17**

**Figure 17.1.**

*Outlook 97 gives you lots of contact data fields.*

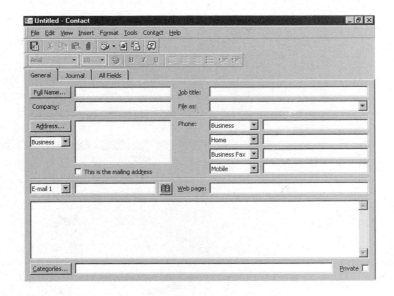

 **TIP**

The contact's data page acts like an Internet Web page browser as well as a repository for contact data. A *browser* is a program that displays Internet Web pages. If a contact has a Web page, enter that Web page's address at the Web page prompt. When you return to the contact information and click the toolbar's Explore Web Page button, Outlook 97 locates and displays the contact's Web page using whatever Web browser (such as Internet Explorer) is installed on your system.

 **NEW TERM**     A *browser* is a program, such as Microsoft's Internet Explorer, that lets you search Internet Web pages.

 **NOTE**

If you use Microsoft Exchange to track names and e-mail addresses, click the address-book button (to the left of the Web page field) to import an e-mail address from your Exchange address book.

Be on the lookout for shortcuts as you work with Outlook 97. Generally, you can drag and drop information instead of re-entering data when you need to transport information from one Outlook 97 area to another. For example, suppose you wrote yourself a quick note with a new client's name and phone number with Outlook 97's notes (you learned how to take notes with Outlook 97 in the previous hour). You can transfer the client's information from the note to your contact list by dragging the note to the Outlook bar's Contacts icon. Outlook 97 sets up the initial client name and number information, to which you then can add.

When you close the Contact dialog box, your first contact will appear in Outlook 97's address book like the one shown in Figure 17.2. After you enter several contacts, click the alphabetic tabs to the right of the address book to locate specific contacts.

**Figure 17.2.**

*Your contact appears in Outlook 97's address book.*

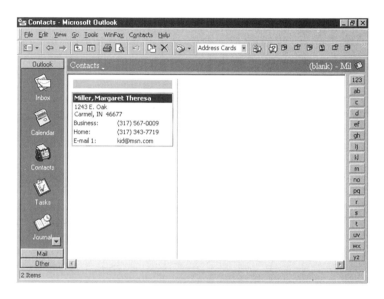

To select a contact, display the contact name in the address book. Here are a few things you can do after you select a contact:

- [ ] Directly edit the addresses, phone numbers, and e-mail addresses displayed on the page by clicking the appropriate fields.
- [ ] Double-click the name to open the contact's Contact dialog box, which displays the contact information, allowing you to edit or view more detail.
- [ ] Right-click the contact name, select AutoDialer, and dial the contact's phone number from the New Call dialog box shown in Figure 17.3. If you click the Journal Entry option, Outlook 97 adds the call to this contact's journal; the journal records the call! The next section explains all about Outlook 97's journal feature.
- [ ] Right-click the contact name and select Explore Web Page to see the contact's Web page from within your Web browser.

**17**

☐ Right-click the contact name and select the New Contact from same Company option. Outlook 97 creates a new contact entry and transfers all of the business-related addresses and phone numbers to the new contact. You only need to fill in the new contact's name and other specifics. Likewise, Outlook 97 lets you create an employee contact list easily by transferring similar company data to each new employee you enter.

**Figure 17.3.**

*Outlook 97 will automatically dial your contact.*

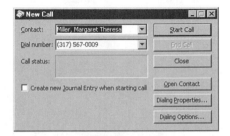

## Keeping a Journal

The Outlook 97 *journal* keeps track of all your interactions with contacts, Outlook 97 items, and activities. Although you can make manual journal entries, the real power of Outlook 97's journal appears when you automate Outlook 97 to record the following kinds of journal entries for you:

☐ Track and record all items (such as e-mail) that you send to and receive from contacts. Depending on the option you selected when you set up a contact, the Outlook 97 journal can automatically record all interactions with that contact, or you can record interactions selectively.

☐ Keep track of all Office 97 documents that you create or edit. Browse the journal to find a summary of the documents you created and the order in which you created (and edited) them.

☐ Track all meetings automatically.

☐ Track all appointments and tasks manually. (Outlook 97 does not track appointments and tasks automatically.)

☐ Manually record *any* activity in your Outlook 97 journal, including conversations around the water cooler.

 The Outlook 97 *journal* keeps track of all your interactions with contacts, Outlook 97 items, and activities.

 **TIP**

Have you ever wished that you had recorded a complaint call you made when you got a bad product or service? Let Outlook 97 track *all* your calls automatically! The journal will record times, dates, and people called. As you use Outlook 97 to make calls, record notes about the calls and track those notes in your Outlook 97 journal.

When you open Outlook 97's journal by clicking the Outlook bar's Journal icon or selecting Journal from the Folder list, you'll probably see a blank journal entry such as the one shown in Figure 17.4.

**Figure 17.4.**

*Your journal starts out blank.*

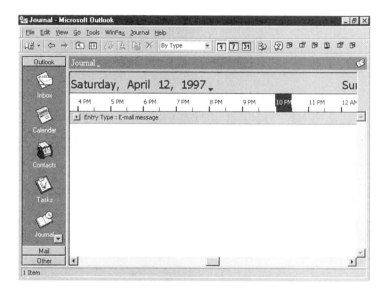

The first thing you'll want to do with your journal is designate all items that you want the journal to track. Select Tools | Options and click the Journal tab. Select each item from the list that you want Outlook 97 to track. For example, select e-mail message, fax, meeting request, and meeting response if those are the items you want the journal to track automatically. In addition, select one or more contacts from the contact list, and Outlook 97 will record all activity for those specific contacts.

If you want Outlook 97 to track document files from another program, such as Word 97, simply select that program from the list. Outlook 97 tracks all Office 97 document activity (if you select this option) as well as other Office 97–aware software documents and data files. Although not all Windows programs are Office 97–aware yet, many more vendors will begin to include this journal-tracking feature as Office 97 gains popularity.

After you set up the automatic recording, Outlook 97 begins logging those activities. When you open the journal for days during which there was an activity of any kind, you'll see the journal entry.

As mentioned earlier in this section, the Outlook 97 journal cannot automatically record all activity in your life. However, you can add manual entries for any activities you want recorded in your journal. If you want to record an appointment, open that appointment (from within the calendar). If you want to record an item not related to Outlook 97, such as a conversation, create a note for that item (see the last hour's chapter, "Outlook 97 Basics," for help with Outlook 97's note feature) and transport the information from the note to the journal. To record a manual journal entry (such as a conversation's notes), perform these steps:

1. Double-click the item you want to record to display the item's edit dialog box.
2. Select the item's Tools menu, then select the Record in Journal option. The journal will now contain an icon that represents the item. Double-click the journal's icon to display the item's details.

Suppose you wrote a letter to your phone company, and you want to record the complete document in your journal. If you've set up your journal to track all Word 97 documents automatically, the document will appear in your journal. If, however, you have not set up the journal to track Word 97 documents automatically, simply display the document's icon in the Outlook bar's My Computer window and drag the document to the Outlook bar's journal icon.

**NOTE**

You can add a new journal entry of any item type without first creating the item. Display your journal and select File I New. Select Journal Entry to display Figure 17.5's Journal Entry dialog box. Type a subject and select the type of journal entry. When you click the Save and then the Close buttons, Outlook 97 saves your entry in the journal.

**Figure 17.5.**

*Manually enter a new journal entry.*

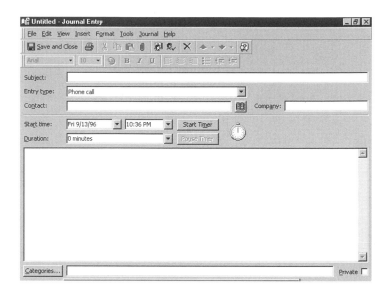

# Mastering Outlook 97 Mail

When you click the Outlook bar's Mail button, the Outlook bar displays the following labeled icons:

- ☐ Inbox—Holds your incoming e-mail and faxes.
- ☐ Sent Items—Displays mail items you've sent to others.
- ☐ Outbox—Holds items you've queued up to send.
- ☐ Deleted Items—Holds items you've deleted but not removed from Outlook 97's recycle bin. Select Tools|Empty Deleted Items Folder to remove the Deleted Items folder contents. When you remove an item from the Deleted Items folder, Outlook 97 does *not* send the item to the Windows recycle bin; Outlook 97 deletes the item completely from your system.

**NEW TERM**  The *Inbox folder* holds your incoming messages, even those you've read.

**NEW TERM**  The *Outbox folder* holds all your outgoing messages until you send them.

**NEW TERM**  The *Deleted Items folder* holds items you've deleted from Outlook 97 but not completely erased from the disk.

One task you'll perform quite often is sending a message to a recipient across the Internet. To create a message, perform these steps:

**17**

1. Click the Outlook bar's Mail button.

2. Select File|New|Mail Message to display Figure 17.6's Message dialog box.

3. Enter the recipient's names in the To (your primary recipient) and Cc (the copy if you want to send to multiple recipients) fields. Click these buttons if you want to select a contact in your contacts list (highly recommended because your contacts list holds e-mail addresses). If you have not entered the recipient in your contacts list, add the information now, then close the contacts list to return to the mail message.

4. Enter the message subject. Your recipient will see the subject in the list of messages that he or she receives.

5. Type your message in the large message area at the bottom of the message dialog box. Although Outlook 97 uses Office 97's spell checker, it does not work automatically as you type the message. To spell check your message, type your message, click your cursor at the top of the message, then select Tools|Spelling.

6. Click the Options tab to select certain message options (such as the message importance level and a delivery date). The recipient, like you, will be able to order received mail by importance level when reading through the messages.

7. Click the Send button. Outlook 97 sends the message to your folder named Outbox.

8. Select Tools|Check for New Mail to send your Outbox messages. Not only will Outlook 97 send your Outbox messages, but it will also collect any incoming messages waiting for you. Therefore, always check your Inbox for mail after sending mail from the Outbox.

**Figure 17.6.**

*Enter the message you want to send.*

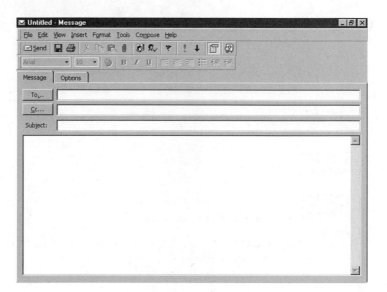

To attach another document file to your message, such as a Word 97 or Excel 97 document, click the Insert File toolbar button and select a document file from the Open dialog box that appears. Any text that you typed will be followed by the file that you attached.

Regularly, you'll need to check your Inbox folder to see what items await you. As Step 8 just mentioned, you must select Tools|Check for New Mail to send Outbox items and receive Inbox folder items. Outlook 97 will log you onto your Internet provider if needed. Your Outlook bar's Inbox folder displays a number if you have unread messages that require your attention.

When you display your Inbox folder (by clicking the Outlook bar's Inbox icon), you'll see a list of incoming message headers like the ones shown in Figure 17.7.

**NOTE**

If you only see headers (with no text), select View | Current view | Messages with AutoPreview. The AutoPreview view lets you read the first few lines of each message in addition to showing the message header.

**NEW TERM**

*AutoPreview view* is the Inbox folder's mode that displays each message's subject as well as three lines from each message.

**Figure 17.7.**

*Read the AutoPreview to get a glimpse of each message.*

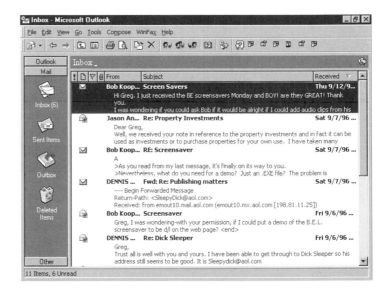

**NOTE**

As you read each message, the message icon changes to show that the message has been read. Revert the read message flag back to an unread state by right-clicking the message and selecting Mark as Read from the pop-up menu.

To read a message, simply double-click it. To reply to the sender (in effect, sending a new message to your Outbox folder), click the toolbar's Reply button and enter a reply. You can reply to the sender and all Cc recipients of the sender's message by clicking the Reply All toolbar button.

# Calling Someone

To make a call from anywhere inside Outlook 97, display the Tools menu and select Dial. If you select New Call, Outlook 97 displays Figure 17.8's New Call dialog box, from which you can select a contact to dial or manually enter a number. If you have not set up automatic journal recording for the call's recipient, click the option labeled Create new Journal Entry when starting the call. If you recently called the recipient, click Tools | Dial | Redial and select from the list of recently called numbers.

**WARNING**

You must have a modem connected to your computer before Outlook 97 can dial a number.

**Figure 17.8.**
*You can place a call from Outlook 97 at any time.*

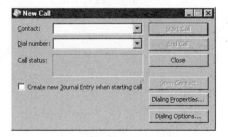

# Summary

This hour explains the remaining Outlook 97 features. You now understand contacts and the importance of entering as much information as you can about your contacts into Outlook 97. All Office 97 products use the contacts list for names and addresses. When you automate your journal, the journal contains all contacts you've elected to track.

One of the busiest Outlook 97 areas is the messaging Inbox and Outbox folders. Outlook 97 organizes incoming and outgoing messages, and makes it easy for you to respond to messages that you receive.

The next hour, "Access 97 Basics," begins exploring Access 97, the Office 97 database that is arguably the most useful and powerful personal-computer database available today.

# Q&A

**Q  What if I don't have a Web browser?**

**A** You *do* have a Web browser because Office 97 comes with one. You may not have any Internet access, however. You must sign up with an Internet provider to use any Internet-based features.

**Q  How does a message reply differ from a forwarded message?**

**A** When you reply to a message, you create a brand new message that responds in some way to your recipient's original message. If you forward a recipient's message, you send the message exactly as you first read it to another recipient (or to a list of recipients).

**Q  Why does Outlook 97 not send my messages as soon as I complete outgoing messages and send them?**

**A** Outlook 97 does not send messages until you select Tools|Check for New Mail (F5 is the shortcut key). Dialing and logging on takes time. Instead of logging into your Internet provider every time you create an Outbox folder message, Outlook 97 waits until you request the check for new mail to get your waiting mail and to send your outgoing mail. By waiting, Outlook 97 only has to log on to the Internet one time to send all your messages.

**17**

# PART VI

# Tracking with Access 97

# Hour

# Hour **18**

# Access 97 Basics

This hour introduces you to the world of databases with Access 97. The nature of databases makes Access 97 one of the more involved programs in the Office 97 suite of programs. Generally, people find that they can master Word 97, Excel 97, PowerPoint 97, and Outlook 97 more quickly than they can Access 97. Access 97 is not difficult to learn and use, but you must understand the structure of database design before you can truly understand Access 97.

A *database* is an organized collection of data. You'll learn to set up databases, enter and edit database data, search for data within the database, and report database contents after you master data organization. Access 97 is called a *database management system* because it lets you create, organize, and manage data stored in databases.

 **New Term** A *database* is an organized collection of data.

 **New Term** A *database management system* is a program, like Access 97, that lets you create, organize, and manage your data stored in databases.

The highlights of this hour include

☐ What a database is

☐ Which database-related objects Access 97 manages

☐ Why databases contain tables

☐ What fields and records are

☐ How to create and modify tables

# Database Basics

Whereas previous hours of this book begin by showing you how to start the program, this hour begins by explaining the database concept. You need to learn a little about how a database management system organizes data before using Access 97.

Everyone trudges through data at work and at home. A database manager, such as Access 97, lets you organize your data and turn raw facts and figures into meaningful information. Access 97 processes data details, so you can spend your valuable time analyzing results. Say your company keeps thousands of parts in an Access 97 inventory database, and you need to know exactly which part sold the most in Division 7 last April. Access 97 can find the answer for you.

**WARNING**

Database experts have written complete books on database theory. This hour won't give you an extremely in-depth appreciation for databases, but you'll learn enough to get started with Access 97.

A database typically contains related data. In other words, you might create a home office database with your household budget, but keep another database to record your rare-book collection titles and their worth. In your household budget, you might track expenses, income, bills paid, and so forth, but that information will not overlap the book collection database. Of course, if you buy a book, both databases might show the transaction, but the two databases would not overlap.

When you design a database, define its scope before you begin. Does your business need an inventory tracking system? Does your business need an electronic general-ledger system? If so, an Access 97 database would work well. Only you and your accountants can decide whether the inventory should be part of the general-ledger system. The database integration of inventory into the general ledger will require much more work to design, but your financial requirements may necessitate the integration.

**18**

**NOTE**

> Not all database values will directly relate to one another. For example, your company's loan records do not relate to your company's payroll, but both probably will reside in your company's accounting database. Again, you'll have to decide on the scope when you design your database. Fortunately, Microsoft made Access 97 extremely flexible, so you can change any database structure when you begin using your database. The better you analyze the design up front, however, the easier your database will be to create.

## Database Tables

If you threw your family's financial records into a filing cabinet without organizing them, you would have a mess. That's why most people organize their filing cabinets by putting related records into file folders. Your insurance papers go in one folder; your banking records go in another.

Likewise, you cannot throw your data into a database without breaking the data into separate related groups. These groups are called *tables*; a table is analogous to a folder in a filing cabinet.

**NEW TERM**    A *table* is a collection of data about a specific topic.

A database might contain many tables, each being a further refinement of related data. Your financial database might contain a table for accounts payable, a table for customer records, a table for accounts receivable, a table for vendor records, a table for employee records, and a table for payroll details, such as hours worked during a given time period. The separate tables help you eliminate redundant data; when you produce a payroll report, Access 97 retrieves some information from your employee table (such as name and pay rate) and some information from your time tables (such as hours worked).

**NOTE**

> Access 97 is a *relational database*. That means Access 97 uses data from multiple tables instead of requiring you to duplicate data in two or more places. Therefore, if you increase a customer's discount, you only need to change the discount in one customer table instead of in the customer table, the pricing table, and the sales table.

**NEW TERM**    A *relational database* relates data from multiple tables instead of requiring you to duplicate data in more than one location.

18

Access 97 stores all of a single database's tables in one file that ends with the .mdb extension. By storing the complete database in one file, Access 97 makes it easier for you to copy and back up your database. You'll never have to specify the .mdb extension when you create a database. As with all the Office 97 data files, a database is referred to as a *document* when you want to open the database from the Office 97 shortcut bar and menus.

 **TIP**

> You can import data from an Access 97 document (database table) into a Word 97 document. This makes creating and reporting data simple.

## Tables Have Records and Fields

To keep track of table data, Access 97 breaks down each table into *records* and *fields*. In a way, the table structure looks a lot like an Excel 97 worksheet. As Figure 18.1 shows, a table's records are the rows, and a table's fields are the columns. Figure 18.1 shows an electronic checkbook register table; you usually organize your real checkbook register just like the computerized table, so you'll have no problem mastering Access 97's records and fields.

**NEW TERM**  A *record* is a row from a table.

**NEW TERM**  A *field* is a column from a table.

**Figure 18.1.**

*Tables have records (rows) and fields (columns).*

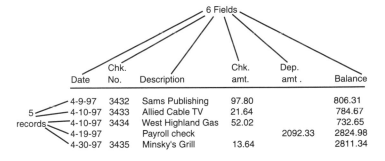

Your table fields contain different data types. As Figure 18.1 shows, one field might hold a text description, while another holds a dollar amount. Every *item* within the same field must be the same data type, but a table might contain several fields that differ in type. When you design your database, you are responsible for telling Access 97 which data type you want for each field in your database tables.

**18**

Here are the types of data that you can store in an Access 97 database table:

☐ Text—Text data consists of letters, numbers, and special characters. You only report text data; you cannot calculate with it. A balance-due field would never be a text data type, but addresses, names, and Social Security numbers are examples of text fields. Generally, you'll store short text items (names, addresses, cities, codes, product names, and part codes) in text fields.

☐ Memo—The memo field can hold an extremely large amount of text, including paragraphs. Memo fields consume lots of space, and not all tables require memo fields.

☐ Number—A number field holds numbers; use this field to calculate values.

☐ Date/Time Fields—These fields hold date and time values (similar to Excel 97's date and time format). Access 97 lets you enter data into date and time fields using many formats. Additionally, Access 97 respects your Windows international settings, so you'll be able to enter a date in your country's format.

☐ Currency—This field holds dollar amounts. Access 97 keeps the dollar amounts rounded to the proper decimal alignment. Access 97 recognizes your Windows international settings, and uses international money amounts when needed.

☐ AutoNumber—This field holds sequential numbers, one number for each record in the table.

**NEW TERM**    *AutoNumber* refers to a field data type that holds sequential numbers, one for each record in the table. Access 97 automatically adds the AutoNumber data to tables as you add records to a table.

☐ Yes/No—These fields hold Yes and No (or true and false) two-pronged values to indicate the existence or absence of an item or to indicate the answer to an implied question.

☐ OLE object—This is an embedded object, such as a graph you create in Excel 97. Your Access 97 databases can hold any kind of OLE-compatible embedded object.

**NEW TERM**    *OLE*, which stands for *Object Linking and Embedding*, refers to objects from another program that you can insert into an Access 97 table.

☐ Hyperlink—This is an Internet Web-page site address.

**NOTE**

Office 97's Internet integration extends to Access 97. When you click a hyperlink Internet Web-page address in a table, Access 97 sends you to the Web page, logging you in to your Internet provider if necessary.

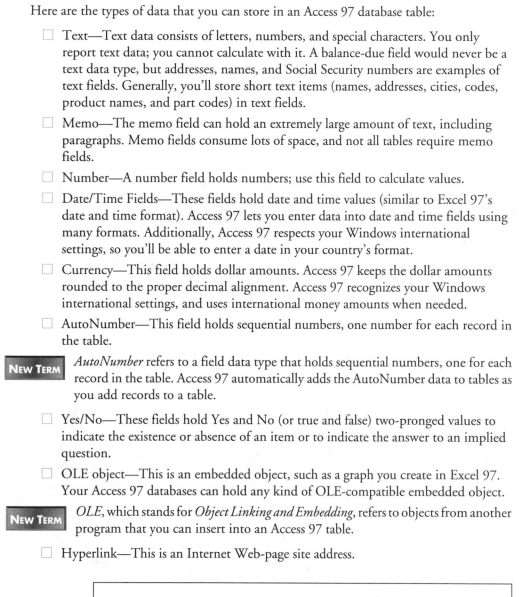

18

## Use a Key

Every Access 97 table requires a *primary key field*. The primary key field (often just called a *key*) is a field that contains no duplicate entries. Whereas a table's city field might contain multiple occurrences of the same city name, a key field must be unique for each record. You can designate a field as a key field, or you can let Access 97 add a key field to tables for you.

 **TIP**

> If you access a particular field very often, designate that field as an *index field* in the Design view property settings. Access 97 creates an index for every database and locates the index fields in that index. Just as an index in the back of the book speeds your searches to particular subjects, the index field will speed searches through that field.

If you were creating a table to hold employee records, a good key-field candidate would be the employee's Social Security number because every person's Social Security number is unique. If you're not sure that your data will contain unique information in any field, let Access 97 create a key field. Access 97 will assign an AutoNumber format to the key field to ensure that each key field contains a different value.

Access 97 uses the key field to find records quickly. For example, when you want to locate an employee's record, search by the employee's key field (the Social Security number). If you search based on the employee's name, you might not find the proper record; two or more employees might be named *John Smith*, for example.

 **NOTE**

> The reason so many companies assign you a customer number is because the customer number uniquely identifies you in their database. Although today's computerized society sometimes makes one feel like "just another number," such a customer number lets the company keep your records more accurate and keep costs down.

# Getting Acquainted with Access 97

You start Access 97 when you do one of these things:

☐ Click the Office 97 Shortcut bar's New Office Document button and double-click the Blank Database icon to create a new Access 97 database. (If you don't see the Blank Database icon, click the General tab.)

☐ Click the Office 97 Shortcut bar's Open Office Document button and select an existing Access 97 database that you want to edit.

**18**

- Use the Windows Start menu to start Access 97 by clicking Microsoft Access on the Program menu.

- Select an Access 97 database from the Windows Start menu's Documents option. Windows will recognize that Access 97 created the database and will start Access 97 and load the database automatically. The Start menu's Document option holds a list of your most recent work.

- Click the Office 97 Shortcut bar's Access 97 button to create a blank database. (Depending on your Office 97 Shortcut bar's setup, you might not see the Access 97 button there.)

Figure 18.2 shows the opening Access 97 screen. Your screen might differ slightly depending on the options that the installer set.

**Figure 18.2.**

*Access 97's opening screen when you start Access 97 from the Start menu.*

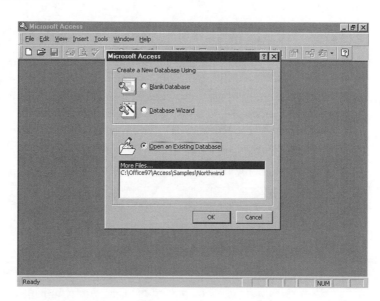

The center of the opening screen contains a dialog box that guides you to your first Access 97 operation. The dialog box lets you do one of the following:

- Create a blank database, which requires that you set up the entire database structure including tables, fields, and other pertinent database-structure information.

- Start a database wizard that walks you through the creation of a database using predefined wizard formats.

- Open an existing database so you can modify the database structure or work with the database information.

When you're finished with Access 97, quit by performing any of the following:

- [ ] Select File|Exit.
- [ ] Press Alt+F4.
- [ ] Double-click the Control icon.
- [ ] Click Access 97's Close Window button.

**WARNING**

> Always quit Access 97 and shut down Windows before turning off your
> computer, or you might lose your work.

# Your First Access 97 Database

While you are learning Access 97, practice designing your early databases without the help of the Access 97 wizards. In most cases, the wizards will not create *exactly* the kind of database you require, and you'll have to change the database structure as soon as the wizard completes the database design and creation. Changing an existing database is difficult when you've never worked with Access 97. The best way to gain Access 97 mastery is to design and create your own database from scratch so you'll better understand the inner workings of data.

After you master Access 97, the wizards will save you lots of time if you find one that creates a sample database that is close to what you need. After the wizard creates the database, you can modify the database to suit your needs.

Here are some of the Access 97 database wizards that you can use after you master Access 97's fundamentals:

- [ ] Address book—This wizard keeps track of names and addresses.
- [ ] Asset tracking—This wizard manages your company's assets.
- [ ] Book collection—This wizard lets you record titles and values for your book collection (you can easily convert this database wizard to a coin collection, baseball card collection, or virtually any other kind of collection you want to track).
- [ ] Donations—This wizard manages donations for nonprofit organizations.
- [ ] Household inventory—This wizard keeps track of your home items for inventory and estate-management purposes.
- [ ] Inventory control—This wizard tracks and manages your company inventory records.
- [ ] Order entry—This wizard is a complete order-entry and transaction system.
- [ ] Students and classes—This wizard is a school or church class planner.
- [ ] Workout—This wizard is a collection of exercise-tracking tables.

In addition to the wizards, Access 97 comes with a comprehensive database called the *Northwind Traders, Inc., Database*, which you can study to learn about advanced database operations.

## The Database Window

When you start Access 97 and see Figure 18.2's opening dialog box, select Blank Database and click OK to create a new database. Access 97 prompts you for a database name (using the default name db1 with the filename extension .mdb, which you should change to something more meaningful). Enter a new name and click the Create button to display Figure 18.3's *Database window*. The Database window title bar includes the name of your database (My First in Figure 18.3) and lists the names of your database *objects*, none of which will exist when you create the database.

 The *Database window* lists your database object names and provides the central control panel for your Access 97 work.

 *Objects* are tables, queries, forms, reports, macros, and modules within your database.

**Figure 18.3.**
*The Database window displays a list of your database objects as you create them.*

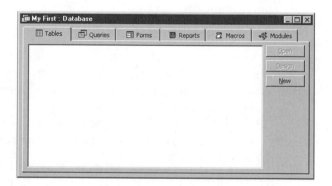

 A database object is a piece of an Access 97 database. For example, a table is an object. A database report that prints database data is an object. Your data, however, is not an object.

As you create your database, you'll add objects to the Database window's six object categories. Any database can contain lots of objects from each category. Here are brief descriptions of the six kinds of Access 97 objects (you've already seen tables in the previous section):

☐ Tables—Related data within a database.

☐ Queries—Stored instructions that select data from one or more tables for reporting, analysis, and data-management purposes.

**NEW TERM**  A *query* is a selection of data from one or more tables.

☐ Forms—Onscreen representations of paper forms that you and other users use to enter data into tables.

**NEW TERM**  A *form* is an onscreen data-entry sheet in which you enter data into tables. Forms often mimic their paper equivalents.

☐ Reports—Printed listings of database data.

**NEW TERM**  A *report* is a printed table output.

☐ Macros—Stored task lists for Access 97 commands.

**NEW TERM**  *Macros* are lists of tasks you want Access 97 to perform.

☐ Modules—Programs written in Visual Basic for Applications (VBA): a powerful (but advanced for nonprogrammers) programming language with which you can automate any database task.

**NEW TERM**  *Modules* are programs you write with the Office 97 VBA language.

As you create your database, you'll create one or more instances of the database objects. For example, you might create 25 tables and 50 reports. When you want to create, edit, or work with one of the database objects, return to the Database window (the toolbar always contains a Database Window toolbar button when you're using Access 97 but not working in the Database window) and click the tab of the object you need to work with.

Generally, you'll select the object category, then click New to create a new object in that category. Or, you might select an object and click Open to work with that object.

**NOTE**

Although you can read Access 95 databases from Access 97, it's best to convert Access 95 databases to Access 97. Do so by selecting Tools I Database Utilities I Convert Database. Access 97 does not let you change the structure of an Access 95 database until you convert it to Access 97.

**18**

# Creating a Table

You must create tables before you can do anything with a database. The tables hold the data on which the other objects operate. As mentioned earlier in this hour, you should begin creating your tables from scratch until you learn more about Access 97 and can modify tables and other database objects generated by the wizards.

To create a table, follow these steps:

1. In the Database window, with the Tables tab selected, click New. Access 97 displays Figure 18.4's New Table dialog box.
2. Select Design View and click OK to display Figure 18.5's Design view dialog box. Describe your table's fields in the Design view dialog box.

 *Design view* displays your table's design showing the individual fields and field properties. Other Database window objects also have Design views to show their structures.

3. Type a field name, such as First Name or Quantity, for the first field in your database. The names have nothing to do with the data type that you'll eventually store in the table's field. The field name lets you refer to the field as you design your table. Only after you completely design the table will you enter data in the table. The order that you add fields does not affect your database use. Even so, try to add the fields in the general order that you want to enter the table data.
4. Press Tab and click the Data Type's drop-down list to select the field's data type.
5. Press Tab and type a description for the field. Some field names are optional and don't require a description, but the more you document and describe your data, the easier it will be to modify your database later.

**Figure 18.4.**

*The New Table dialog box helps you create tables.*

18

**Figure 18.5.**

*Define your table's fields in the Design view dialog box.*

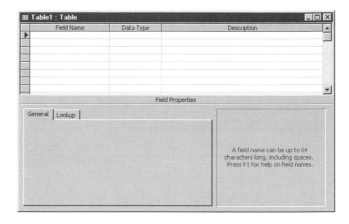

After you enter the first field's name, data type, and optional description, describe the field properties in the lower half of the Design view dialog box. Some fields do not require property settings, but most require some type of setting. The next section describes how to set field property values.

# Setting Field Properties

The lower half of the Design view contains settings for your field property values. Each field has a data type, as you already know. In addition to describing the field's data type in the Design view's upper half, you can further refine the field's description and limitations in the Field Properties section.

You can configure a different set of field property values for each data type. For example, text fields contain properties related to text data, whereas numeric fields contain properties related to numbers (such as decimal positions).

Here are a few common field property values that you might want to set as you create your table:

☐ Field Size—Limits the number of characters the field can hold, thereby limiting subsequent data-entry of field data.

☐ Format—Displays a drop-down list with several formats that the field's data type can take on.

☐ Caption—Holds a text prompt that Access 97 displays when the user enters data into this table's field. If you don't specify a caption, Access 97 uses the field name. Access 97 displays the caption in its status bar when you enter data into the table.

☐ Default Value—Contains the field's default value, which appears when the user enters data into this table. The user will be able to enter a value that differs from the default if desired.

**18**

□ Required—Holds either Yes or No to determine whether Access 97 requires a value in this field before the user can save a table's data record. If you specify a field as the key field instead of letting Access 97 add a key field, your key field *must* contain Yes for the Required property. If you don't want the user leaving a field blank, enter Yes for the Required property.

□ Decimal Places—Holds the number of default decimal places shown for numbers entered into this field.

Figure 18.6 shows a completed table's Design view. The selected field's (the field with the arrow, or *field selector* in the left-hand column) property values appear at the bottom of the dialog box. As you enter your own table fields, edit any information that you type incorrectly by clicking the field name, data type, description, or property value, and moving the text cursor to the mistake to correct the problem.

**Figure 18.6.**

*A more complete table definition.*

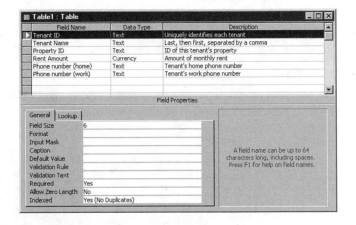

18

## Set the Key and Save the Table

Once you complete your table's fields, you cannot close the table's Design view without designating a field as the table's primary key field. If you do not designate a key and attempt to close the table, Access 97 warns you that no key exists. Access 97 adds a key field and uses the AutoNumber format if your data does not contain a key field.

Consider adding your own key field for tables that you access often. The key field will let you search the table more quickly. The key might be a Social Security number, a phone number, or some other code (such as a unique inventory code or customer number) that will be unique for each record in the table.

To specify a key field, select the table Design view's record by clicking to the left of the field name, then click the Primary Key toolbar button. Access 97 adds a small key icon to the left of the record, indicating the table's key field.

After you add the key field, save the table by clicking the toolbar's Save button. (If you close the table before saving it, Access 97 prompts you for a name.) If you don't specify a new name, Access 97 uses Table1 (and Table2, Table3, and so on as you create additional tables); however, you should use a more meaningful table name, such as Tenants, so you'll easily identify the table.

# The Table Datasheet View

Until now, you've worked exclusively in the table's Design view, which describes the table's fields, properties, and key. If you open the table and click the Datasheet view toolbar button (or select from the View menu), Access 97 changes your table's Design view to the *Datasheet view*, like the view shown in Figure 18.7. The table's Datasheet view remains empty until you type data into your table.

**NEW TERM** The *Datasheet view* displays your table and table data (if the table contains data) in a worksheet-like format.

**Figure 18.7.**

*Use the Datasheet view to see your table's design results and enter data.*

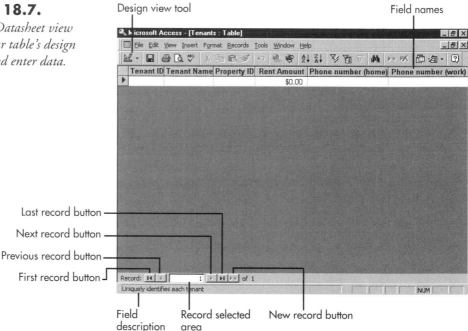

Design view tool Field names

Last record button
Next record button
Previous record button
First record button

Field description Record selected area New record button

The Datasheet view lets you see your table in row and column format, like an Excel 97 worksheet. Until you enter data in the table, the Datasheet view shows only one empty record. As you'll see in this hour's last section, you can enter table data from within the Datasheet

**18**

view. You should familiarize yourself with the Datasheet view screen elements because later parts of this book refer to them.

Although the Datasheet view is not fancy, it lets you quickly see your table's design results and enter data. If you cannot read a full field name, drag the field separator left or right to increase or decrease the field width shown on the screen. You'll learn more about modifying the view in the section titled "Modifying the Table."

**WARNING**

> If you have not saved your table's design from within the Design view, Access 97 prompts you for the table name before showing you the Datasheet view.

Use the toolbar or the View menu to switch back and forth between the two views. As you design a table, the two views help you pinpoint design and data problems.

**NOTE**

> Most Database window objects offer two views: a Design view and another view that displays the final object, such as the Datasheet view and the form's Form view.

**18**

You can even design a table from the Datasheet view, but you'll make more work for yourself if you do. The default Datasheet view field names are Field1, Field2, and so on until you right-click the names and change them. You cannot set specific field properties from the Datasheet view. Use the Datasheet view for simple data-entry and table-design verification unless you create only an extremely simple table.

# Modifying Table Structures

The beauty of Access 97 is that, unlike in other database programs, you can easily change the structure of your Access 97 tables even after you've added data. Access 97 makes it easy to add and delete fields as well as change field properties.

**WARNING**

> Some table-structure changes affect table data. For example, after you add data to a table, you'll lose columns of data if you delete fields, and you'll lose some data through truncation if you limit a field's size property. If you add fields to an existing table, you'll have to add the data for the new fields in every existing record in the table.

To modify a table, switch to the table's Design view. If you've closed the table and returned to the Database window, select the table name (which will now appear in the Database window) and click Design. After you master table design changes, you'll be better equipped to use the database wizards to create initial tables that you can change to suit your specific table requirements.

## Adding Fields

To add a field at the end of your table, simply click the first empty Field Name box and enter the field information as you did when adding the table's initial fields.

To insert a new field between two other fields, select the field that will appear *before* your new field by clicking the selection box to the left of the field name. Next, right-click the row and select Insert Rows. Access 97 opens a new field row and lets you enter the new field information. Figure 18.8 shows a new field being inserted into a table.

**Figure 18.8.**
*The new field will go in the empty space.*

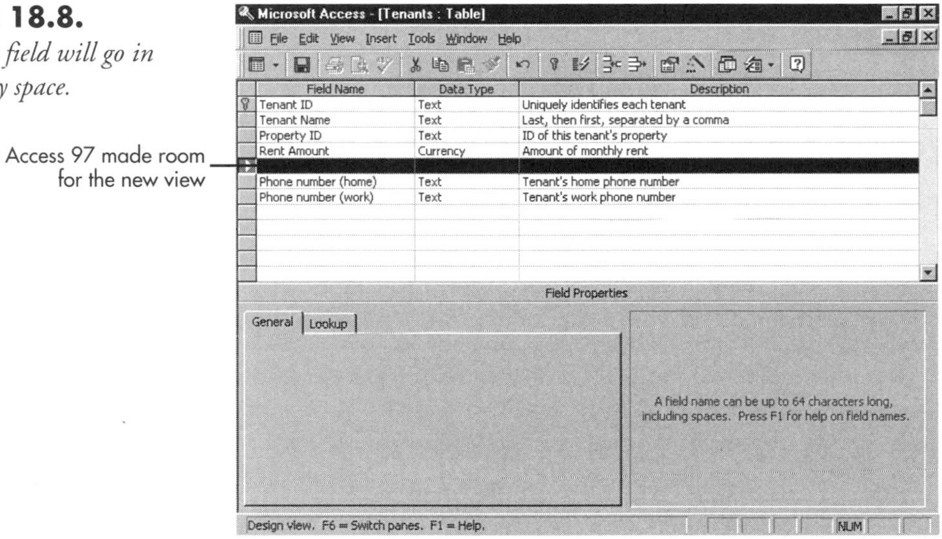

Access 97 made room for the new view
Microsoft Access - [Tenants : Table]
File Edit View Insert Tools Window Help
Field Name
Data Type
Description
Tenant ID
Text
Uniquely identifies each tenant
Tenant Name
Text
Last, then first, separated by a comma
Property ID
Text
ID of this tenant's property
Rent Amount
Currency
Amount of monthly rent
Phone number (home)
Text
Tenant's home phone number
Phone number (work)
Text
Tenant's work phone number
Field Properties
General
Lookup
A field name can be up to 64 characters long, including spaces. Press F1 for help on field names.
Design view. F6 = Switch panes. F1 = Help.
NUM

## Deleting Fields

To delete a field, select the field from within the Design view and press Delete. You can delete fields from either the Datasheet view or the Design view. You can delete several fields in one operation by selecting multiple sections, and dragging your mouse down several fields in the Design view.

**TIP**

Use Undo (Ctrl+Z) to reverse an accidental field deletion.

## Modifying the Table

Use your mouse to make minor adjustments to your table (such as the height of each row and the width of columns). Although the Field Size property determines the exact data storage width of each field in your table, the column widths determine how much of a field you can read while entering and editing table data and the table's structure.

At any time during your table design or data entry, you can drag a column divider left or right to increase or decrease the width of a column displayed. You can also drag a record divider up or down to increase or decrease a record height.

To rearrange the location of a field, either in Datasheet view or in the table's Design view, drag a Datasheet view field name or a Design view field selector to its new location in the table and release the mouse. Access 97 moves the field to the location you select.

18

**NOTE**

The order in which you structure a table's fields has little bearing on the table's use. You can report a table's data in any field order that you want regardless of the physical field order. Order your fields in whatever way makes the most sense to you.

# Summary

This is a theory-based hour because Access 97 requires more preparation than the other Office 97 products. After you learn about tables, records, and fields, the Access 97 mechanics are easy to understand.

To create an Access 97 database, add tables that describe the database data. Each table contains fields and records. When you design a table, tell Access 97 about the field names and data types that the table needs.

Now that you know how to create and edit tables, you are ready to enter data and master forms in the next hour, "Entering and Displaying Access 97 Data." By using forms for data entry and editing, you'll make Access 97 tables easier to manage for you and others who use databases that you create.

# Q&A

**Q Would I ever want to configure a field with the AutoNumber format?**

**A** Your data might require a unique sequential number for each record, like invoice numbers. Most often, however, Access 97 uses the AutoNumber format for the key field that is added when you don't specify a key field.

**Q Can a key field contain duplicates?**

**A** No. If you have to locate records by field and that field is not unique, you cannot make the field a key. You must decide on another key or let Access 97 add the key field. You can speed up the access on the duplicate field by making the field an *index field* in the field's Design view property settings. Access 97 will set up a special quick-find index for that field.

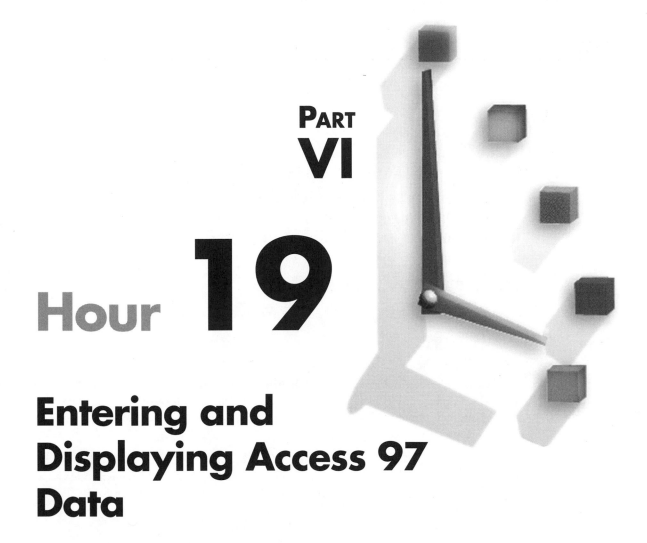

# Hour 19

# Entering and Displaying Access 97 Data

This hour explains how to use the Access 97 tables you learned to create in the previous hour, "Access 97 Basics." After you master this lesson, you'll be able to enter and edit table data.

You'll want to print the data to proofread for accuracy and to keep as a back-up. You don't have to master all of Access 97's reporting tools to print good-looking reports, as you'll learn in this hour.

Finally, this lesson explains how to use the Form Wizard to generate forms that match your data. Forms offer a different data perspective than datasheets. The Access 97 forms you create look like printed forms on the screen.

The highlights of this hour include

- [ ] How to enter data into tables
- [ ] Which table-editing commands Access 97 supports
- [ ] When to use the Form Wizard to generate forms from tables
- [ ] How to use forms for data entry and editing
- [ ] The drawbacks of forms
- [ ] How to print tables and forms

# Entering Table Data

Access 97 gives you these primary means for adding data to tables that you create:

- [ ] Datasheet views
- [ ] Forms

You'll learn more about forms later in this hour's lesson; for now, let's focus on the Datasheet view. The Datasheet view lets you enter, view, and edit several records at one time, and displays many records on your screen. When you use a form, on the other hand, you typically only work with one record at a time.

To enter data in the Datasheet view, simply click the Datasheet view's first field and enter the field information. When you enter data into the first field, Access 97 opens an additional blank record below the one you're entering. Access 97 always leaves room for additional records. As you enter data, press Tab, Shift+Tab, or the arrow keys to move from field to field. You can also click any field into which you want to enter data.

To change a mistake, click in front of the mistake to correct the entry. You can also press the arrow keys to move to any field, and press F2 to edit the field's text. As you enter data, watch the status bar. If you entered a description for a field, Access 97 displays that description in the status bar when you enter data in that field.

**WARNING**

> If you enter data and see a number appear, Access 97 is automatically entering an AutoNumber field (such as a key field).

Figure 19.1 shows a Datasheet view that contains several records. The record pointer always moves as you enter and edit data to show the current record. When the record pointer becomes a pencil, as shown in Figure 19.1, Access 97 is indicating that you are entering data in that record. The asterisk to the left of the empty record indicates a new record into which you can enter data.

**19**

**Figure 19.1.**

*A Datasheet view with several records of data.*

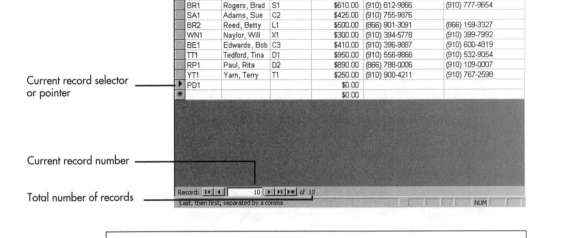

Current record selector or pointer

Current record number

Total number of records

| Tenant ID | Tenant Name | Property ID | Rent Amount | Phone number (home) | Phone number (work) |
|-----------|-------------|-------------|-------------|---------------------|---------------------|
| JJ1 | Johnson, Joan | C1 | $375.00 | (910) 500-7665 | (910) 600-8554 |
| BR1 | Rogers, Brad | S1 | $610.00 | (910) 812-9866 | (910) 777-9654 |
| SA1 | Adams, Sue | C2 | $425.00 | (910) 755-9876 | |
| BR2 | Reed, Betty | L1 | $500.00 | (866) 901-3091 | (866) 159-3327 |
| WN1 | Naylor, Will | X1 | $300.00 | (910) 394-5778 | (910) 399-7992 |
| BE1 | Edwards, Bob | C3 | $410.00 | (910) 396-9887 | (910) 600-4819 |
| TT1 | Tedford, Tina | D1 | $950.00 | (910) 556-9866 | (910) 532-9054 |
| RP1 | Paul, Rita | D2 | $890.00 | (866) 788-0006 | (910) 109-0007 |
| YT1 | Yarn, Terry | T1 | $250.00 | (910) 900-4211 | (910) 767-2598 |
| PD1 | | | $0.00 | | |
| | | | $0.00 | | |

Record: 10 of 10

Last, then first, separated by a comma

---

**TIP** Often, multiple records contain the same data in certain fields (as is the case with city and state names in a table). Press Ctrl+' to copy the previous record's field value into the current field's cell.

As you enter data, take advantage of Office 97's AutoCorrect feature. When you enter AutoCorrect abbreviations and shortcuts, Access 97 substitutes the shortcut with the AutoCorrect correction. Access 97 does not automatically enable the Office 97 automatic spell checker because much of your table data will contain formal names that would appear to the spell checker as misspellings.

When you finish entering or editing a table's data, save the table and click its Close button to return to the Database window. If you've not saved the table before attempting to close it, Access 97 prompts you for a name. By default, Access 97 uses the names Table1, Table2, and so on, but you should rename the tables to reflect the data they contain.

## Dealing with Formats

Access 97 is forgiving when you enter special data such as dates, times, monetary amounts, and memo field values. You can basically enter data in these fields in whatever way seems best to you! For example, you can enter a date in a date field with any of the following formats:

5/12/97
05/12/97

19

```
5/12/1997
May 12, 1997
May 12 1997
```

Access 97 uses a predefined date format to display dates and times in the Datasheet view, so after you type a date, it can be immediately reformatted to match this view. By default, Access 97 uses the date format *mm/dd/yy*.

As with dates, you can enter time in several common ways. Add AM or PM or use 24-hour clock time. Access 97, by default, formats your time values to the *hh:mm:ss* format.

 **TIP** | Press Ctrl+; to enter the current date in a field, and press Ctrl+: to enter the current time. Access 97 gets these values from your computer's clock and calendar setting.

Access 97 currency fields accept a wide variety of formats. You can type a dollar sign (or whatever currency symbol that matches your Windows' international country setting), decimals, and even insert commas in currency values. After you enter a currency amount, Access 97 displays the amount with the default format.

 **NOTE** | If you need to format a currency amount in a different format from your Windows international settings, you can do so by specifying the format in the Design view's property settings.

If you enter a format that Access 97 does not recognize, such as placing two decimal points inside a single dollar amount, Access 97 displays Figure 9.2's dialog box, telling you to correct the value before entering the next field.

**Figure 19.2.**

*Access 97 lets you know if you enter a bad format.*

Access 97 will not let you leave a record that contains a bad format. Therefore, when you close your tables, you can be assured that Access 97 saved all the data with the proper data type.

**19**

# Working in the Datasheet View

All the editing skills you mastered with the other Office 97 products work with Access 97. You can rearrange the order of fields and records by dragging them with your mouse. You can select more than one field or record at a time by dragging your mouse through the record selectors or field names or by holding Shift while you click on record selectors or field names. Press Ctrl+A to select all records in the table.

To delete one or more records or fields, select the records or fields you want to delete and right-click them. Select Delete Column or Delete Record.

 **NOTE**

When you right-click the selected records or fields, the pop-up menu provides quick cut, copy, and paste commands as well as insertion commands for records and fields. Use the Hide command to temporarily hide records and fields (they physically stay in the table) that you want out of the way while you work with other data, and reveal the data when you're ready to work with the entire table again. Additionally, you can *sort* (alphabetize or file numerically) records in *ascending order* (from low to high) or from *descending order* (from high to low) with the right-click's pop-up menu options.

 **NEW TERM** To *sort* is to alphabetize or numerically order table records.

 **NEW TERM** To sort by *ascending order* is to sort from low to high order.

 **NEW TERM** To sort by *descending order* is to sort from high to low order.

 **TIP**

If you often need to adjust the width or height of records and fields, consider changing your table's font size and style (with Format I Font) to fit more data in a smaller screen area.

# Large Tables

Use the record selector at the bottom of the Datasheet view to move through and jump over large blocks of records that don't interest you at the time. The record selector works somewhat like a VCR, letting you move forward and backward through your data.

Here are a few pointers:

☐ Click Next Record to move the record selector to the next record.

☐ Click Previous Record to move the record selector to the previous record.

☐ Click First Record to move to the table's first record.

☐ Click Last Record to move to the table's last record.

☐ Click the Record Number area and type a new record number to jump directly to that record.

# Simple Printing

Access 97 includes powerful reporting tools, but they take some time to master. You'll learn about reporting in Hour 21, "Advanced Access 97," but if you just want to print a listing of your data, you can do so easily from the Datasheet view. Access 97 automatically prints the Datasheet view with field titles.

Perhaps you need to check a table listing for errors, or you want a printed listing (called a *hard copy*) so you can proofread your data. Before printing, display a preview (like the one shown in Figure 19.3) by selecting File | Print Preview. Move the magnifying-glass mouse cursor over any portion of the preview and click to see a close-up.

**New Term**    A *hard copy* is a printed listing of your data.

**Figure 19.3.**

*Get a preview of printed datasheet tables.*

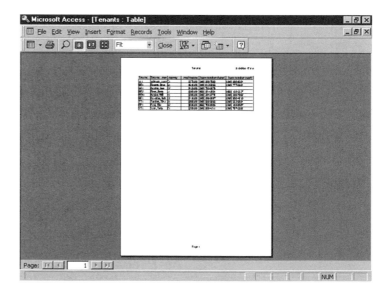

**19**

To print a Datasheet view's table, select File | Print (or click the Printer button on the toolbar).

# Introduction to Forms

When you computerize your records, you want to make it as easy as possible for people to enter, edit, and view data in your database. Often, Access 97 reduces paperwork. For example, a credit agency might use Access 97 to keep track of loan applications that borrowers fill out. As borrowers bring in their completed applications, a clerk types the data from the application into an Access 97 table. Although a Datasheet view would work fine for the data entry, a form works even better! The form can, on the screen, mimic the look and feel of paper forms that many people are accustomed to using. You will not have to keep files of paper forms now that you use Access 97.

You'll probably want to use the Form Wizard to create your first form. The Form Wizard generates simple forms that work well in most cases.

Follow these steps to start the Form Wizard:

1.  Display the Database window.
2.  Click the Forms tab to display the Forms sheet.
3.  Click New to display Figure 19.4's New Form dialog box.

**Figure 19.4.**

*Creating a new form.*

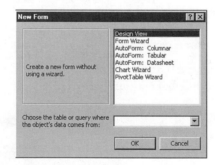

4.  Select the Form Wizard option.
5.  Select the table in the lower part of the dialog box to use as a basis for the form. If your database contains multiple tables, they will all appear in the drop-down list.
6.  Click OK to display Figure 19.5's opening Form Wizard dialog box. This dialog box lists your selected table's fields that you can include in the form.

**Figure 19.5.**

*The opening Form Wizard dialog box showing your selected table.*

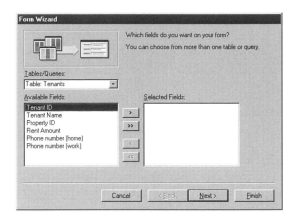

You may or may not want to include every field on every form you create. For example, say you want to create a form for your company's personnel that contains employee names and extension numbers, but not employee pay rates. Therefore, the next step in creating your form is to tell Access 97 which fields to include.

To select table fields for the form, select a field and click the button labeled >. Access 97 adds that field to the selected field list. To include all the fields, click the button labeled >>. The Form Wizard sends all the table's fields to the selected field list.

If you send a field to the form accidentally, select that field and click the button labeled < to remove the field from the form. Clicking << removes *all* the fields, so you can start over if you want to rearrange the fields or copy new ones from scratch.

Click the Next button to display the Form Wizard Layout dialog box, shown in Figure 19.6. Click the different options to see a preview of how that option will change the form's layout.

**Figure 19.6.**

*Select a layout for your form.*

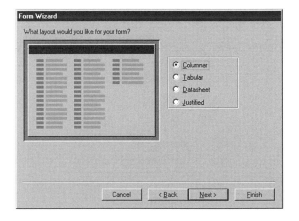

**19**

**NOTE**

The Tabular and Datasheet form layouts are similar to the Datasheet view. The Columnar and Justified layouts look more like typical paper forms.

When you click the Next button, the Form Wizard displays Figure 19.7's dialog box, from which you can select a form style. Click through the style selections to see a preview of the available styles. Many styles have unique personalities that can add eye-catching appeal to an otherwise dull form.

**Figure 19.7.**

*The Form Wizard supports several form styles.*

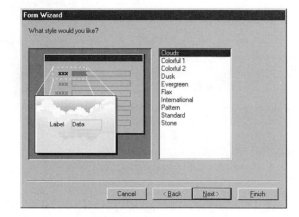

When you click the Next button, you'll see the Form Wizard's closing dialog box, which asks for a form title (the default title is the name of your selected table). Click Finish to generate the form.

**NOTE**

When you learn more advanced Access 97 commands, such as how to use the form-creation and editing tools, you'll be able to open the generated form's Design view and change specific parts of the form. The Form Wizard will generate your form, and you can then modify the form to look exactly the way you want it. For now, the Form Wizard's generated forms work well.

**WARNING**

In some cases, generated forms contain problems. For example, Figure 19.8 shows a generated form with a record's data. The Form Wizard automatically uses field names for the form prompts and data descriptions.

19

If your field names are long, the Form Wizard may not display the entire field name for the prompt. Also, some data does not align properly, such as Figure 19.8's Rent Amount field. In addition, if your table does not contain many fields, the form will not take up the full screen and may look too small. You can maximize the form on the screen.

**Figure 19.8.**

*The Form Wizard generates good forms, but they sometimes have problems.*

Short field numbers

Value appears too far to the right

Figure 19.8 shows the form in Access 97's Form view. The *Form view* displays records in the form-like format. Access 97 also contains a form's Design view (not unlike the table's Design view), with which you can edit the form and change its appearance.

 *Form view* is Access 97's display of forms with record data appearing in the form fields.

## Moving Around with Forms

Forms typically show only single records. Unlike the Datasheet view, the form is a much better tool for working with single records. On the Datasheet view, you can often see many records but not all the fields in those records because the fields rarely fit on the Datasheet view screen. The form shows only a single record, but often manages to include all fields from the records because of the form layout.

Access 97 offers several ways to move through records in the Form view. Use Up Arrow, Down Arrow, Tab, and Shift+Tab to move from one field to another. Use PageUp and PageDown to move to the preceding and next table record, respectively. The record number appears at the bottom of the form window's record selection control. As with the Datasheet view, you can click the record selection control to move from record to record.

**TIP**  To jump to a record quickly, press F5, type a record number, and press Enter. F5 sends the cursor to the record selector so you can find a different table record.

You can quickly change from the Form view to the Datasheet view by clicking the View toolbar button's down arrow and selecting Datasheet View. By switching between the views, you can see multiple records (in the Datasheet view) and single records (in the Form view), depending on your needs.

As you move through the form records, feel free to change data in the record. The record selector arrow changes to an editing pencil to show that you're editing the record. If you use Tab or Shift+Tab to move from field to field, press F2 when the highlight appears over the field you want to edit. When you change data from within the Form view, Access 97 changes the data in the underlying tables.

All Yes/No data-type fields will appear with an x to indicate the Yes value. For example, if you name a rental property's tenant field Pet Deposit? And assigned the Yes/No data type to the field, those owners who pay a pet deposit will have an x for this field value.

Memo fields can hold a lot of data. If you use a memo field, keep typing when the text cursor reaches the right side of the field, and Access 97 will scroll the field to let you continue. Form views display memo fields with scrollbars so you can look at all the data in the fields.

Finally, if you select File | Print from the Form view, Access 97 prints the forms. Unlike the onscreen Form view, Access 97 prints as many forms on the page as will fit (select the File | Print Preview to see what will print, like the preview shown in Figure 19.9).

**19**

**TIP**  To add records from the Form view, click the record selector's New Record button (the button with the arrow and asterisk on it at the bottom of the Form view) to display a new record that you can fill out.

**Figure 19.9.**

*Access 97 prints multiple records per form.*

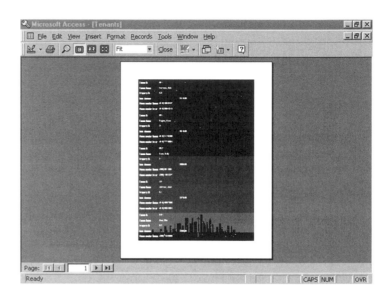

# Summary

This hour extended your Access 97 knowledge by showing you how to enter data, print data, and create and use forms. Access 97 replaces the paper forms you are used to and provides a form-like approach to data-entry and editing.

The Form Wizard quickly generates nice forms for you from your table data. The Form Wizard is a great place to start designing your forms because it analyzes your table and generates a form based on that analysis.

Next hour's chapter, "Queries on Your Data," teaches you how to filter data and use queries so that you can work with subsets of table data.

# Q&A

**Q When I open a table's Datasheet view, why does the data appear in a different order from the order in which I entered it?**

**A** Access 97 sorts data, in an ascending order, according to the table's selected key field. Your Datasheet views always appear in the order sorted by the key field unless you change the sort order by right-clicking the field you want to sort by. Access 97 uses the key field to locate records quickly when you search for data.

**19**

**Q Why should I use the Form Wizard but not the Table Wizard when I begin learning Access 97?**

**A** You must understand tables, records, and fields before you use the Table Wizard to generate tables because you'll almost always have to modify the Table Wizard's generated table to suit your exact needs. Therefore, it helps, when starting out, to create tables from scratch and learn how tables work. After you learn how to use the table's Datasheet and Design views, you are better equipped to edit tables generated with the Table Wizard.

The Form Wizard looks at tables that *you* generated and creates simple data-entry forms with the format and layout that you request. Forms require less editing when you generate them from the Form Wizard than tables do. You'll be pleased with the Form Wizard from the moment you create your first form.

**Q Can I edit the AutoNumber field?**

**A** If you let Access 97 create and enter your table's key field, let Access 97 maintain the AutoNumber that Access 97 enters for you. When you create reports, you'll be able to hide the AutoNumber field so that the field does not appear with the data that others see. The AutoNumber field is Access 97's bookkeeping field when you fail to designate a key. Access 97 keeps the table sorted in the key order, and you should not bother with this field. If you want, rearrange the table to move the AutoNumber field to the far right side of the Datasheet view. Then you'll rarely see the field when you work with the data.

19

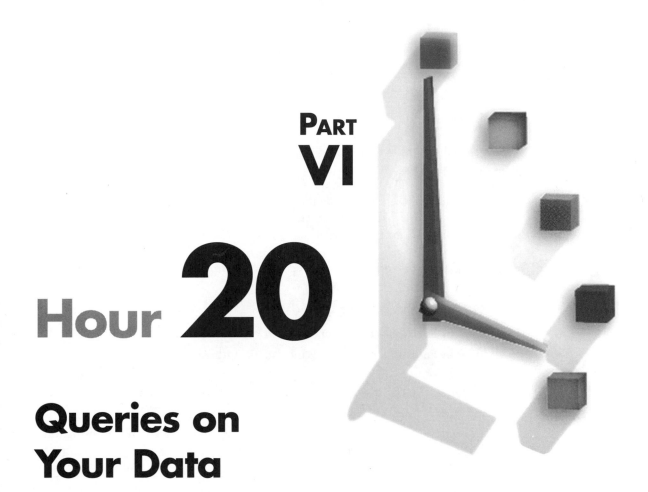

# Hour 20

# Queries on Your Data

This hour teaches you about Access 97 filters and queries. Although your database contains much data, you'll rarely want to see all that data at one time. Generally, you'll want to see only data subsets. Filters and queries produce those subsets for you.

When you view data subsets, you prevent unwanted data from getting in the way of the information that you need to work with. The power of queries is that you can select records and fields from multiple tables and view that selected data subset from within a single Datasheet or Form view.

The highlights of this hour include

- ☐ What a filter is
- ☐ Why you sometimes use Filter by Selection and sometimes use Filter by Form
- ☐ When a filter limits you
- ☐ Why queries are more robust than filters
- ☐ How to use the query wizards
- ☐ How to use the Query Design view to create and edit queries
- ☐ Where to specify advanced selection criteria

# Data Filters

A *filter* is a subset of data from a table. Suppose you want to see only certain records from a table, such as all customers who are past due. Instead of hiding the records that you don't want to see, create a filter. The filter removes unwanted records from view. The records don't go away, and you don't have to unhide the records later (as you do when you actually hide records). A filter works like a short-term record hider, putting certain records out of the way while you work with the filtered data.

**NEW TERM**   A *filter* temporarily creates a subset of records from a table.

Access 97 supports three filtering approaches:

☐   Filter by Selection—Filters data based on selected table data

☐   Filter by Form—Lets you choose the data fields that you want Access 97 to use for filtering

☐   Advanced Filter/Sort—Controls advanced filtering options from the Access 97 menu bar

The easiest and most common filter options are Filter by Selection and Filter by Form, which the following two sections describe.

**WARNING**

Access 97 includes an Advanced Filter/Sort option on the Records | Filter menu, but you'll almost always prefer creating a query over the advanced filter.

## Filter by Selection

Filter by Selection works by example. Suppose you want to display only those table records that contain a specific field value; for example, you need to work only with customer records from Brazil. If your customer table contains a Country field with scattered Brazil entries, you can filter out all those records that do *not* contain Brazil in their Country fields.

Perform the following steps to design such a filter:

1.  Display the customer table's Datasheet view.
2.  Locate one record with Brazil in the Country field.

**20**

3. Double-click the entire field to select it. If you select only the first part of the field, such as the B, you filter all records that do not start with B.

4. Click Filter by Selection on the toolbar. Access 97 filters out all records that don't match your selected criteria. The term *criteria* refers to a specific request pattern that you want Access 97 to use to find a value. Figure 20.1 shows a filtered Datasheet view that displays only records containing a Brazil entry in their Country field. Before the filter, this Datasheet view held 91 records.

 **NEW TERM** The term *criteria* refers to a specific request pattern that you want Access 97 to use to find a value.

5. To return to the full Datasheet view, click the toolbar's Remove Filter button.

As you can see, a filter removes unwanted records; Access 97 filters those unwanted records from view.

> **TIP**
> To filter all records that contain your selected values, leaving all those that *don't* contain the selected value, select Records | Filter | Filter Excluding Selection. The Filter Excluding Selection option works like a reverse filter.

**Figure 20.1.**

*Filter by Selection filters out all unwanted records.*

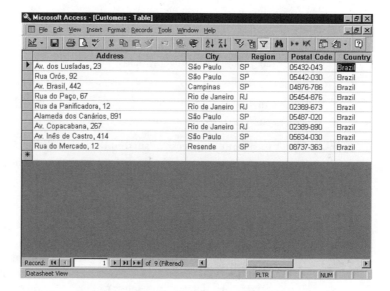

**20**

**TIP**  You did not first have to locate a customer record from Brazil to create the previous list's filter. If you right-click any field value in the table, then type a value in the pop-up menu's Filter For text box, Access 97 applies the Filter by Selection command to your entered filter value. Therefore, you could type Brazil in the Filter For text box, press Enter, and more quickly create the same filter that the previous steps created.

## Filter by Form

Filter by Form lets you filter by multiple values instead of by only one value. Filter by Forms can be performed from the Datasheet and Form views.

Perform these steps to use Filter by Form:

1. Click the Filter by Form button. Access 97 displays a single blank record.
2. Scroll to the field you want to filter by and select the empty field.
3. Click the field's drop-down arrow that appears. Access 97 displays a scrolling drop-down list of every value (without duplicates) that appears in that field.
4. Select the value you want to filter by.
5. Optionally, click another empty field value and select from that field's drop-down list of available values. You can select as many filtering field values as you need. Unlike the Filter by Selection, which lets you filter only by one field value, Filter by Form lets you filter by several fields.
6. Click the Apply Filter button to display the filtered records.
7. Click the Remove Filter button (this button is called the Apply Filter button before you begin filtering) when you are ready to return to the full-record view.

If you filter by a date field, Access 97 surrounds the filtered value with pound signs (#). You'll often see pound signs around dates, such as #7/4/1998#; this allows Access 97 to distinguish the date from a formula.

**TIP**  Access 97 can perform an *Or* filter, meaning that Access 97 filters to find all records that include one or more of your selected filter field values. For example, if you want to find all customers who live in New York or who live in Maine, select New York, click the Or tab at the bottom of the Filter by Form window, and select Maine. You can continue adding *or conditions* to select from one of several fields.

**20**

**NEW TERM** An *or condition* occurs when Access 97 performs a search or filter on one or more value matches at the same time.

**WARNING**

Although Access 97 uses an or condition to select from one of several field values, Access 97 uses an *and condition* to select across fields. That means that if you select Brazil for the Country field filter and Rio for the City field filter, Access 97 filters to find all records with *both* Brazil as a country *and* Rio for the city. If a record contains the country Brazil but Sao Paulo for the city, such a filter would not keep that record.

**NEW TERM** An *and condition* occurs when Access 97 performs a search or filter on multiple value matches at the same time.

# Queries

A *query* is really nothing more than a question you ask Access 97 about your data. Access 97 does not understand questions the way you generally ask them, so you must ask your question with Access 97's special query format.

**NEW TERM** A *query* is a stored set of database record selection commands.

A query is an object, just like tables and forms are objects. Therefore, you'll see the Query object page on the Database window and you'll create, edit, and execute queries from this page. As with other objects, queries have names that you give them. Many queries are nothing more than filters; however, filters go away when you are finished with them, whereas you can recall a query by its name later. Instead of re-creating it, you'll only need to refer to the query by name to execute it subsequently. If you want to reapply a filter, however, you must reproduce the filter.

**TIP**

Although you cannot name filters, you can turn a Filter by Form request into a named query. When you enter the Filter by Form request, click the Save as Query toolbar button. Access 97 prompts you for a query name and stores the filter as a query. Often, creating a named query from a Filter by Form is faster than generating a new query from scratch if you only want to create a simple query that filters records.

20

Queries are often much more advanced than filters. A query lets you specify selected records from a table or from another query. You can create a query that selects records and fields from multiple tables. The data subset that a query generates often becomes a table-like Datasheet view from which you can report. For example, you can build a query that extracts certain records and fields from three tables, then generate a report from those extracted records and fields.

Not only can you create a query that extracts fields and records, but you can specify the exact order of the resulting data subset, sort the subset, and use powerful extraction criteria to select data based on very specific requirements.

Although you can build a query from scratch, the Query Wizard does the dirty work for you in most cases.

**NOTE**

| The created data subset is sometimes called a *dynaset*. |
|---|

NEW TERM

## Creating a Query with the Query Wizard

Access 97 includes these four query wizards:

- ☐ Simple Query Wizard—Extracts fields from one or more tables and from other queries
- ☐ Crosstab Query Wizard—Creates a worksheet-like query that summarizes field values and cross-tabulates matching values
- ☐ Find Duplicates Query Wizard—Creates a data subset from two or more tables or queries that contain matching values in one or more fields that you select
- ☐ Find Unmatched Query Wizard—Creates a data subset from two or more tables or queries that contain no duplicate records

You'll use the Simple Query Wizard most often due to its general-purpose design. When you create a new query by clicking New on the Queries Database window page, Access 97 displays Figure 20.2's New Query dialog box.

**20**

**Figure 20.2.**

*Begin creating your query at the New Query dialog box.*

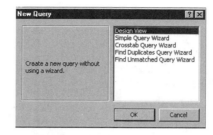

Follow these steps to build your first query using the Simple Query Wizard:

1.  Select the Simple Query Wizard from the New Query dialog box. Access 97 starts the wizard and displays the Simple Query Wizard dialog box shown in Figure 20.3.

2.  Select a table (or an existing query) to hold the data you want the query to extract. Access 97 displays fields from the selected table (or query) in the Available Fields list.

3.  Select one or more fields and click the button labeled >. Access 97 includes these fields in the resulting query data subset. For example, if you want the query to extract all customer names and balances from a customer table, select those two fields and click > to send them to the Selected Fields list. The Selected Fields list is the query's resulting structure, and holds a description of the data subset that the query will eventually produce.

4.  Optionally, select another table or query from the Tables/Queries drop-down list and add more fields to the Selected Fields list. If Access 97 prompts you to create a relationship between the tables, click Yes to create the relationship. Access 97 relates the tables automatically if you've created the relationship link elsewhere. You are now building a query that extracts data subsets from multiple sources. If you send the wrong field to the Selected Fields list, select the incorrect field and click < to remove it. To remove all your selected fields and begin again, click the button labeled <<.

5.  Click Next to select either a detail or summary query. A detail query includes every field of every record; a summary query does not show duplicate selected records, and includes summary statistics if you select them by clicking the Summary Options button.

6.  Click Next and select a title for the query. Access 97 bases the default name for the new query on the first selected table or existing query.

**20**

7. Click Finish to complete the query. Access 97 builds the query and displays the selected records from the query in the Datasheet view. When you close the Datasheet view, you'll see the new query listed on the Database window's Queries page.

**Figure 20.3.**

*Use the Simple Query Wizard to generate your first query.*

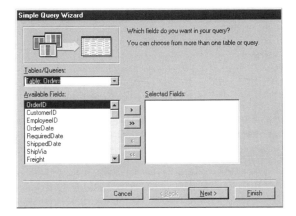

Take a moment or two to reflect on what you just did. For the first time, you have the power to extract records from multiple tables to create a new Datasheet view.

You can also create a new form (using one of the form wizards) to display the results of a query. When you created a new form in the previous hour, "Entering and Displaying Access 97 Data," you knew only to create forms from single tables. If multiple tables contain data you want to display in a form, however, create a query to extract from the two tables and base the form on that query.

**WARNING**

To synchronize a multiple-table query, all tables must have a common field (such as a customer number) or you must use advanced Access 97 commands to relate the two tables in some way. Without a relationship, such as a common field, the query does not know how to combine the fields from the two tables.

Access 97 does not save your query *results*. Therefore, if you want to see a data subset twice, you must open the Database window's Queries page, select the query, and click Open to generate the query extraction once again. Although the extraction requires a little time to generate (usually the speed is negligible unless the tables contain many records), the query is always fresh. If you change one value in any table and open the query again, your most recent table edit appears in the query.

Another advantage of generating the query every time you need to use the data subset is that Access 97 does not have to store the data twice (once in the source tables and once again in the query).

**TIP**

Here's a *real* query advantage: If you edit data from the resulting query's Datasheet view (or from the query's Form view), Access 97 updates the data in the original tables! Suppose you want to edit every employee's pay rate who works in your company's Northeast division; simply create a query to extract only the Northeast division employees, make the edits, and close the query. Find and edit the Northeast employees' pay rates without the other employee records getting in the way.

## Using the Query Design View

When you edit a query or create a query from scratch, you'll use Access 97's Query Design view (shown in Figure 20.4).

**Figure 20.4.**

*The Query Design view lets you create powerful queries.*

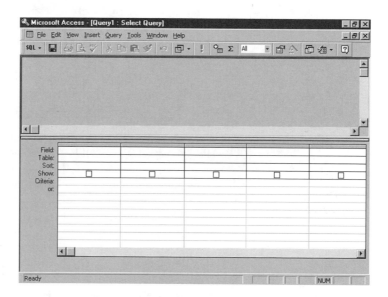

Although the Query Design view looks somewhat strange at first, the view's design is logical. The top of the Query Design view contains the source tables and queries, and the bottom of the Query Design view displays the criteria (the query-selection commands).

You'll use the Query Design view when you must:

☐ Create an advanced query that the query wizards cannot create

☐ Edit an existing query

When you learn to create a query with the Query Design view, you'll also understand how to use the Query Design view to edit existing queries.

## Creating a Query

To use the Query Design view to create a query, follow these steps:

1. Display the Queries sheet inside the Database window.

2. Click the New button to open the New Query dialog box.

3. Select Design View and click OK to open the Query Design view. Access 97 displays Figure 20.5's Show Table dialog box.

**Figure 20.5.**

*Selecting tables and queries for the new query.*

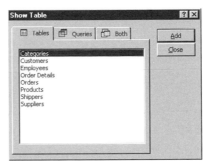

4. Click tables that you want to add to the query and click Add. As you add tables to the query, Access 97 displays a new table in the Query Design view showing in the background. If you want to base your new query on an existing query, click the Queries tab to display your database's queries, then add the new query. If you want to add tables and queries, click the Both tab to display all your database tables and queries, then select the ones you need.

5. Click Close to close the Show Table dialog box.

You have yet to build the entire query, but you have selected tables, existing queries, or both, on which to base your new query. Next, enter the query's criteria so that Access 97 knows which records and fields to select from your tables and existing queries.

**20**

Figure 20.6 shows the start of a new query. This query will extract from two tables, one named Customers and one named Orders. Access 97 drew the line from the Customers table to the Orders table. The line indicates the table relationship that Access 97 found. The table boxes include all the fields from each table, and the two tables share a common field: Customer ID. You'll recall from the previous section that Access 97 must base queries on related tables and queries, and the common field relates the two tables.

**TIP**

Think of the top half of the query's design window as starting the request, "given these tables and queries... " and the lower half of the window as finishing that request, "...extract all data that meets these conditions." The Query Design view contains your instructions when you want Access 97 to extract data from one or more tables or queries and display the result in a table subset.

Each column in the Query Design view's lower half will contain the resulting query's fields. Therefore, if you want the resulting data subset to contain four fields, you'll fill in four of the Query Design view's lower columns. These columns will contain the instructions that tell the query how to extract the data.

**Figure 20.6.**

*This query will extract from two related tables.*

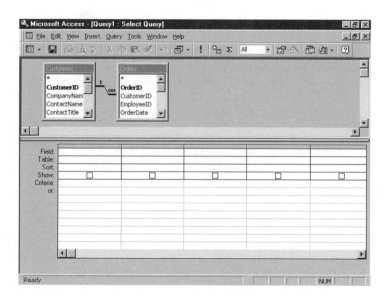

20

## Increasing the Query's Power

To finish the query, follow these steps:

1. Click the first column's row labeled Table and select the table that contains the resulting query's first field. For example, if you want the query's data subset to start with a field from the Customers table, select Customers from the drop-down list.

2. Click the first column's row labeled Field and select the field that you want to place first in the resulting data subset. For example, you might select Customer ID from the list.

3. If you want to sort the resulting query's subset based on the first field, select either Ascending or Descending from the row labeled Sort. You don't have to sort on the first field that you add to the query; you can sort on any field that you add. The query will sort all the resulting data based on the value of the field that you sort by. If you sort on two or more fields, Access 97 sorts the data in the left-most Sort column first.

4. Leave the Show option checked if you want the field to appear in the resulting query's data subset. Generally, you'll want the field to appear. If you want to sort the subset on a field but not send that sort field to the resulting extracted subset, uncheck the Show option for that field.

5. Click the first column's row labeled Criteria and enter a criterion. If you type a value, such as 101, Access 97 will extract only those records with a field containing 101. You can continue adding criteria values beneath the first one. For example, you could type the values 102, 103, 104, and 105 for five rows of criteria (still in the first column). This is like asking Access 97 to extract only those customers whose Customer ID is 101 through 105. If the field is a text-data type, Access 97 encloses the criteria in quotes, as shown in Figure 20.7. Access 97 encloses dates inside pound signs (#1/6/98#, for example) if you enter dates in the criteria.

6. Here's where it gets fun. Instead of selecting the field from the second column's drop-down list labeled Field, drag the field name from a table in the Query Design view's upper half (such as the Orders table's Order Date field). Access 97 automatically fills in the table and field name in the query's second column!

7. Enter the selection criteria for the new field. The criteria will tell Access 97 exactly how you want to pull records from the table. If you want to extract all the records (all that fall within the first field's criteria that you've entered), leave the second field's criteria blank. You can further limit the extraction by entering an additional criterion for the second field. Suppose you not only wanted customers with the IDs listed in the first criteria but also wanted to limit the selection to any of those five who have an order date of January 6, 1998. You would enter #1/6/98# for the criteria.

8. Continue adding fields that you want to appear in the resulting query. When you execute your query, these fields will appear in the resulting table.

**Figure 20.7.**

*This query must match several criteria values for Customer ID.*

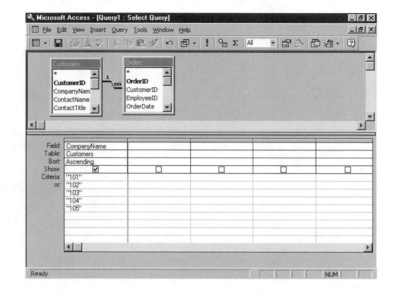

As you work with the query, you might want to add more tables. Add the tables in the Query Design view by selecting Query|Show Table. Add as many tables (or queries) as you like to the query from within the Query Design view, but remember that the tables and queries must relate somehow. Remove a table or query from the Query Design view by right-clicking the table name and selecting Remove Table.

All the cut, copy, and paste methods that you learned earlier in the book work for the query-extraction fields. For example, you can move a field from one location to another by selecting, cutting, and pasting it. Resize column widths by dragging the field column edges. Change any value by clicking that value in the Query Design view.

If you really want to get fancy, use Table 20.1's relational operators to add to your extraction power.

**20**

## Table 20.1. Access 97's relational operators improve extraction power.

| Operator | Description |
| --- | --- |
| > | Greater than |
| < | Less than |
| >= | Greater than or equal to |

*continues*

**Table 20.1. continued**

| Operator | Description |
|----------|-------------|
| <= | Less than or equal to |
| <> | Not equal to |
| = | Equal to (not needed for simple matches) |

Suppose you want to include customer-order details in a query, but you only want to include orders with more than 20 units. Enter >20 for the Quantity field's criteria to limit the selection to those records that match the other criteria and that have order quantities of more than 20 units. The relational operators work with numbers, text values that fall within a range of words, and dates.

The Between keyword is useful if you want to extract values that fall between two other values. For example, if you type Between #1/1/97# And #1/31/97# for a date criteria, Access 97 extracts only records whose date falls between 1/1/97 and 1/31/97 (including the days 1/1/97 and 1/31/97).

Access 97 uses an implied Or when you specify multiple criteria. For example, instead of entering the five criteria lines described earlier for Customer IDs (101, 102, 103, 104, and 105), you could enter 101 Or 102 Or 103 Or 104 Or 105. (Of course, entering Between 101 And 105 would even be easier.)

Figure 20.8 shows a completed (and fairly complex) query.

**Figure 20.8.**

*A completed query that contains lots of extraction criteria.*

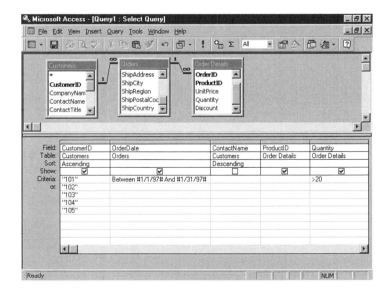

**20**

Be sure to save your query when you finish with it. Click the Query Design view's Close Window button and name the query so you'll be able to refer to it later. When you select the query and click Open from the Database window's Queries page, Access 97 runs the query, extracts the data, and displays the result in your Datasheet view.

# Summary

This hour showed you how to narrow your data and form subsets. Often, a table contains many more fields and records than you want to work with at any one time. Access 97's filter and query powers let you create subsets of data to make your work more manageable.

Filters provide quick subsets, but queries provide much more power. After you run a filter or query to create a subset of your data, you can make changes to the subset and *still* be changing the underlying tables. Although the Query Design view takes some getting used to, it lets you specify powerful query extraction criteria so that Access 97 searches for and finds the data you need to work with.

Now that you can produce subsets of data, you need a way to report that data. The next hour, "Advanced Access 97," explores some of Access 97's reporting capabilities. The Report Wizard makes quick work of report generation from your tables and queries.

# Q&A

**Q  Should I use a filter or a query?**

**A**  When you quickly want to see a subset of a table, use a filter. However, you'll sometimes use the subset in another way (as input to a report, for example), so creating a query that you can name and execute makes more sense (except in the case of one-time extractions to a Datasheet view).

**Q  If I save a filter as a named query, what will the query's Query Design view look like?**

**A**  Filters are much less powerful than queries, but they are easier to designate. As you create more queries and get used to your data needs, you'll find that many of your queries are little more than filters. Instead of messing with the Query Design view to design the query, generate a simpler Filter by Form filter and save it as a query. If you then want to modify the filter-based query or add more complex criteria, open the query's Query Design view and you'll see that Access 97 selected the proper source table and field names for you. You then can add to the criteria lines and request additional fields if you like.

20

**Q  Does the row on which I place criteria make a difference?**

**A**  Yes, although you're getting into some confusing logic. The way you specify criteria between two fields often indicates how you want the combined criteria to work. If you place one field's criteria on the same row as another field's, an implied and relation takes place, and Access 97 extracts only those records that contain a match for both criteria values. If you place one field's criteria on a different row from another field's, an implied or relation takes place between them.

**Q  How can I see my data in two ways, say, with the field names arranged alphabetically and with the fields arranged in the order of my table's design?**

**A**  Create a query that extracts all the fields from your table. The query's output, or data subset, will contain all data that the original table contains (the subset will be the same size as the table). Set up the query's output for ordering the fields alphabetically. Queries aren't just for creating smaller subsets of tables; you can create a query to report table data in an order that differs from a table's original design order.

# Hour **21**

# Advanced Access 97

This hour shows you how to create custom reports. Access 97 includes several reporting tools, both automatic and manual, that produce complex reports. You can create a simple report by clicking a toolbar button. If you spend a little time developing the report with a report wizard, it can look extremely nice.

You will not have to master the Report Design view, an extensive report-creating tool, to create most of your reports. Some people have never designed an Access 97 report from scratch because of the report wizards' power. The report wizards give you complete control over a report's design.

The highlights of this hour include

- ☐ Why you should preview reports
- ☐ Where you can get the source for your reports
- ☐ How AutoReport creates simple reports
- ☐ Which report wizards Access 97 supports
- ☐ When to request summary statistics
- ☐ How to use the main report wizard to generate virtually any report you'll need by making a few selections

# Introducing Access 97 Reports

You'll often want printed listings of your data, and the Access 97 reporting tools let you produce professional reports with ease. This hour explains how to use the report wizards and discusses the different reporting styles and options available. You learned how to produce printed listings in Hour 19, "Entering and Displaying Access 97 Data"; now you'll learn how to add flair to your reports.

Unlike forms, a report often displays multiple records in a view that resembles the Datasheet view. The difference between the Datasheet view and a printed report is that the report provides summary statistics, fancy headings, footers, page numbers, and styles that accent your data.

 **NOTE**

> A *report* is not just a listing of multiple data records. Any time you need to send Access 97 data to paper, you must create a report. Therefore, a report might be a series of checks or mailing labels that you print.

Before you print any report, use Access 97's print preview to see the report on your screen. Often, you'll notice changes that you need to make, so previewing a report can save you time and paper. Your computer's print *spooler* (the memory area where Windows sends printed output before the output goes to paper) is too difficult to stop quickly, so you'll usually end up printing the first few pages of a report even if you attempt to stop the printing.

 **NEW TERM**   The *spooler* is the Windows memory area where Access 97 sends your report before the report goes to paper. The spooler frees up your program while the printing continues.

When you are about to print a report, Access 97's Database window's Report sheet lets you preview any report by clicking the Preview button. As Figure 21.1's report preview shows, Access 97 can generate fancy reports.

 **TIP**

> You'll be surprised at how little Access 97's report wizards differ from Access 95's. Except for some dialog box format changes, you'll be familiar with every report wizard dialog box. If you've mastered the ins and outs of Access 95 reports, you may want to skip to the next hour, "Office 97's Synergy."

**21**

**Figure 21.1.**

*Access 97's report preview shows how Access 97 formats your report.*

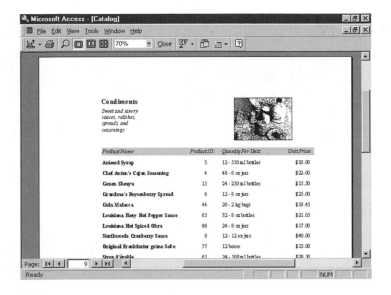

# Reports and Queries

Rarely will you report all the data from a single table. Except for detailed reports, such as inventory listings and master customer listings, you'll almost always report part of a table or values from more than one table.

Therefore, almost all reports that you generate will get their data from queries that you've created. If you need to report from part of a table's data or from multiple tables, create a query on which to base the report. Your queries can order the data however you want to see it, and Access 97 can then print your query's results.

# The Simplest Reports: AutoReports

Access 97 includes an *AutoReport* feature, which quickly generates reports from your Datasheet views. As Figure 21.2 shows, the AutoReport feature is simply a listing of field names and their corresponding field values.

 *AutoReport* is Access 97's automatic reporting tool that creates simple reports from your Datasheet views.

**21**

**Figure 21.2.**

*AutoReport does not generate extremely fancy reports.*

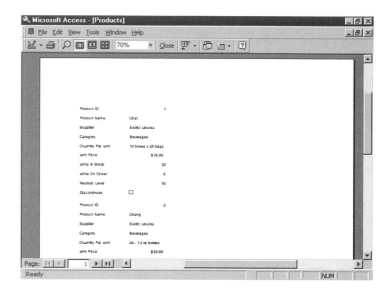

Unlike the printed listings you get with File | Print, AutoReport formats your data in a readable manner without squeezing too much information on a single page. If you need to run a quick report from a table, follow these steps to let AutoReport generate the report:

1. Display your data in a Datasheet view. If you want to report from a subset of data or from a collection of multiple tables, display the query's Datasheet view.

2. Click the down arrow next to the AutoForm button on the toolbar. Some toolbars already show the AutoReport button, depending on your last Access 97 task.

3. Select AutoReport from the button's drop-down list. Access 97 generates a report from the current Datasheet view and shows a preview of the report, as shown in Figure 21.2.

4. If the preview shows what you want, click the preview's Print icon to print the report.

5. Click the Close button to close the AutoReport preview. Access 97 displays the Report Design view shown in Figure 21.3. The Report Design view can be difficult to understand when you first see it. For now, don't worry about the contents. AutoReport created the report's design and saved you from having to use the Report Design view.

6. Close the Report Design view and enter a report name if you want to save the AutoReport's design. If you think you'll edit the AutoReport design later or generate the report often, save the report. Generally, you'll use AutoReport only to produce quick reports and use the report wizards (described next) to generate more standard reports.

**21**

**Figure 21.3.**

*AutoReport keeps you
from having to mess
with the Report Design
view.*

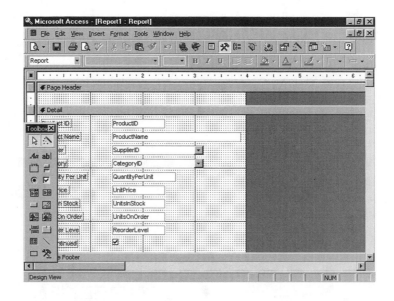

**TIP**
AutoReport generates reports using Access 97's report-designing tools. After you learn how to modify a Report Design view, you will be able to use AutoReport to generate the foundation of a report, then change the report to fit your exact needs.

If you like AutoReport for quick reports, check out the AutoForm feature. AutoForm creates fast and simple forms from your Datasheet views.

# Using the Report Wizards

Access 97 includes several report wizards that design reports for you. Select one of the report wizards by opening the Database window, clicking the Reports tab (which displays the database reports), and clicking New to create a new report. The New Report dialog box lets you access the following reporting components:

☐ Design View—A blank Report Design view on which you can add a new report's headers, footers, detail, and summary requests. When you want to generate a report from scratch, use the New Report dialog box's Design View.

**NEW TERM**   A *summary* is a subtotal, total, average, minimum-value search, or maximum-value search that Access 97 performs when printing your reports.

☐ Report Wizard—Walks you through the report-generation process by letting you select the source tables and queries as well as the fields that you want in the final

**21**

report. You'll run Report Wizard the most often because it generates less-specific reports than other reporting wizards.

☐ AutoReport: Columnar—Generates a report that contains all the fields from the underlying table or query. The columnar report looks much like the AutoReport, except that the columnar report makes better use of your report's page space and designs a more routine report. As Figure 21.4 shows, a columnar report can include titles and special fonts, and can emphasize field data.

**Figure 21.4.**

*Columnar reports look much better than AutoReports.*

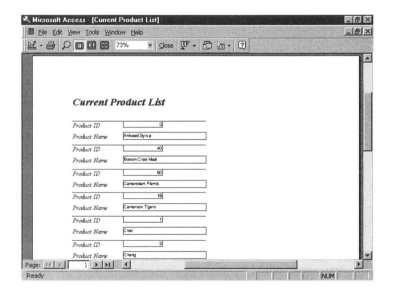

☐ AutoReport: Tabular—Generates a report that displays each source table's or query's record on a single line by adjusting the font size to fit your report page. The tabular report looks much better than a simple Datasheet view, and is often more useful than the generic AutoReport you learned about in the previous section. Figure 21.5 shows a sample of the wizard's tabular report.

☐ Chart Wizard—Produces graphs from your data. Access 97 graphs resemble Excel 97 graphs, and you can control the format and style of the graph as well as the table from which Access 97 graphs.

☐ Label Wizard—A generic mailing-list report that produces mailing labels for all common labels. The mailing label industry has a standard numbering system (the *Avery numbering system*, after the company that is perhaps best known for computerized mailing labels). Most office-supply stores sell mailing labels with an official Avery number, so you can format a report for your labels.

**NEW TERM**    *The Avery numbering system* is an industry-standard mailing-label numbering system. You can request an Access 97 mailing-list report that works with your labels by matching the Avery numbers.

**21**

**Figure 21.5.**

*Tabular reports produce good-looking listings of your data.*

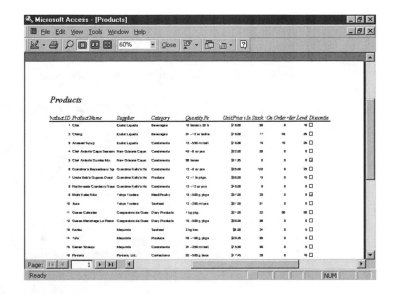

# The Report Wizard

The second New Report dialog box option, Report Wizard, is probably the most common selection you'll make when you generate customized reports. The Report Wizard walks you through a series of steps to create a custom report from your tables and queries, and it includes many common reporting styles and special features that you'll need.

**WARNING**

> You must create a named query before generating a report from that query.

To start the Report Wizard, follow these steps:

1. Display the Database window.
2. Click the Reports tab to display your Database reports.
3. Click the New button to display the New Report dialog box.
4. Select Report Wizard.
5. Open the New Report's drop-down box to select from a list of tables and queries that reside in your database. You're not limited to this single table's or query's data.
6. Click the OK button to display the Report Wizard's field-selection dialog box, shown in Figure 21.6.
7. Select the fields that you want in the final report by highlighting the field in the Available Fields list and clicking > to send the field to the Selected Fields list. As

21

you can see when you open the Tables/Queries drop-down list box, you can select fields from several tables and queries in addition to the primary source you selected in Step 5.

8. After you select the fields for the report, click Next.

**Figure 21.6.**

*Select the fields you want for your report.*

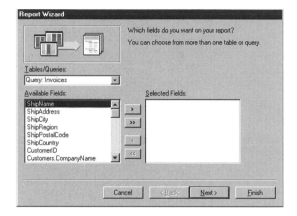

## Grouping Report Summaries

Now that you've selected the report fields, you must tell Access 97 how to summarize the report. Rarely will you want to print a data listing without requesting a summary. Depending on the type of fields you select for your report, the report wizard will prompt you for subtotal and total summary information or grouping information. If your report contains numeric data, the report wizard shows you its Summary dialog box, shown in Figure 21.7. This dialog box explains how you want Access 97 to group your report. If Access 97 does not display Figure 21.7, the report wizard will prompt you for grouping information, and you can select the field on which you want Access 97 to group your data.

**WARNING**

> Access 97 can group the report on numeric fields, not text fields. The numeric fields let the report wizard produce subtotals and total summaries, whereas no such summaries are possible with text fields.

Select only those numeric fields that will produce proper subtotals. For example, if you report a division number field and that field is numeric, you wouldn't want Access 97 to subtotal and total the division number. If, however, you printed a report with customer past-due balances, you would want to print a subtotal for each customer and an overall grand total of past-due balances.

**21**

**Figure 21.7.**

*Tell Access 97 how to produce the subtotals and totals.*

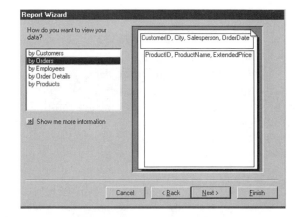

The grouping field should be groups, such as customer IDs, that you are printing a detailed list for. Although the same customer might appear on several report lines, you want Access 97 to subtotal only when the customer ID changes to the next customer in the report. Access 97's grouping capability will keep multiple customer IDs from appearing down the column when you print multiple records for the same customer.

As you click each field that you selected, the grouping dialog box displays a preview of your report, showing how the grouping will fall out. Generally, Access 97's grouping options and preview will give you enough information to decide on a grouping scheme. If you need more control over the grouping, click the cross-reference labeled Show me more information, and read the dialog box presented. If you *still* need verification, click the cross-reference labeled Show me examples, and Access 97 provides examples of different grouping options using your database's data.

Figure 21.8 shows one such example and gives you visual feedback on how the report will look given the selected grouping options.

**Figure 21.8.**

*Preview a sample of one grouping option.*

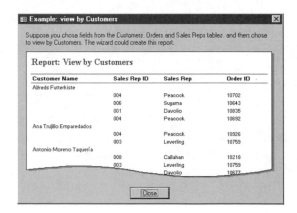

21

Click Close until you return to the grouping dialog box, then select your grouping preference. Access 97 displays the grouping level dialog box.

If you want to group on multiple fields, the group order you select determines the priority that Access 97 uses to group the data. The highest priority grouping level (if you select multiple groups) appears on the left of the report, the second grouping level appears to the right of the first one, and so on. Generally, multifield grouping gets confusing. If you want to add such grouping levels, click every group level from the series of fields that Access 97 displays. The report wizard will prioritize the multifield groups in the order you select the fields.

**WARNING**

> You can group by a maximum of four field-grouping levels. If you need to group by more than four fields, you'll have to edit the report design or create a report from scratch. Rarely will you need more than four groups.

If the report wizard has presented you with the grouping view dialog box instead of the subtotal and total summary dialog boxes described here, you only need to click the field you want to group the report by. For example, if you are producing a customer balance report, the report wizard might let you group by either the Customer ID field or the Customer Order Number field.

When you've set up the grouping levels that you need, click Next to select a sort and summary order for the report.

# The Report's Sort and Summary Order

When you see Figure 21.9's sorting and summary dialog box, you're almost done creating your report. Select between one and four fields that you want Access 97 to use for sorting your data. If you're reporting from a query that already contains sorted data, and if you generate the report so that the data groups in the order of those sorted fields, don't select any fields by which to sort. If, however, you want to sort by one or more fields that do not enter the reporting system already sorted, select up to four fields and click the button labeled AZ to sort in ascending order.

**NOTE**

> The AZ button changes to ZA when you click it, so you can then select a descending sort.

**21**

**Figure 21.9.**

*Select one to four fields by which to sort.*

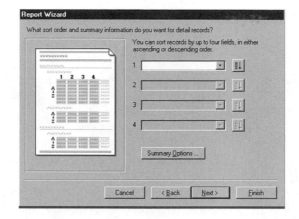

Whether or not you select a sorting option, click the Summary Options button to display the report wizard's Summary Options dialog box. Each of your report's numeric fields appears in the box, so you can select any or all of these summaries for that field:

☐ Sum—Requests a total for the field.

☐ Avg—Requests an average for the field.

☐ Min—Requests that Access 97 highlight the minimum value in the field.

☐ Max—Requests that Access 97 highlight the maximum value in the field.

**WARNING**

> You cannot display summaries if your report has no numeric fields or if you are grouping by the numeric fields.

# Finishing Your Report

Click OK to close the Summary Options dialog box, then click Next to choose a report layout. Click through the various layouts to select one that fits your needs. As you click layouts, Access 97 displays thumbnail sketches of that layout. For example, if you click the Block style, you'll see that Access 97 displays boxes around your report fields.

After you select the layout, click Next to select from the report wizard's Style dialog box, shown in Figure 21.10. The Style dialog box adds the finishing touches to your report.

Click Next, enter a report title if you don't want to use the original source table or query name, and click Finish to generate the completed report. Sometimes Access 97 takes several minutes

**21**

to generate the report, especially if the source tables and queries contain several records and your report contains several grouping levels. When finished, Access 97 prints a preview of your report so that you can look at your handiwork.

**Figure 21.10.**
*The Style window determines your report's overall appearance.*

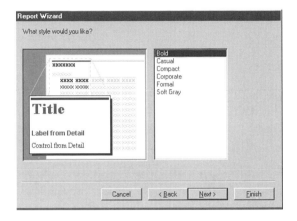

## Summary

Access 97 is certainly a powerful program. Despite its ease, Access 97 does take some getting used to before you fully master all its features. You'll probably use the Access 97 wizards more than any other wizard in Office 97.

At this point, you are ready to begin generating sample databases and practicing with Access 97. As you create more databases, you'll learn how to partition your data properly into tables and generate data-entry forms and reports.

The next hour begins the part of the book that explains how the Office 97 programs work together to help you with your data-processing requirements.

## Q&A

**Q How does the toolbar's AutoReport differ from the AutoReport entries I see on the report wizard's opening dialog box?**

**A** The AutoReport entries on the Report Wizard's opening dialog box create more finished reports than the AutoReport toolbar button. Use the AutoReport toolbar button to quickly generate a report from your Datasheet and Form views. Use the report wizard AutoReport entries to produce more complete reports without taking the time to set up summary and sorting features. Not all reports require summaries, and the two AutoReport wizards suffice for many reports that you generate.

**21**

**Q  Do I subtotal on numeric fields or fields that I want to group by, such as Customer ID numbers?**

**A**  When you specify grouping instructions, the field that you group by will usually be a non-numeric field, such as a Customer ID field. Access 97 collects all the customer ID records together and reports each customer's information in one group. When Access 97 finishes reporting a customer's records (when the ID changes), Access 97 subtotals the numeric fields in that group before starting the next group.

**21**

# PART
# VII

## Putting Things Together

## Hour

# Hour **22**

# Office 97's Synergy

This hour begins exploring how Office 97 products work together and how they work with other Windows programs. Office 97 programs integrate so well that it's hard to know where to start describing the possibilities. Generally, if you need to work with two or more Office 97 program documents together, you'll be able to load or embed one document within the other even though the Office 97 programs that created the two documents are completely different.

This hour and the next two describe scenarios in which you can combine Office 97 products to produce a synergistic power. From inserting a Bookshelf Basics definition into a Word 97 document to combining an Access 97 table and an Excel 97 worksheet into a PowerPoint 97 presentation, Office 97 supplies the combining tools you'll need.

The highlights of this hour include

- ☐ Which common terms describe program integration and data sharing
- ☐ How you can grab a definition from Bookshelf Basics while working in Word 97
- ☐ Why drag-and-drop operations work so well between Office 97 programs

☐ How to control a drag-and-drop operation to produce a copy, a move, a link, or a shortcut

☐ How to edit and break links between Office 97 documents

☐ What requirements a Word 97 document must meet to serve as a PowerPoint 97 presentation

☐ Which steps you must take to import Access 97 data into Word 97

# Terminology

Fully integrated software has been the dream of software developers for years. Perhaps you've heard the terms *OLE*, *COM*, and *ActiveX*. These buzzwords describe the ways software developers have attempted to integrate different software products and data files.

 *OLE* stands for *Object Linking and Embedding*, and describes the technology that lets Windows applications seamlessly share data files.

 The term *ActiveX* refers to controls, such as command buttons and check boxes, that let software programs interact with one another. ActiveX controls replace older Visual Basic controls (*VBXs*). VBX was an earlier cross-application control standard. When you view a Word 97 document from Internet Explorer's Internet browser software, Internet Explorer uses a Word 97 ActiveX control to let you see the document.

**NEW TERM** *COM* stands for *Common Object Model*. COM is a low-level specification that lets OLE and ActiveX objects communicate with each other.

You don't have to master the terminology to integrate Office 97 products with each other and with other products. Don't worry about whether you're embedding an OLE link or working with an ActiveX control. Just concentrate on your application's needs, and Office 97 (along with this book!) will be there to help.

# Bookshelf Basics and Word 97

In Part I of this book, you learned how to access Bookshelf Basics by itself so that you could look up definitions, synonyms, and quotes. The real power of Bookshelf Basics comes into play when you need a Bookshelf Basics item while writing in Word 97 or using other Office 97 products.

For example, suppose you're typing a meeting report from your boss's handwritten notes and you run across the word *praenomen*. Since you're unsure of the spelling (and perhaps the meaning), why not use Bookshelf Basics to verify the boss's writing? Type and select the word, then choose Tools | Look Up Reference. Word 97 displays Figure 22.1's Look Up Reference dialog box.

**22**

**Figure 22.1.**

*The Look Up Reference dialog box.*

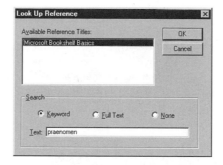

**NOTE**

> The Look Up Reference dialog box's Keyword option limits the search to Bookshelf Basics article titles, whereas the Full Text option searches through the text of all the Bookshelf Basics articles for your term. The full-text search takes longer to complete, and often returns more information than you need.

Press Enter to start Bookshelf Basics's search. In a moment, Bookshelf Basics will display *praenomen*'s definition, as shown in Figure 22.2.

**Figure 22.2.**

*Bookshelf Basics displays a definition for praenomen.*

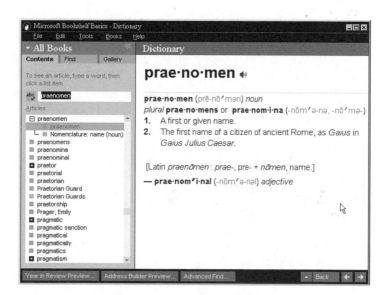

The Tools | Look Up Reference option is available on all of Office 97's menus.

**TIP**

If you select Edit | Copy (or press the Ctrl+C shortcut key) while in Book-shelf Basics, Office 97 copies the complete article (definition, quote, or synonym list) to the Windows clipboard. When you paste the clipboard contents to another Office 97 program (or to any other Windows program that accepts pasted text), Windows pastes the entire article.

# Sharing Data Between Applications

Office 97's cornerstone is data sharing among its programs. Office 97 offers several ways to share data between products. The following sections explain the most common methods.

## Drag and Drop

Suppose you want to use part of an Excel 97 worksheet inside a Word 97 document. If you've got both Excel 97 (with the relevant data loaded) and Word 97 running at the same time, perform these steps to drag the worksheet to the Word 97 document:

1. Arrange your program windows so that you can see both the *source document* (the Excel 97 worksheet) and the *destination document* (the Word 97 document).

2. In the Excel 97 worksheet, select the cells that you want to transfer to Word 97.

3. Hold the Ctrl key and drag the edge of the highlighted cells to the location in your Word 97 document where you want to place the table.

4. Release your mouse to anchor the table. Figure 22.3 shows the result of such a copy.

**WARNING**

If you did not first press Ctrl before dragging the cells, Excel 97 would have *moved* the table from the Excel 97 worksheet to the Word 97 document instead of copying the table.

**TIP**

Depending on the size and style of your Word 97 document, you might want to format the copied table differently from Excel 97's format. Right-click the table and select Format Object to display Figure 22.4's Format Object dialog box. You can apply colors, lines, shading, and other formatting attributes to the copied object from the Format Object dialog box.

**22**

**Figure 22.3.**

*The table came from Excel 97.*

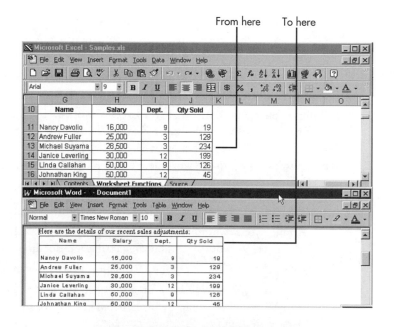

**Figure 22.4.**

*You might want to format the table when it arrives in Word 97.*

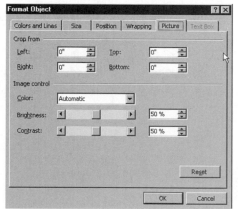

# Creating Links

Suppose you create a monthly sales report using the same Word 97 document and the same Excel 97 worksheet every time. Only the details in the Excel 97 worksheet change (obviously, you've created templates for these files long before now). You don't have to drag the updated Excel 97 table to your Word 97 document before printing the Word 97 document each month. Instead of copying or moving the cells, you can create a *link* to the cells.

**NEW TERM** A *link* is a cross-reference to another file. Instead of copying or moving the contents of one file to another, the link maintains a live connection to the other file. Therefore, if the source file changes, the destination file always displays those changes. The destination file does not actually hold the source file's data, but displays the data as though it resides in the destination file.

As long as you've inserted a link to the Excel 97 worksheet, you only have to change the Excel 97 worksheet each month, start Word 97, load the report document, and print the document. You won't have to copy or move the actual Excel 97 cells into the report. The report always points to the worksheet cells via the link that you inserted when you created the Word 97 document.

To create a link, perform these steps:

1. Arrange your two program windows so that you can see both the source document (the Excel 97 worksheet) and the destination document (the Word 97 document).

2. Select the cells in the Excel 97 worksheet that you want to transfer to Word 97.

3. *With the right mouse button*, drag the edge of the highlighted cells to the location in your Word 97 document where you want to place the table.

4. Release your right mouse button. Word 97 opens a pop-up menu with these options: Move Here, Copy Here, Insert Excel Object Here, and Create Shortcut Here.

5. Select Insert Excel Object Here to let Word 97 know that you want an object link (as opposed to a move or a copy of the cells). While the cells appear as though Office 97 copied them into the Word 97 document, the cells represent only the link that you created between the Excel 97 source and Word 97 destination document.

**WARNING**

> The destination document (in this case, the Word 97 document) will always reflect the most recent changes to the source document (in this case, the Excel 97 worksheet). Therefore, if you must keep archives of old reports with the previous monthly values, you'll want to copy the cells instead of creating a link.

To see the interactive nature of the links, change a value in the source Excel 97 worksheet. The Word 97 document in the lower window will immediately reflect your change as soon as you make it.

**22**

**TIP**
After inserting one or more links, select Edit | Links to display Figure 22.5's Links dialog box. The Links dialog box contains every link in your document and lets you change, break, or lock any link. When you break a link, the data becomes embedded in the document and no longer updates when you update the source. When you lock a link, you temporarily prevent the link from being updated when its source is updated.

**22**

**Figure 22.5.**
*Use the Links dialog box to manage your document links.*

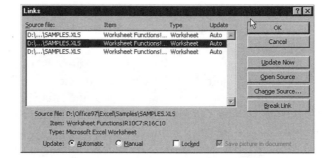

### Step-Up

A link might even point to an Internet address that resides on the other side of the world. Internet links are extremely useful for companies that keep constant Internet connections to other company sites. A central repository of data at the corporate offices might provide several links for the satellite divisions.

## Creating Shortcuts

Instead of inserting a copy or a link, you can insert a *shortcut* in the destination document.

**New Term** A *shortcut* appears as an icon that represents data from a document stored elsewhere.

You'll probably use shortcuts less often than links and embedded copies when producing reports because the reports must show actual data and not icons. However, if you often work with data from one program while in another program, the shortcuts are nice. The data does not get in your way until you're ready to work with it because you'll see only icons that represent the shortcut data.

**WARNING**

If you create a shortcut from one Office 97 program to another, Office 97 actually displays the data and does not display a shortcut icon. If you double-click the data, Office 97 opens the appropriate program and lets you edit the original data using the source program that created the data. If, however, you were to insert a shortcut into a non-Office 97 program, Office 97 would insert a shortcut icon that represents the data. If you double-click the icon from within the other program, the appropriate Office 97 program will begin, and you can edit the data.

Consider this scenario: You're working in Excel 97, modifying weekly salary figures for a large worksheet that you maintain. Each week you must study the salary amounts and enter a 10-line explanation of the salaries. Instead of typing the definition each week or (worse) using Excel 97 as a limited word processor and editing the text each week, you could embed a shortcut to a Word 97 document that contains a template for the text. When you double-click the shortcut, Excel 97 starts Word 97, which automatically loads the template. You can create the final text in the template, then copy the Word 97 text into your salary worksheet (replacing the shortcut), and save the worksheet under a name that designates the current week's work.

To insert a shortcut, perform these steps:

1. Arrange your program windows so that you can see both the source document (the Word 97 template document) and the destination document (the Excel 97 worksheet).

2. Select the Word 97 template text that you want to use for the shortcut. (Press Ctrl+A if you want to select the entire Word 97 template document.)

3. *With the right mouse button*, drag the edge of the highlighted template text to the location in your Excel 97 worksheet where you want to place the shortcut.

4. Release your right mouse button.

5. Select Create Shortcut Here from the pop-up menu. Office 97 creates the shortcut. As with a link, the shortcut data does not actually appear in the destination document. Unlike a link, you can drag the shortcut to your Windows desktop, to Explorer, or to another program to create additional copies of the shortcut.

**TIP**

Before inserting an Access 97 table into another Office 97 program, run a query to filter data that doesn't interest you. In most cases, you'll want to use Word 97's special Access 97 Database Insert feature to load Access 97 data into a Word 97 document. Later in this hour, the section titled "Using Word 97 and Access 97" describes how to insert Access 97 data into a Word 97 document.

# PowerPoint 97 and Word 97's Special Link

Word 97 and PowerPoint 97 share a special link that allows you to turn a set of notes into a presentation. Before creating your notes, be sure to use the Heading 1 through Heading 5 styles. PowerPoint 97 will use the Heading 1 style for each slide's title and will use the Heading 2 through Heading 5 styles for the slide's subsequently indented text.

**NOTE** If your Word 97 document contains other styles, PowerPoint 97 will ignore those paragraphs.

You can easily apply Heading 1 through Heading 5 styles to a Word 97 document that you've already created by clicking a paragraph, pressing Ctrl+Shift+S, and selecting Heading styles from the drop-down list box.

After you create the Word 97 document, open it from PowerPoint 97 or click Word 97's Present It toolbar button to create the presentation. Depending on your Word 97 customization, you might not see the Present It toolbar button until you add it (use the Tools | Customize menu).

# Using Word 97 and Access 97

A database can be extremely large with many tables. Often, you'll want to export a portion of an Access 97 database to a Word 97 document. The drag-and-drop method does not always offer exactly what you need to get exactly the data you want into a Word 97 document.

**TIP** If you want to use an Access 97 table in a PowerPoint 97 presentation, load the table into a Word 97 document, then convert the Word 97 document to a PowerPoint 97 presentation as described in the previous section.

To load Access 97 data into a Word 97 document, perform these steps:

1. Display Word 97's Database toolbar (select View | Toolbars and click the Database option).
2. Click the Insert Database toolbar button. Word 97 displays Figure 22.6's Database dialog box.

**Figure 22.6.**

*Use the Database dialog box to load Access 97 data into Word 97.*

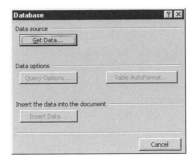

3. Click the Get Data button and locate the database you want to import. Word 97 will *not* import the data yet, but you must locate the database before specifying the data to be imported. To display Access 97 databases, select MS Access Databases (*.mdb) from the list box labeled Files of type. Word 97 displays Figure 22.7's dialog box, which contains a list of every table and query from the selected database.

**Figure 22.7.**

*Tell Word 97 exactly which table to use.*

4. Select the table or query that you want to load into the Word 97 document and click OK to return to the Database dialog box.

5. Click the Query Options button if you want to limit the table's records or fields. If you don't select the Query Options button, Word 97 imports the entire table. Word 97 displays an Access 97 query window, from which you can select records and fields using normal Access 97 database-selection criteria. You can add tables if you want Word 97 to import data from multiple tables. Instead of generating a query, you can select the rows and records you want to import.

6. Select File | Return Data to Microsoft Word.

7. Click the Insert Data button to insert your selected data.

8. You now can format the data and use it in your Word 97 document as though you typed the data yourself.

**22**

# Summary

This hour describes how to integrate Office 97 products by sharing data files between the programs. One of the most elegant ways to copy or move data from one Office 97 program to another is to use drag and drop. By holding your right mouse button, you can control how the drag-and-drop operation sends the data from one document to another.

Word 97 and PowerPoint 97 share data files easily as long as you use the proper heading styles. Presenters often use Word 97 documents as a basis for a presentation, and you'll appreciate the automation Office 97 provides. Once you convert your Word 97 document to a PowerPoint 97 presentation, you can adjust the presentation's format and add slides if you wish.

When importing Access 97 data into Word 97, you must be selective. Databases are often huge, and you'll usually want to import only a small part of the database into your Word 97 document. First, tell Word 97 what data from what table you want to import so that you get only the data you need.

The next hour, "Office 97's Drawing Tools," describes the ways you can add art to your Office 97 documents. Today's data requirements include both text and graphics. Office 97's integrated art tools let you use a common interface for graphics creation and editing.

# Q&A

**Q  Can I import references into Office 97 programs from the full Microsoft Bookshelf or only from the Bookshelf Basics that comes with Office 97?**

**A**  As soon as you upgrade to Microsoft Bookshelf, all of Microsoft Bookshelf's references will be at your fingertips. For example, say you are writing a report on a foreign city. You can use the Microsoft Bookshelf atlas to point the way to the city when you click the city name and select Tools | Look Up Reference to display the atlas's information.

**Q  What format does my data take when I drag and drop something from one Office 97 product to another?**

**A**  Office 97 provides excellent intuitive conversions when you combine data from more than one Office 97 product. For example, when you drag a worksheet from Excel 97 to Word 97, the worksheet becomes a Word 97 table. You can then use all the standard table-editing tools in Word 97 to modify the appearance of the worksheet. Excel 97 converts Word 97 text to text-cell entries. Excel 97 converts Access 97 table data to worksheet cells, respecting the data types when possible (so the numbers stay numbers and the dates stay dates).

**Q  What is the advantage of a shortcut over a link?**

**A**  If you're sticking with Office 97 products only, you'll probably want to use links to embed live connections from one document to another. However, if you share Office 97 documents with other programs, those programs will probably recognize shortcuts and present your Office 97 document as an icon. For example, if you use a standalone e-mail program (such as Eudora) to send a Word 97 document, the Word 97 document will appear in your e-mail note as a Word 97 icon. If you double-click that icon (or if your e-mail recipient double-clicks the icon after receiving the e-mail), Word 97 will start (assuming Word 97 resides on the system), and you (or the recipient) will be able to edit the document.

**Q  Why would you ever want to copy data and not create a link to another document?**

**A**  When you copy data, that data is copied into the destination document, so the data resides in both the destination document and the source document. If you were to take the destination document to another computer, the document could not access its original link (if you had used a link). In addition, you may not want the destination document's data being hooked "live" to the source data. For example, if you are creating archive files of older data, you will want to always copy the data and not form a link or shortcut to the original source data.

**Q  True or False: PowerPoint 97 can turn a Word 97 document into a presentation.**

**A**  True, as long as you use the proper heading styles.

**Q  Why would you not import a complete database into Word 97?**

**A**  A complete database would contain tables, queries, reports, forms, macros, and modules, and all those items would make little sense in a Word 97 document. If you need to report data using the entire Access 97 database, use Access 97 to generate reports. Word 97 is useful for printing database subsets. If you want to include part of an Access 97 database table in a Word 97 report, you can easily send the table's data into Word 97 using the tools described in this lesson.

**22**

# Hour 23

# Office 97's Drawing Tools

This hour discusses Office 97's art-based tools. After you master this hour's material, you'll be able to insert graphics in your Office 97 documents, as well as draw your own graphics. (If you're like me, you may not know art, but you know what you like!)

The Office 97 products come with a complete line of drawing tools. Although Office 97 does not compete with a dedicated art program (such as CorelDRAW), Office 97's tools offer more than enough drawing features to create most of the art you'll ever need for your Office 97 documents. Also, Office 97 includes all the tools you need to insert virtually any kind of existing image file into Office 97, including any art masterpieces you want to include in your Office 97 documents.

The highlights of this hour include

- ☐ Why the Clip Gallery does not provide every art feature you'll need
- ☐ What to do to add your own art (or sound or video) clip files to Office 97's Clip Gallery

□ When the AutoShape toolbar comes in handy

□ How to select WordArt styles when you want to add fancy text titles and banners to your Office 97 documents

□ Which option to use when you want to scan pictures into Office 97 documents

□ When to use Microsoft's Web site to access graphic images

□ How to add text to your Office 97 drawings

□ Why Microsoft decided to completely rewrite Office 97's drawing tools

# Non-Office 97 Objects

Office 97 lets you insert and work with data that is not created by Office 97. For example, if you have a CorelDRAW! image that you want to insert in a Word 97 document, go right ahead! Graphics spruce up newsletters and other documents that require eye-catching images.

In Hour 15, "Advanced PowerPoint 97 Power," you learned how to use the Clip Gallery to insert images, sounds, and videos into presentations. If you select Insert | Picture | Clip Art from any of the Office 97 products, Office 97 displays the same Clip Gallery dialog box you used in Hour 15.

In addition to producing the Clip Gallery, the Insert | Picture option produces a menu with the following options:

□ From File—Lets you insert an image from any graphics file. Use this option when you don't want to confine your images to the ones supplied in the Clip Gallery.

□ AutoShapes—Inserts one of Office 97's *AutoShapes*, which you can manipulate.

**New Term** *AutoShape* is a ready-made shape that you can use in a document. After you insert a shape, you can resize, rotate, flip, color, and combine that shape with other shapes. The Drawing toolbar contains an AutoShape section, which produces the AutoShape floating toolbar. Use the AutoShape floating toolbar to insert and edit AutoShapes.

□ WordArt—Displays Figure 23.1's *WordArt* gallery of WordArt styles.

**New Term** *WordArt* lets you convert text into shapes. Despite its name, WordArt is available from all Office 97 products, not just Word 97.

□ From Scanner—Lets you scan an image into the Office 97 document. You must have a TWAIN-compliant scanner attached to scan images into Office 97. (Most scanners follow the PC scanner standard called *TWAIN*; your scanner's documentation should let you know if your scanner is TWAIN-compliant.)

**23**

**Figure 23.1.**

*You can select a WordArt style from the WordArt gallery.*

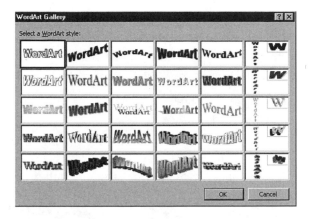

23

☐ Organization Chart—Starts an Office 97 add-in application that creates organizational charts (available only in Excel 97).

☐ Chart—Displays a small Excel 97-like worksheet (called a datasheet) in which you can enter data. The datasheet offers a sample set of cells in which you can enter your own values or import data from Excel 97. When you close the datasheet, the resulting bar chart appears in your document (available only in Word 97).

The next three sections describe the most common graphic insertions you'll make into your Office 97 documents from the Insert | Picture menu.

## Inserting Images from Files

To add an image (or sound or video) clip-art file to a document, select Insert | Picture | From File to display the Insert Picture dialog box. Locate the image on your disk (or on your network, or the Internet by selecting the source from the Look in list box) and click OK to insert the image.

**NOTE**

To insert a link to the clip art instead of embedding the art in your document, click the Link to file option before selecting the image.

**TIP**

Uncheck the Float over text option if you want to place the image on the same layer as the text. Leave the Float over text option checked if you want to place the image on a special art layer. Use the Draw menu to place text on top of or underneath the art image.

If you often insert the same image, sound, or video clip, consider adding the clip to your Office 97 Clip Gallery. The Clip Gallery makes common clips easy for you to find, thus eliminating the need for you to search your disk drive every time you want to insert a clip file.

To add a clip file to your Clip Gallery, perform these steps:

1. Display the Clip Gallery by selecting Insert | Picture | Clip Art.
2. Click the Import Clips button.
3. Locate the clip-art file you want to import. When you locate the file and press Enter, Office 97 displays Figure 23.2's Clip Properties dialog box, which shows a thumbnail sketch of the image along with the image's details.

**Figure 23.2.**

*Enter a frequently used image into the Clip Gallery category so you can quickly find the image later.*

4. Select the category and add a keyword or two (to help with subsequent searches for the image).
5. Press Enter to add the image to the proper Clip Gallery category.

## Inserting AutoShapes

The AutoShapes toolbar that appears when you insert an AutoShape provides numerous drawing tools for creating line drawings inside Word 97, Excel 97, or PowerPoint 97. When you click one of the toolbar options described next, Office 97 opens a set of drawing tools for that option. For example, if you click the Basic Shapes tool, Office 97 displays a drop-down selection box of about 30 shapes. After you select a shape, you can continue drawing with that shape until you select a different shape or another AutoShape tool. To draw a shape, drag your mouse over the editing area.

Here is a description of the AutoShape tools you'll find on the AutoShape toolbar:

☐ Lines—Provides straight, curved, and free-form lines that you can draw with your mouse.

☐ Basic shapes—Provides circles, ovals, rectangles, and other shapes that you can select and draw with.

☐ Block arrows (Word 97 only)—Provides several connecting arrows that you can use for linking parts of a drawing to other parts.

☐ Flowchart—Draws various flowcharting symbols.

☐ Stars and Banners—Places stars and various banners on your editing area.

☐ Callouts—Draws spoken and bubble-thought cartoon callouts so that the figures you draw can speak.

☐ Connectors (Excel 97 only)—Draws special connecting lines from one AutoShape image to another.

Figure 23.3 shows several AutoShape images placed on a Word 97 document.

**Figure 23.3.**

*A sample of AutoShape images.*

AutoShape offers two ways to add text to your image:

☐ Placing text in a callout—As soon as you add a callout AutoShape to your drawing, Office 97 lets you enter text for that callout.

☐ Placing text anywhere on the AutoShape image—Right-click anywhere over the AutoShape area and select Add text to place text on any AutoShape image.

> **TIP**
>
> When you click any AutoShape image that you draw, resizing handles appear so you can resize the image. In addition, you'll see the image's yellow *adjustment handle*.

 Drag the yellow *adjustment handle* to change the shape's most prominent feature, such as the smile on the happy face.

When you add an AutoShape to your document, Office 97 displays the Drawing toolbar on your screen. Select from the Drawing toolbar to change the orientation of any selected AutoShape image. For example, you can vertically or horizontally flip an image. Any text you've placed on the image retains its original orientation.

## Inserting WordArt

WordArt displays text in several shapes, colors, and styles to add pizzazz to your documents. For example, you can add an eye-catching title at the top of an Excel 97 worksheet to grab the reader's attention.

To add a WordArt image, perform these steps:

1. Select Insert | Picture | WordArt to display the WordArt Gallery dialog box (refer to Figure 23.1).
2. Select the WordArt style you want to use by double-clicking the style. Office 97 displays Figure 23.4's Edit WordArt Text dialog box.

**Figure 23.4.**

*You need to tell WordArt which text to format.*

**23**

3. Enter the text you want to format as WordArt and select the proper font and point size. The WordArt style that you select will follow your font and size request as closely as possible.

4. Click OK to insert the WordArt text. Office 97 displays resizing handles around the WordArt image, which you can use to resize or move the WordArt image. In addition, the WordArt toolbar that appears provides several editing techniques that you can apply to the WordArt image, such as rotation and color.

Figure 23.5 shows a sample WordArt image inserted at the top of a small Excel worksheet.

**23**

**Figure 23.5.**

*Here's a sample of WordArt's appeal.*

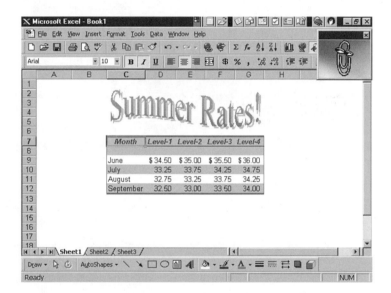

## Inserting Other Objects

If you want to insert objects other than the typical clip art, sound, or video clips, select Insert | Object to display Figure 23.6's Object dialog box.

**NOTE**

The Insert Object dialog box inserts OLE objects, which can be any kind of OLE-compatible object created from non-Office 97 Windows programs.

**Figure 23.6.**

*You can create objects*
*from scratch if they do*
*not yet exist.*

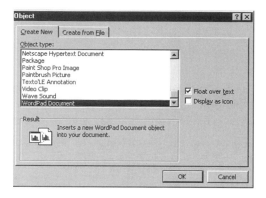

If the object already exists, click the Create from File tab and select the object that you want to insert from Figure 23.7's dialog box. Office 97 will start the appropriate program to load the file. For example, if you want to insert a new Microsoft Paintbrush file in an Excel 97 worksheet, Office 97 will start Paintbrush on top of your Office 97 application.

**Figure 23.7.**

*Create Word 97 objects*
*from existing OLE*
*source files.*

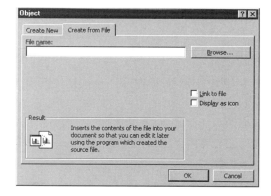

Office 97 will either insert the object or a link to the object depending on the option you check. You can control how the object inserts over text. Also, you can control whether the object itself appears, or whether an icon representing the object is displayed.

When you look at the document, you'll see either the object or an icon representing the object. Office 97 will not be able to edit the object (you can only resize some objects and delete the objects from within the Office 97 document). However, when you double-click the object or icon, the original program that created the object appears on top of your Office 97 program space. You can use that program's tools to edit the object. When you finish editing the object, close the program to return to Office 97.

**23**

**TIP**

By clicking the Clip Gallery's Internet button, you can log on to Microsoft's Office Internet Web site (see Appendix B for the other Microsoft-related Internet sites), and access Microsoft's *Clip Gallery Live*, where Microsoft stores over 2,000 clip files (including art images, sound, video, and background graphic files). Microsoft offers these clip files free of charge.

# Some Words About Office 97's Art Features

This entire section will improve your day if you remember how sluggish previous Office drawing tools were. Office 97 introduced a completely revamped set of *OfficeArt* tools. Instead of simply upgrading previous Office drawing tools, Microsoft rewrote them for Office 97 to improve performance.

 *OfficeArt* is the general term applied to the Office 97 drawing tools such as AutoShape and WordArt.

OfficeArt provides a single drawing interface for all the Office 97 programs. If you learn how to use AutoShape inside PowerPoint 97, you'll also know how to use AutoShape in Excel 97. Although you might expect such an integrated and consistent drawing system, Office 97 is the *first time* Microsoft successfully integrated one consistent drawing interface into all the Office 97 products.

**NOTE**

Outlook 97 contains no OfficeArt tool support.

**TIP**

OfficeArt's drawing tools work with all the applicable Office 97 features. Therefore, you can spell check the text in an AutoShape drawing.

Not only did Microsoft help you learn the OfficeArt tools more quickly, but Office 97 includes only one set of OfficeArt code. Therefore, whether you install only Word 97 or the entire set of Office 97 programs, Office 97 installs a single shared copy of the OfficeArt code. As a result, Office 97's drawing tools work quickly, efficiently, consuming much less disk space than they would consume if each Office 97 program contained its own drawing code.

# Summary

This hour explains how to use Office 97's graphics-related tools to insert art and draw pictures inside your Office 97 documents. As you might expect, the Office 97 tools are easy to use and show themselves (along with their toolbars) when you request them.

When you need to insert a graphic image, first check out Office 97's Clip Gallery to see if you can find an appropriate image. If you do not see an image you want, perhaps you know of a graphics clip-art file elsewhere on your system that you could insert. You can even insert clip-art files from another networked computer or directly from the Internet.

If you cannot find an image that you want to use, try drawing one yourself with the AutoShape tools. AutoShape provides several free-hand drawing tools with several standard shapes that you can use to draw on your screen. In addition, you can spruce up your text graphically with WordArt.

The next hour completes this 24-hour session by showing you how to combine the Office 97 products with the Microsoft Binder. In addition, you might find Office 97's mail-merge feature handy when you send form letters or print mailing labels.

# Q&A

**Q  What is the difference between AutoShape, WordArt, and OfficeArt?**

**A**  AutoShape is the general term applied to all the drawing tools provided when you insert an AutoShape picture into an Office 97 document. The AutoShape toolbar appears when you draw AutoShape graphics to help you with free-form drawings and to supply common shapes that you might need. WordArt is a system that manipulates and colors text to turn standard text into various eye-catching 3D colorful styles. The term *OfficeArt* is a general term applied to all the graphics and drawing tools you'll find in the Office 97 suite of products.

**Q  Why would I want to enter values into a datasheet to produce a Word 97 bar chart instead of creating a fancier graph in Excel 97 and importing the Excel 97 graph into my Word 97 document?**

**A**  If you only want a simple bar chart, Word 97's datasheet-based chart is simple and efficient. You won't have to start Excel 97 and follow Excel 97's charting wizards to generate a graph in Word 97. Excel 97 can create much more complicated charts, so if that's what you require, simply use Excel 97 and drag the chart into Word 97.

**Q  Why does the Clip Gallery include sound and video files?**

**A**  The most common non-Office 97 file you'll insert into an Office 97 document will be a graphic image. However, with the World Wide Web so prevalent these days,

**23**

you might be creating a Web page with Word 97. Web pages often contain sounds and even videos. In addition, sound and video clips are the second and third most common kinds of files inserted into today's word-processed files (after graphic images).

The Clip Gallery, therefore, gives you the ability to insert sound and video clip files into any Office 97 document. The sound and video clips insert as icons. When you (or another user) click one of these icons, you'll hear the sound or watch the video using a helper application such as Windows Media Player application. Office 97 automatically starts Media Player so you can hear the sound or watch the video.

**Q Why would you ever want to add a clip file to the Clip Gallery?**

**A** If you insert the same clip art (or sound or video clip file) very often, consider putting that clip file in Office 97's Clip Gallery. The Clip Gallery categorizes all images, and you can search the Clip Gallery by keyword when looking for a particular subject.

**Q Why is Office 97's OfficeArt more efficient than its predecessors?**

**A** Microsoft completely rewrote the OfficeArt code so that all Office 97 OfficeArt graphics tools share a common interface and code. Only one copy of OfficeArt resides on your computer regardless of how many Office 97 products are installed. Therefore, the OfficeArt tools load more quickly and consume less disk space.

**Q Why can't you simply drag and drop non-Office 97 objects into Office 97 documents?**

**A** Office 97 cannot possibly understand the format of every kind of file in existence. Therefore, Office 97 cannot handle the transfer of some objects with drag-and-drop operations. Nevertheless, using OLE and ActiveX features, you can usually insert any kind of non-Office 97 file as an object into an Office 97 document.

**Q True or False: Outlook 97 contains no OfficeArt tools.**

**A** True. Outlook 97 does not support OfficeArt directly, but if you choose Word 97 as your e-mail editor, you will have access to the OfficeArt tools through Word 97 when creating messages for Outlook 97.

**Q True or False: WordArt works for Word 97 but not for Excel 97.**

**A** False. WordArt works across all the Office 97 products except Outlook 97.

**Q What is the difference between an adjustment handle and a resizing handle?**

**A** Adjustment handles change the form of shapes, while resizing handles change the size of shapes.

# Hour 24

# Really Use Office 97!

The more you use Office 97, the more ways you'll find to use the Office 97 products together. This chapter completes your 24-hour tutorial by showing you a few ways to integrate the Office 97 suite of programs to accomplish common tasks.

Office 97's Binder program consolidates multiple Office 97 documents into a single project file. From inside the Binder, you can switch back and forth to work among the documents *even if you used different programs to create those documents*. The Binder gives you the ability to publish the entire project at once when you finish the project.

Word 97 works well with Outlook 97, Access 97, and Excel 97 to perform mail merging. Office 97's mail-merge feature produces customized form letters, catalogs, membership lists, and more. Instead of typing a separate document for each customer, you need only type a single form document. Let Word 97 fill in the blanks to personalize each letter.

If you don't need the full mail-merge power, you can learn how to use Word 97 to print a single envelope. Word 97 can grab the envelope's address information from your Outlook 97 address book.

The highlights of this hour include

- [ ] How to collect documents for your Binder projects
- [ ] Why the Binder integrates well with the Internet
- [ ] Which data Word 97 uses for mail-merging names and addresses
- [ ] How to set up a mail-merge main document and data source
- [ ] Why you must distinguish between fields and main-document text
- [ ] How to print single envelopes and labels from inside Word 97

# Try the Binder

The Office 97 Binder helps users who work with many types of document files to build a single project. Although each of the Office 97 programs lets you work with multiple files and each Office 97 program lets you insert files from the other Office 97 programs, only the Binder lets you collect different kinds of document files and use them collectively in a single project.

**NOTE**

> Microsoft used the traditional three-ring Binder and the Binder clip symbols for the Office 97 Binder design.

After you create a new Binder project, you can easily create, collect, edit, print, and distribute document collections from a variety of Office 97 sources into a single file called a Binder file. For simplicity, I'll keep calling the Binder file a *project*.

**NOTE**

> In Office 97, the Binder lets you set global document settings for all project files and use consistent headers across documents. You can also view all of a project's files together in a single Print Preview and then print the entire Binder project file in one step.

If you often create similar Binder projects, consider creating a Binder template file. Microsoft supplies three pre-defined Binder templates, but you'll probably want to create your own templates after you master Binder.

**24**

## Setting Up a Binder Project File

You have two options for creating a Binder project file:

- ☐ Collect existing Office 97 document files that relate to your project and store them in a Binder project.
- ☐ Create a new Binder project and add the Binder's individual files one at a time as you create the files.

You can begin working in Word 97 or Excel 97. If you find that the files would be more manageable in a bound project file, simply add those files to a new Binder project that you create.

## Creating a New Binder Project

To create a Binder project, simply start the Microsoft Binder program by selecting Microsoft Binder from your Start menu. Binder automatically starts with a new Binder project file named Binder1 (Binder files end with the .OBT filename extension). Create additional new Binder projects by selecting File | New.

## Adding Sections

The empty project is useless until you add Office 97 document files. Binder creates a new *section* for each document you add to the project.

 A *section* is an individual Binder document file.

When you work with Microsoft Binder, the File menu options apply to *every* document section in the entire project. The Section menu options apply only to an individual section (the highlighted one) within the project. Your Binder screen is normally divided into left and right panes. The left pane displays icons for each document section, and the right pane displays your activity as you work on one of the sections.

### Adding Existing Files to a Project

You can add an existing Office 97 document to your Binder using drag and drop or using the Binder's menu options. If you've opened a file-folder window such as the Windows Explorer window or the My Computer window, you can drag files from the window to

Binder. Binder does not have to be open on the screen at the time; if you've minimized the Binder application to the Start menu's taskbar, you can drag the file to the taskbar's Binder button to drag the file to Binder's current project.

Surprisingly, the Binder's main-menu bar does not contain a way for you to add a document to the project. However, if you right-click the left pane and select the pop-up menu's Add from File option, Binder opens an Add from File dialog box from which you can select a document.

**TIP**

Press Ctrl while selecting more than one file in the Add from File dialog box to add multiple documents to the project in one step.

Here's the neatest thing about Binder: When you add one or more documents to the project and click one of the document's icons, Binder opens that document's parent program (such as Access 97 or PowerPoint 97) and lets you edit the document *in place* inside Binder's right window pane. Figure 24.1 shows three documents (three sections) stored in a single project: two Word 97 documents and an Excel 97 document. The Excel 97 document's icon is highlighted, so you see Excel 97 in the right pane with that document open.

**Figure 24.1.**

*A project with three sections; the Excel 97 document is loaded.*

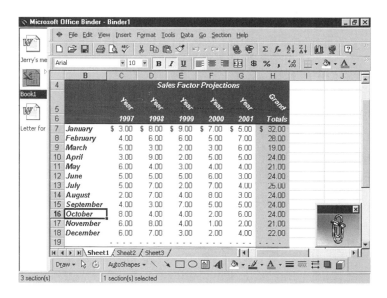

**TIP**

Drag the left pane's icons up or down to rearrange them. You'll probably want to place the project documents that you access most often at the top of the icon list.

Notice that the application menu now contains a mixture of Binder and Word 97 options. Word 97's menu bar does not normally contain a Section option. If you click one of Binder's Word 97 sections, Word 97 replaces Excel 97 in the right pane.

**NOTE**

The ActiveX control mentioned in Hour 22, "Office 97's Synergy," makes this in-place editing of Binder project sections possible.

As you work with the project, you can continue adding sections from existing Office 97 documents and inserting new ones (see the next section). Temporarily hide the left pane if you want more room for an application by clicking the Show/Hide Left Pane button (this button appears to the left of the File menu option).

## Adding New Files to a Project

Right-click the left pane and select Add to create a new section from scratch. Binder displays Figure 24.2's Add Section dialog box, from which you can create a new Office 97 file. As you might expect, you can create the new file from a template if you wish.

**Figure 24.2.**

*Creating a new Binder project file section.*

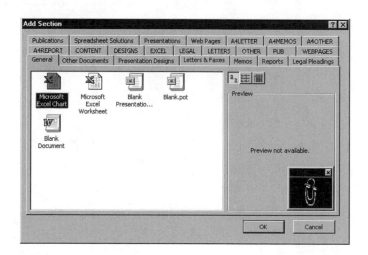

# Working with Binders

To preview the Binder's printed output, select File | Binder Print Preview. Binder displays a preview of the first Binder section, and you can select from the floating menu to see subsequent Binder sections or exit the preview. To preview only a single Binder section, select Section | Print Preview.

If you want to work with Binder sections outside Binder, select the section, choose Select | Save as File, and enter a new filename. The file resides both in the Binder and in the designated Office 97 product, and you can work with the file both inside and outside the Binder by starting its parent application.

If you select Section | View Outside, Binder starts the selected section's parent application and lets you edit the section without interference from Binder. Figure 24.3 shows an editing session with a Word 97 section being edited outside Binder. Binder is still in control (you can see Binder in the figure's background), but a standalone version of Word 97 has been started, and the section has been placed inside for editing. The Word 97 menus are true Word 97 menus, not the combination of Word 97/Binder menus you would have if you edited a Word 97 document inside Binder.

**Figure 24.3.**

*Binder opened a section separate from the project.*

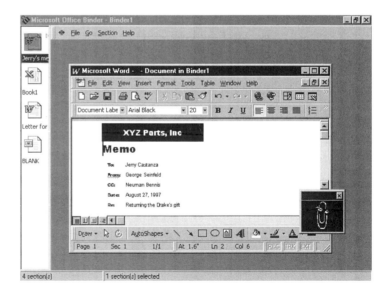

**WARNING**

Until you close the outside section, Binder does not let you edit the section in Binder. When you open a section outside Binder, Binder displays the message `The section is currently in view outside mode.` All Binder files reside on your disk even if you edit them outside Binder. Therefore, you cannot edit the same Binder document both inside and outside Binder at the same time.

After you create your Binder project, be sure to save the Binder file so you can access the project later. As you save the file, Binder gives you a chance to rename the project.

## The Web and Binder

If you want to store Binder projects on the Internet, the Binder's File | Open Binder option lets you open the Binder from a Web or FTP site. You can also open Binder projects from your network or intranet. In addition, Binder lets you save projects to remote sites.

Display the Web toolbar to easily browse Internet documents and document files that contain hyperlinks. The Web toolbar keeps a list of the last 10 documents you accessed via the Web toolbar or through hyperlinks, so you can easily return to those documents by opening the drop-down list of sites.

# Word 97, Outlook 97, and Mail Merge

Office 97's capability to print on envelopes and to create form letters and mailing labels makes it a great tool for your mass-mailing needs. Word 97 supplies the primary mail-merge engine, and you can use Outlook 97, Access 97, or Excel 97 as the *mail merge's data source*.

 *Mail merge* refers to Word 97's capability to send personalized form letters and work with mailing labels and envelopes.

 *Data source* refers to the supplier of names and addresses used in the mail-merge process.

Due to Outlook 97's contact-management strength, Office 97 users will generally select Outlook 97 as their mail-merge data source. As you add names and addresses to your Outlook 97 contact list, you'll build a comprehensive Outlook 97 data source for your mailings.

Some people have unique mail-merge requirements that necessitate the use of Access 97 or Excel 97 as the data source. Not every mail-merge letter will be a letter that you mail to a person. Perhaps you need to print descriptive inventory forms from your company's Access 97 database. Word 97's mail-merge capabilities let you specify non-Outlook 97 data sources such as an Access 97 database or an Excel 97 worksheet.

Generally, however, Office 97 users use Word 97's mail-merge function to print personalized form letters to personal or business contacts stored in Outlook 97. The next sections describe how to do just that.

**TIP**

> The more you use Outlook 97, the more amazed you'll be by its integration in other Office 97 products. Outlook 97 works extremely well—not only for office users, but also for people who travel a lot. Outlook 97 outputs its information in popular paper-planner formats as well as to a personal digital assistant (PDA). Outlook 97 even supports the Timex® DataLink watch by downloading its appointment and contact information to the watch.

## The Items You Need

As you know, you need a data source that supplies the mail merge's personalized details. For each set of mailings you make, you also need a *main document* that acts as the mail-merge template. As Figure 24.4 shows, the mail-merge process sends a copy of your main document to each person in the data source by producing personalized *form letters*.

**Figure 24.4.**

*Mail merge combines data-source details with a main document to produce form letters.*

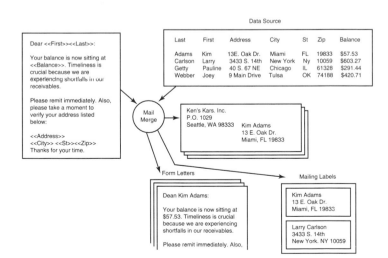

**24**

A *main document* is a single document that acts like a template or form. Special fields in the main document tell Word 97 where to place the data-source details.

 *Form letters* are personalized letters that Word 97 produces. They contain the main document's text, but the fields are replaced with data-source details.

## Generating the Mail Merge

Word 97 makes generating mail merges simple by providing a wizard-like set of dialog boxes that walk you through the process. To begin, select Tools | Mail Merge. Word 97 displays Figure 24.5's Mail Merge Helper dialog box.

**Figure 24.5.**

*Starting the mail-merge process.*

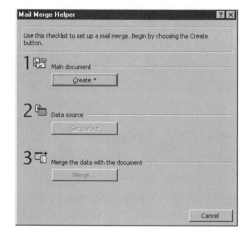

### Generating the Main Document

Click the Mail Merge Helper dialog box's Create button to create the main document. A drop-down menu appears with the following selections:

- ☐ Form Letters—Generates personalized form letters
- ☐ Mailing Labels—Generates mailing labels to be printed on adhesive labels
- ☐ Envelopes—Generates a document sized for selected standard envelopes
- ☐ Catalog—Creates catalogs (such as sales catalogs), membership directories, parts lists, and similar documents

Obviously, you'll select Form Letters to generate form letters. Word 97 displays a dialog box that asks whether you want to use the current document or create a new document for the main document. If you created or opened a main document before you started the mail-merge process, click the Active Window button to use the document currently in memory. Click New Main Document to create a new main document.

## Selecting the Data Source

If you select the mail-merge data source before creating the main document, Word 97 will be better prepared to help you create the main document. Therefore, click the Get Data button to display the following options:

☐ Create Data Source—Lets you create and use an internal Word 97 database for the data source

☐ Open Data Source—Lets you select a Word 97, Access 97, or Excel 97 data document for the data source

☐ Use Address Book—Allows you to select between Schedule+ Contacts, Personal Address Book (from Microsoft Exchange), or Outlook Address Book (see Figure 24.6)

☐ Header Options—Lets you specify two different documents: one for the form-letter headers and one for the form-letter body

### Figure 24.6.

*Select from an existing data source.*

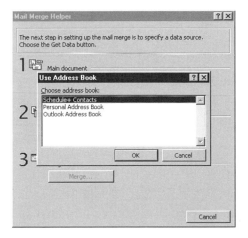

You'll usually select the Use Address Book option and choose Outlook 97 as your data source. To create catalogs or other merged documents that don't fit the form-letter style, select Open Data Source.

After you select a data source, Word 97 analyzes your open document. If have not yet created a document or if your created document has no field names, Word 97 reminds you to edit the main document. Click Edit Main Document to edit your main document.

## Editing the Main Document

When you return to edit the main document, you'll see the Mail Merge toolbar on the editing window. The Mail Merge toolbar helps you add fields to the main document.

**24**

You can now type your main document. Any text that you type will appear on *every* form letter that you print. Any field that you add will be replaced with the data-source details. The field will contain a name that will match the Outlook 97, Access 97, or Excel 97 field name for that data source. In other words, if you want to use the City field from Outlook 97, type <<City>> where you want mail merge to place each record's city on each form letter. The angled brackets around the field name let you and Word 97 know that the item is a field and shouldn't be printed as regular text.

Instead of having to remember the name of every field, click the Mail Merge toolbar's Insert Merge Field button to display Figure 24.7's drop-down list, which contains every field in your selected data source.

**Figure 24.7.**

*Select the field name you need from the field list.*

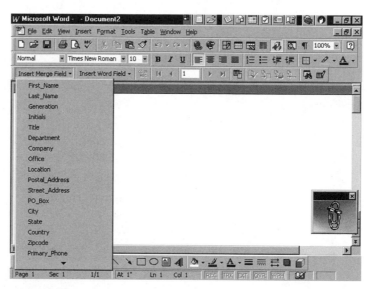

**NOTE**

If you selected an Access 97 or Excel 97 database, the Insert Merge Field displays all the field names from the data source.

Figure 24.8 shows the first part of a main document. The main document contains several fields from the selected data source.

**TIP**

Notice the comma between the return address's city and state in Figure 24.8. That comma will appear between each form letter's city and state. If you apply bold, italics, or any other format to a field, the resulting form letter's detail will contain that same style.

**Figure 24.8.**

*A sample main document with several field names embedded in the text.*

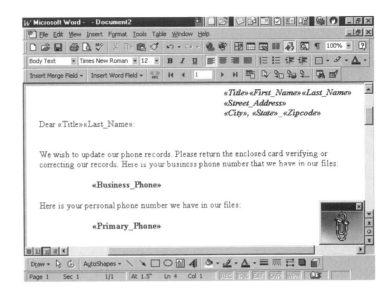

 **TIP**

As you edit the main document, click the View Merged Data button to see the first data-source record's details appear in place of the field names. This allows you to see how the final form letter will look with live data. Click the Mail Merge toolbar's First Record, Mail Merge Previous Record, Mail Merge Next Record, and Last Record buttons to step through the data-source details. Watch Word 97 replace the data-field names with the actual data in the data source's records.

When you finish creating the main document, click the Mail Merge Helper toolbar button to return to the Mail Merge Helper dialog box. You are now ready to merge the data and produce the form letters.

## Generating the Form Letters

To generate the form letters, click the Mail Merge Helper dialog box's Merge button to display Figure 24.9's Merge dialog box.

**Figure 24.9.**

*Selecting mail-merge options.*

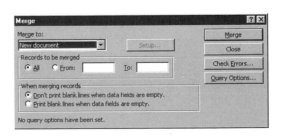

**24**

The following options are available to you from the Merge dialog box:

- ☐ Merge to—Lets you direct the resulting form letters to a new document (named Form Letters1), the printer, electronic mail addresses, or electronic fax. If you select Electronic Mail, click the Setup button to let mail merge know which field to use for the e-mail addresses. Mail merge will send a separate form letter to each e-mail address in the data source. If you select Electronic Fax, click the Setup button to let mail merge know which field to use for the fax numbers. Mail merge will send a separate form letter to each fax number in the data source.

- ☐ Records to be merged—Lets you select all the data-source records or the starting and stopping record numbers.

- ☐ When merging records—Lets you specify whether you want blank lines to print if an empty field would result in a blank line. For example, some of your data-source records might have information in a second address line while others leave the second address line blank. Instead of printing a blank line, let mail merge squeeze the line from the resulting output.

- ☐ Merge—Click this command button to start the mail-merge process.

- ☐ Close—Click this command button to halt the mail-merge process. You can return to the main document, edit the data source, or cancel the mail merge by closing the Merge dialog box.

- ☐ Check Errors—This command button produces Figure 24.10's Checking and Reporting Errors dialog box, which indicates how mail merge should handle common problems.

- ☐ Query Options—This command button produces a Query Options dialog box from which you can filter and sort data-source records.

**Figure 24.10.**

*Decide how mail merge is to handle errors that often occur.*

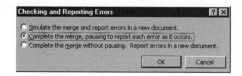

Much of the time, you'll prepare your printer and click Merge to start the mail merge and printing of the form letters. After you execute the mail merge, save your main document so you can use it another time.

# Envelopes and Labels

Although you can execute a mail merge to envelopes and labels, one of the most forgotten Word features is its ability to print a single envelope or label. Some people dedicate an entire printer to envelopes and labels so they can print them when needed.

 **NOTE**

> It seems as though the only time an office regrets replacing its typewriters with word processors is when someone needs a single envelope or label printed! Word 97 tries to alleviate that loss.

When you select Tools | Envelopes and Labels, Word 97 displays Figure 24.11's Envelopes and Labels dialog box. From this dialog box, you can fill in the information for a single envelope or label.

**Figure 24.11.**

*Word 97 lets you easily define a single envelope.*

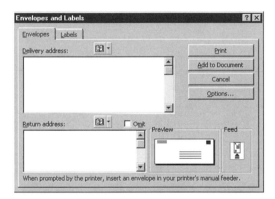

Type a delivery and return address or click the address-book icon next to the address areas to select an address from your address book. The Feed area shows how to feed the envelope so that Word 97 prints the addresses in their correct locations. When you click Print, Word 97 prints the envelope.

 **NOTE**

> Some printers prompt you for the next envelope, depending on how that printer is set up.

Instead of printing the envelope, you can add the envelope to the top of the current document. This allows you to create the envelope before writing a letter and print both of them later. The Options button produces Figure 24.12's Envelope Options dialog box. The dialog box contains a drop-down list of industry-standard envelope sizes, as well as mailing and font options.

> **TIP**
> Word 97 supports delivery-point bar codes and facing identification marks if you use bulk mailing discounts.

**Figure 24.12.**
*Determine how the envelope appears.*

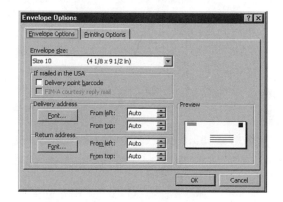

You can also click the Options tab to change the envelope-orientation settings.

If you want to print a label instead of an envelope, click the Envelopes and Labels dialog box's Labels tab. Type your label information or select an address from the address-book icon. The Print area controls the printing of an entire sheet of mailing labels (all with the same information) or a single label. Click the Options button to change the label options (such as the label's style or size).

# Summary

This hour wraps up the book by presenting a few ways to apply your Office 97 skills. The Binder program helps you manage projects that contain multiple Office 97 documents, including documents you created with more than one Office 97 program. Working in the Binder will help you be better equipped to handle large Office 97 projects.

Office 97's mail-merge capability is one of its cornerstone features. Although mail merging has been awkward in the past, Office 97's Mail Merge Helper dialog box walks you through every step of the process. You'll easily select a data source and create the main document.

Word 97 makes it easy for you to print single envelopes and labels if you don't need the full mail-merge power. The Envelopes and Labels dialog box asks for everything Word 97 needs to produce the envelope or label you need.

# Q&A

**Q  Why would I want to print an entire Binder project?**

**A**  Binder's File menu option applies to the entire project, not just the selected section's document. Therefore, if you select File | Print, Binder prints every file in the project (in the order of the left pane's section icon list).

Printing the entire project file makes a lot of sense in many cases. For example, a comprehensive year-end report might require text from Word 97, data from Access 97, and worksheets from Excel 97. Instead of starting each of these programs and printing the documents one at a time, you can print them all from Binder in one easy step.

**Q  Why would I ever use Access 97 as mail merge's data source?**

**A**  Outlook 97 is great for names, addresses, phone numbers, and personal contact information. However, mail merge is not just for envelopes and form letters. Combining a formatted catalog page with an inventory database table allows you to print comprehensive inventory reports. Any time you need to integrate descriptive text with an Access 97 database, consider using mail merge. Although the Access 97 reports are powerful and often generate the only reports you'll need, mail merge's simplicity, combined with Word 97's powerful document-creation tools, makes mail merge a strong competitor to Access 97's report wizards.

**Q  True or False: *Section* is another name for a Binder project document.**

**A**  True.

**Q  How can I add multiple sections to a Binder in one step?**

**A**  Add multiple sections to a Binder by dragging documents from a file-folder window (such as Explorer). Hold Ctrl to select multiple documents to send to Binder.

**Q  How can I store Binder projects on the Internet?**

**A**  Use Binder's File | Save option to select the appropriate Internet Web or FTP site in which to store your Binder project.

**Q  How can mail merge reduce mailing costs?**

**A**  Mail merge prints bar codes on your envelopes and labels for a bulk mailing discount.

**24**

**Q** **Should I use mail merge or the Envelopes and Labels dialog box to print labels from Outlook 97 for holiday greeting cards?**

**A** It depends on who will receive the cards! The mail-merge feature works best for printing labels to each record in an Outlook 97 contact list. Use the Envelopes and Labels dialog box when printing single envelopes and labels.

24

# PART
# VIII

## Appendixes

# Appendix A

# Bonus Hour: Using the IntelliPoint Mouse

No mention of Office 97 would be complete without discussing the new IntelliPoint mouse, the first new mouse style from Microsoft in several years. As figure A.1 shows, the IntelliPoint mouse includes a new center wheel, which adds another dimension to mouse navigation in Windows programs.

**Figure A.1.**

*The IntelliPoint mouse comes with a wheel and wheel button.*

**NOTE**     When you press the wheel, you'll hear a click. The wheel becomes a
             wheel button when you press it.

The IntelliPoint mouse allows you to:

- ☐ Scroll documents without clicking scrollbars.
- ☐ Pan, or move your screen around your document's viewing area.
- ☐ Adjust a document's zoom level so you can see more or less document detail.
- ☐ Expand and collapse structured data, such as outline views and Internet newsgroups.

The Office 97 suite of products takes full advantage of the IntelliPoint mouse, but other programs may not be able to until their software makers rewrite the application's mouse interface. In addition, Microsoft built the IntelliPoint mouse support directly into Internet Explorer 3.0, Microsoft Works, and several other Microsoft programs whose release dates fall after the release of Office 97.

# Installing the IntelliPoint Mouse Hardware

Many readers only have to turn off their computer, unplug their previous mouse, and plug in the IntelliPoint mouse. Windows's Plug and Play (PNP) feature should recognize the IntelliPoint mouse.

If your system does not recognize the IntelliPoint mouse, perform these steps:

1. Open the Windows Control Panel.
2. Select Add New Hardware.
3. Let Windows search for all devices (this takes a while, depending on your computer's speed).
4. Windows may need to be restarted to read the mouse properly.

**A**

**NOTE**

> Although the wheel and wheel button do not operate in MS-DOS and pre-Windows 95 systems, you can use the mouse as a standard two-button mouse in these environments. Therefore, if you use your mouse on several different systems, the IntelliPoint mouse will work but you won't be able to use the wheel or wheel button. You may have to restart Windows after you turn on your laptop if your IntelliPoint mouse does not work properly because some energy-saving laptop tricks mask the new IntelliPoint mouse features until you reboot from a power-off state.

# Installing the IntelliPoint Mouse Software

After you install the IntelliPoint mouse, perform these steps to install the IntelliPoint mouse software:

1. Insert the IntelliPoint mouse software disk in your diskette drive.
2. Display the Start menu. If you use a version of Windows NT prior to 4.0, display the Program Manager's File menu.
3. Click Run.
4. Type a:\setup and press Enter. Use a different drive name if your diskette drive is not named a.

If you ever need to uninstall the IntelliPoint mouse, you'll have to reinstall your previous mouse software if you want to go back to the older mouse.

The Setup program installs the IntelliPoint mouse support on your system and provides you with the IntelliPoint mouse setup options on your Windows Control Panel. To modify the IntelliPoint mouse settings, perform these steps:

1. Display the Start menu.
2. Select Settings|Control Panel.
3. Double-click the Mouse icon to display the IntelliPoint Mouse Properties dialog box. Pre-4.0 NT users should double-click the Program Manager's Control Panel Mouse icon to see the Properties dialog box.

The IntelliPoint Mouse Properties dialog box lets you modify the behavior and customize the sensitivity of the IntelliPoint mouse. Before you make any changes, try the IntelliPoint mouse for a while to make sure that you need to change settings from their default values. Generally, the IntelliPoint mouse is fine-tuned to work well for applications that support it.

# A Quick IntelliPoint Mouse Tutorial

You'll quickly master the IntelliPoint mouse. Here are a few guidelines to get you started.

## Scrolling

To scroll down a document to see pages that are not in view, roll the IntelliPoint mouse wheel instead of clicking the scroll bars. The IntelliPoint mouse software simulates the scrolling and sends your screen up or down the document until you stop rolling the wheel.

When you roll the wheel forward, you scroll up; when you roll the wheel backward, you scroll down. Obviously, if no scroll bar appears on your screen, the IntelliPoint mouse will do nothing when you attempt to scroll.

## Panning

Use the IntelliPoint mouse to *pan*, or scroll in any direction, by holding down the wheel button and moving your IntelliPoint mouse in the direction you want to pan. If, for example, you're working with a large Excel 97 worksheet, you can bring the far-right portions of the worksheet into view by panning with the IntelliPoint mouse. Previously, you had to combine the vertical and horizontal scroll bars to simulate a panning of your worksheet.

## Zooming

Instead of selecting View | Zoom, then clicking the Percent value every time you want to adjust the zoom settings, use the IntelliPoint mouse. Any time you need to zoom a document into view, hold your Ctrl key and roll the IntelliPoint mouse wheel. Windows adjusts the document's view as you roll. When you stop rolling the wheel, Windows anchors to the zoom value in effect.

## Data Zooming

When you work in an outline view, such as the one in Figure A.2, let the IntelliPoint mouse expand and collapse heading levels. If you want to see more detail, press the Shift key while rolling the IntelliPoint mouse wheel. You'll expand or collapse as much as the application allows.

**TIP**  Use this data-zooming feature to view more detail in help screen Contents sheets.

**A**

**Figure A.2.**
*Use the IntelliPoint mouse to expand and collapse outline details.*

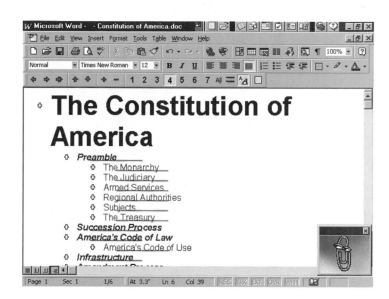

# Appendix B

# Other Office 97 Resources

As you explore Office 97's advanced features, you're sure to have questions that go beyond the scope of this book. Following are some resources that might come in handy.

## Books

*Microsoft Office 97 Unleashed*, 2nd Edition, by Paul McFedries and Sue Charlesworth (Sams Publishing ©1996).

*Access 97 Unleashed*, 2nd Edition, by Dwayne Gifford et al (Sams Publishing ©1996).

*Teach Yourself Access 97 in 14 Days*, 4th Edition, by Paul Cassel (Sams Publishing ©1996).

# Microsoft's Internet Sites

Microsoft's general software Internet address is

```
http://www.microsoft.com
```

Microsoft's Office Internet address is

```
http://microsoft.com/office/
```

Microsoft's technical-support address is

```
http://microsoft.com/technet/
```

# Online Services

These online services provide help for Office 97 users. In addition, you can access the Internet through these services.

America Online—Dial 1-800-827-6364 for sign-up information.

CompuServe—Dial 1-800-848-8199 for sign-up information.

Microsoft Network (MSN)—Dial 1-800-426-9400 for sign-up information.

Prodigy—Dial 1-914-448-8000 for sign-up information.

**B**

# INDEX

A V I A C O M  S E R V I C E

# The Information SuperLibrary™

**Bookstore**  **Search**  **What's New**  **Reference**  **Software**  **Newsletter**  **Company Overviews**

**Yellow Pages**  **Internet Starter Kit**  **HTML Workshop**  **Win a Free T-Shirt!**  **Macmillan Computer Publishing**  **Site Map**  **Talk to Us**

## CHECK OUT THE BOOKS IN THIS LIBRARY.

You'll find thousands of shareware files and over 1600 computer books designed for both technowizards and technophobes. You can browse through 700 sample chapters, get the latest news on the Net, and find just about anything using our massive search directories.

*All Macmillan Computer Publishing books are available at your local bookstore.*

We're open 24-hours a day, 365 days a year.

You don't need a card.

We don't charge fines.

And you can be as **LOUD** as you want.

The Information SuperLibrary
http://www.mcp.com/mcp/    ftp.mcp.com

Copyright © 1996, Macmillan Computer Publishing-USA, A Simon & Schuster Company

# GET CONNECTED
## to the ultimate source of computer information!

# *The MCP Forum on CompuServe*

Go online with the world's leading computer book publisher!
Macmillan Computer Publishing offers everything
you need for computer success!

*Find the books that are right for you!*
A complete online catalog, plus sample
chapters and tables of contents give
you an in-depth look at all our books.
The best way to shop or browse!

➤ Get fast answers and technical support for
MCP books and software

➤ Join discussion groups on major computer
subjects

➤ Interact with our expert authors via e-mail
and conferences

➤ Download software from our immense
library:

   ➢ Source code from books
   ➢ Demos of hot software
   ➢ The best shareware and freeware
   ➢ Graphics files

## Join now and get a free CompuServe Starter Kit!

To receive your free CompuServe Introductory Membership, call **1-800-848-
8199** and ask for representative #597.

*The Starter Kit includes:*
➤ Personal ID number and password
➤ $15 credit on the system
➤ Subscription to *CompuServe Magazine*

*Once on the CompuServe System, type:*

# GO MACMILLAN

*for the most computer information anywhere!*

MACMILLAN
COMPUTER
PUBLISHING

CompuServe

# Microsoft Office 97 Unleashed, Second Edition

*—Paul McFedries and Sue Charlesworth*

Microsoft has brought the Web to its Office suite of products. Hyperlinking, Office Assistants, and Active Document Support lets users publish documents to the Web or an intranet site. It also completely integrates with Microsoft FrontPage, making it possible to point-and-click a Web page into existence. This book details each of the Office products—Excel, Access, PowerPoint, Word, and Outlook—and shows the estimated 22 million registered users how to create presentations and Web documents. This book also demonstrates how to extend Office to work on a network as well as the various Office Solution Kits and how to use them. The CD-ROM includes powerful utilities and two best-selling books in HTML format.

Price: $35.00 USA/$49.95 CDN    User Level: Accomplished–Expert
ISBN: 0-672-31010-4    1,200 pages

# Teach Yourself Access 97 in 14 Days, Fourth Edition

*—Paul Cassel*

Through the examples, workshop sessions, and Q&A sections in this book, you can master the most important features of Access. In just two weeks you'll be able to develop your own databases and create stunning forms and reports. *Teach Yourself Access 97 in 14 Days, Fourth Edition* covers wizards, tables, data types, validation, forms, queries, artificial fields, macros, and more. You'll learn how to program with Access Basic and Access lingo.

Price:$29.99 USA/$42.95 CDN    User Level: New–Casual
ISBN: 0-672-30969-6    700 pages

# Access 97 Unleashed, Second Edition

*—Dwayne Gifford, et al.*

Access, one of Microsoft's database managers for Windows, has become one of the most accepted standards of database management for personal computers. The *Unleashed* format for this book allows current and new users to quickly and easily find the information they need about new features. It also serves as a complete reference for database programmers who are new to Access. Readers learn advanced techniques for working with tables, queries, forms, and data. *Access 97 Unleashed, Second Edition* shows you how to program Access and how to integrate your database with the Internet. The CD-ROM includes Access utilities and applications as well as an electronic Access reference library.

Price: $49.99 USA/$70.95 CDN    User Level: Accomplished–Expert
ISBN: 0-672-30983-1    1,100 pages

# Microsoft Internet Explorer 3 Unleashed

*—Glenn Fincher, Joe Kraynak, et al.*

This comprehensive guide to Internet Explorer 3 fully exploits the complete Microsoft Internet Explorer and ActiveX environment. It details the steps for using Internet Explorer to get around the Internet as well as for sending and receiving e-mail and news, using FrontPage and the Internet Assistants to create Web pages, and adding interactivity to Web pages with VBScript and JavaScript. The CD-ROM includes source code from the book as well as powerful utilities.

Price: $39.99 USA/$56.95 CDN    User Level: Accomplished–Expert
ISBN: 1-57521-155-6    1,008 pages

# Microsoft FrontPage Unleashed

*—William Stanek, et al.*

FrontPage technologies have recently been acquired by Microsoft, who immediately reduced its retail price from a staggering $695 to $150, making FrontPage affordable for thousands of hackers and professionals. Microsoft is also launching FrontPage as its point technology for its suite of Internet products, which will undoubtedly increase demand. With that new demand in mind, this book gives readers of all levels the information they need to succeed in Web publishing with FrontPage. This book explains how to add interactivity to Web sites and shows how to integrate CGI scripting with FrontPage. The CD-ROM includes all the examples and source code from the book.

Price: $49.99 USA/$70.95 CDN     User Level: Casual–Accomplished
ISBN: 1-57521-140-8     1,032 pages

# Laura Lemay's Web Workshop: Microsoft FrontPage

*—Laura Lemay & Denise Tyler*

This is a hands-on guide to maintaining Web pages with Microsoft's FrontPage. Written in the clear, conversational style of Laura Lemay, it is packed with many interesting, colorful examples that demonstrate specific tasks of interest to the reader. The CD-ROM includes all the necessary templates, backgrounds, and materials.

Price: $39.99 USA/$56.95 CDN     User Level: Casual–Accomplished
ISBN: 1-57521-149-1     672 pages

# Laura Lemay's Web Workshop: Creating Commercial Web Pages

*—Laura Lemay*

Filled with sample Web pages, this book illustrates how to create commercial-grade Web pages using HTML, CGI, and Java. In the classic clear style of Laura Lemay, this book details not only how to create the page, but how to apply proven principles of design that will make the page a marketing tool. This book illustrates the corporate uses of Web technology, such as how to use your Web page as a catalog as well as for customer-service and product-ordering purposes. The CD-ROM includes all the templates in the book, plus HTML editors, graphics software, CGI forms, and more!

Price: $39.99 USA/$56.95 CDN     User Level: Accomplished
ISBN: 1-57521-126-2     528 pages

# Teach Yourself Web Publishing with HTML 3.2 in a Week, Third Edition

*—Laura Lemay & Brian K. Murphy*

This is the updated edition of Lemay's previous best-seller, *Teach Yourself Web Publishing with HTML in 14 Days, Premier Edition*. In it, readers will find all the advanced topics and updates—including adding audio, video, and animation—to Web-page creation. This book explores the use of CGI scripts, tables, HTML 3.2, Netscape and Internet Explorer extensions, Java applets and JavaScript, and VRML.

Price: $29.99 USA/$42.95 CDN     User Level: New–Casual–Accomplished
ISBN:1-57521-192-0     624 pages

# Add to Your Sams Library Today with the Best Books for Programming, Operating Systems, and New Technologies

## The easiest way to order is to pick up the phone and call

# 1-800-428-5331

### between 9:00 a.m. and 5:00 p.m. EST.

### For faster service please have your credit card available.

| ISBN | Quantity | Description of Item | Unit Cost | Total Cost |
|---|---|---|---|---|
| 0-672-31010-4 | | Microsoft Office 97 Unleashed, Second Edition (Book/CD-ROM) | $35.00 | |
| 0-672-30969-6 | | Teach Yourself Access 97 in 14 Days, Fourth Edition | $29.99 | |
| 0-672-30983-1 | | Access 97 Unleashed, Second Edition (Book/CD-ROM) | $49.99 | |
| 1-57521-155-6 | | Microsoft Internet Explorer 3 Unleashed (Book/CD-ROM) | $39.99 | |
| 1-57521-140-8 | | Microsoft FrontPage Unleashed (Book/CD-ROM) | $49.99 | |
| 1-57521-149-1 | | Laura Lemay's Web Workshop: Microsoft FrontPage (Book/CD-ROM) | $39.99 | |
| 1-57521-126-2 | | Laura Lemay's Web Workshop: Creating Commercial Web Pages (Book/CD-ROM) | $39.99 | |
| 1-57521-192-0 | | Teach Yourself Web Publishing with HTML 3.2 in a Week, Third Edition | $29.99 | |
| ❏ 3 ½" Disk | | Shipping and Handling: See information below. | | |
| ❏ 5 ¼" Disk | | TOTAL | | |

Shipping and Handling: $4.00 for the first book, and $1.75 for each additional book. Floppy disk: add $1.75 for shipping and handling. If you need to have it NOW, we can ship the product to you in 24 hours for an additional charge of approximately $18.00, and you will receive your item overnight or in two days. Overseas shipping and handling adds $2.00 per book and $8.00 for up to three disks. Prices subject to change. Call for availability and pricing information on latest editions.

**201 W. 103rd Street, Indianapolis, Indiana 46290**

**1-800-428-5331 — Orders    1-800-835-3202 — Fax    1-800-858-7674 — Customer Service**

Book ISBN 0-672-31009-0